ECONOMICS
REIMAGINED

Nature, Progress, and Living Standards

RICK TELLER

For information about this title or to order other books and/or electronic media, contact the publisher:
Omyac Publishing Co.
www.rickteller.com
info@rickteller.com

ISBN:
979-8-9883077-2-3 Hardcover
979-8-9883077-0-9 Softcover
979-8-9883077-1-6 eBook

Printed in the United States of America
Cover and Interior design: 1106 Design

Math makes a research paper look solid, but the real science lies not in math but in trying one's utmost to understand the real workings of the world.

—KIMMO ERICKSSON

There once was a time when everything was cheap,
But now prices nearly puts a man to sleep.
When we pay our grocery bill,
We just feel like making our will.
Tell me how can a poor man stand such times and live?

I remember when dry goods were cheap as dirt,
We could take two bits and buy a dandy shirt.
Now we pay three bucks or more,
Maybe get a shirt that another man wore.
Tell me how can a poor man stand such times and live?

—BLIND ALFRED REED, 1929

TABLE OF CONTENTS

• • •

INTRODUCTION

• • •

W E LIKE TO THINK we have complete control over our own lives. Yet what we do for a living, how much we make, what taxes we pay, what we earn on our savings, how much we can borrow, and what interest rate we pay when we do—all these things are affected, or completely controlled, by the decisions of macroeconomists.

Knowledge of macroeconomics (macro) seems extensive. Interest rates, stock prices, government deficits, unemployment, tax policies, and other topics are regularly in the news and discussed widely.

Nevertheless, the immense power that leading economists have been given nearly everywhere in the world is barely noticed and never debated. It is universally accepted that economies need expert management by economists working at the Federal Reserve Bank (the Fed) in the US, and at the various central banks of other countries.

Without their intervention, the economy is thought certain to misbehave badly, giving us financial crashes, depressions, out-of-control inflation, rising poverty, or other disasters. Except, even with that supposedly expert management, we get all those things anyway, just not when the leading economists anticipate them.

What happens in the economy is often surprising. For more than a decade after the collapse of the US housing bubble in 2007-08, inflation indices showed barely any increases, and the Fed was constantly talking about ways to get inflation up to the 2% per year level that was and still is its goal. Then, predicted by no mainstream economist even well into 2021, including the top leaders of the Fed, prices took off. By 2022, inflation indices hit the highest rate in 40 years, more than four times the Fed's 2% goal.

In an earlier surprise to macroeconomists, at the top of the housing bubble in 2006-07, the head of the Fed expressed confidence that house prices would not decline and, if they somehow did, it would pose no risk to the financial system. In almost no time at all, both those problems showed up in a massive way.

Why are the top economists regularly blindsided by events? If they don't understand their field well enough to anticipate what is about to happen, why do we continue to give them so much power? Can this be fixed by replacing the current powerful batch of economists with a different batch, or is the problem deeper than that?

My answer is that mainstream macroeconomics is fundamentally flawed and cannot do what it has promised. Economists themselves are well meaning, and almost all of them are very smart, but the economy is more complex than any single one of them, or even a group of the very smartest economists, can possibly manage in a way that produces better results than if it were left to its own devices, unmanaged.

Complex doesn't mean confusing. The basic principles are not hard to understand. Mainstream macro looks at the world using faulty ideology and flawed conceptual tools, and, as a result, gets cause and effect wrong. This book will explain why they are wrong and show you a better way to understand what happens in the economy. You won't need an economics degree to follow along.

The other major area of study within economics is microeconomics (micro), which covers how individuals and businesses interact in the economy, including what determines prices, how people decide what to buy or where to work, how businesses decide whether to invest or hire, and what they can afford to pay workers, among other things. While people are very interested in their own and others' experiences in their roles as consumers, employees, and/ or employers, very rarely will any commentator discuss micro theory, because it is so predictable as to be not worth mentioning.

We are almost never surprised by anything related to micro, such as when a clothing store puts bathing suits on sale near the end of the summer, because we expect them to do just that. We are also never surprised that a hot new car sells at list price or even higher, because we all know that an excess of demand over supply means sellers have no reason to offer discounts.

Have you ever wondered why micro is so much more predictable than macro? The answer is that micro is a science, a very settled one, to use the popular phrase. There could be ten million clothing stores in the world, and except for ones in a country with runaway inflation, a grand total of none of them would ever raise the price of bathing suits near the end of the summer, just as no car company that has a new car selling out fast would ever slash the price.

The reason micro is predictable is that it is based on human nature. What? Isn't human nature infinitely variable? Isn't it very dependent upon the customs of the society in which a person lives? Even within a given society, aren't people wildly different in many ways?

Yes, all true, but **not** when it comes to how we interact with each other in the economy. It doesn't matter which society you live in, or whether you are alive now or lived thousands of years ago. When buying something, you always want to pay less for it rather than more. When selling something or getting a salary, you would always rather be paid more than less. When investing your own money, you would always prefer to invest in something you expect to provide a high return and a low risk of loss, not the other way around.

When engaging in transactions with others, the price we agree upon will reflect our sense of the balance of supply and demand, with relative increases in demand likely to move prices up and relatively more supply likely to move them down.

People universally respond to incentives and disincentives, not in a lockstep, predictable fashion, but we at least take them into consideration, which is why you are more likely to buy something when it goes on sale, and less likely to ignore the setting on your heat or air conditioning if energy prices are soaring. People, no matter where or when, obey the Law of Diminishing Returns: that someone who already has plenty of something will lose much of their desire to get more, not counting collectors looking for a complete set.

Also, people, regardless of the society in which they live, have similar hierarchies for the beneficiaries of their decisions. Working hard to benefit oneself and one's family and friends nearly always has a higher priority than helping strangers far away.

These rules don't all apply to every single person 100% of the time. The Law of Diminishing Returns often has exceptions, such as people who have amassed more wealth than they could possibly use or give away but who still work hard for more. Some people don't always place themselves and their families as the most important beneficiaries of their efforts, such as soldiers with families who don't want them harmed, yet who still fight and die for their countries.

There can be other exceptions. Some clothing stores might feel it diminishes the good name of their store or its bathing suit lines to discount, so they just pack away unsold suits at the end of the season and pray they are still in style next year. For some products where buyers are uncertain about their quality, price can sometimes convey useful information. A person might prefer to buy a more expensive wine or watch, thinking it might be better than a less expensive one. But these are trivial exceptions, and once one has chosen the wine or watch they want, no one would turn down a discount if offered.

Because of these universal characteristics, the patterns of behavior that comprise micro do not change, because human nature regarding economic choices hasn't changed in all of human history. It is the same under any economic system or social system. It doesn't matter who runs the government. That makes micro closer to physics and other established sciences. Predictions based on micro laws are not certain to be exactly correct, as is the case in physics, but are likely to come close.

Macro couldn't be more different. There are no established relationships between the concepts it uses. One can't say that an X% increase in inflation will cause a Y% change in short-term interest rates, or vice versa, or cause some change in Gross Domestic Product (GDP), employment, or anything else. The only causes of anything in the economy are human decisions. People take economic data into account, but only as one of many factors.

A person thinking of quitting their job might be concerned about a high unemployment rate. A contractor bidding on a construction job that won't get started for a year will ponder the inflation rate. People consider interest rates, trends in the economy, and so forth, but also many other factors related to their personal situation, some rational, some emotional, some even subconscious.

An economist is not a mass mind reader and will never know the extent to which a change in inflation or any other concept in economics will affect the decisions people make. Inherently unpredictable relationships between economic concepts mean that, if a macro model of the economy seems to work for a little while (few even do that), it is more likely a matter of luck than anything else.

This is important, because every country in the world has given massive power to economists on the grounds that macro is a science and that economists are the experts at applying the science to the particulars of the economy at that time. Neither of these beliefs is true.

The main concentration of economists' power in the US is at the Fed, which lacks any serious oversight by elected officials. It is considered impertinent for laypeople to even question their decisions. They swear they know what they are doing, and we are expected to take that on faith. We never explicitly voted to give economists so much power, nor has there ever been an election in which an issue of great importance was whether economists should be given such a dominant position in our society. They have it, and that is how it is. Very few people even ask why.

This book argues that mainstream macro is not just randomly wrong due to inability to guess how people will respond to complex and changing circumstances, but also consistently wrong to the extent that it makes false assumptions about human nature, ignores constraints of the real world, and uses inherently flawed concepts that aren't really saying what economists think they do.

If you are not a macroeconomist, you may wonder: Who am I to judge? Actually, everyone has standing to judge. The history of ideas is full of examples where an elaborate intellectual construct was developed and widely adopted, and yet was wrong, not because of some subtle point that only the most sophisticated experts in the field eventually detected, but because one or more of the basic assumptions underlying the edifice were wrong, something that non-experts were open minded enough to notice. Think of "The Emperor's New Clothes". Such is the case with macro.

That is good news for me as the author and you as a reader. We all happen to be experts at human nature, being humans ourselves. Even those with no knowledge of economics or statistics have the skills to recognize what is wrong with an economic theory when it is based on assuming that people behave in a certain way that we all know they never have and never will.

An example exists in every civilized country of how non-experts can examine evidence, think about cause and effect, and apply what we know about human nature in order to make important decisions. And even though in doing so we make no use whatsoever of mathematics, computer models, or formulas, it is generally agreed that the decisions, while occasionally faulty, are the correct ones most of the time.

I'm referring to the court system, both civil and criminal. Adversaries show up in court with professional advocates. Each side presents evidence and testimony, which usually contradict each other on many points, or the two sides would have settled and wouldn't be in court. Each side gets to present a narrative, a story of cause and effect that paints its own side as having the best explanation of what really happened, while pointing out the flaws in the other side's case.

The judge or jury then considers the evidence and arguments, and more than anything else, applies what they know about human nature to understand the testimony, character, and motivations of the witnesses. They decide whose story makes the most sense. If the losing side feels strongly that justice was not done, there are appeals mechanisms that can reverse or ameliorate the outcome.

The law and the court system are both based upon the fact that any member of a jury, regardless of education level or whether they have had any formal training in psychology, is perfectly qualified by their life experiences to size people up and decide who is right, or at least more believable. The same applies to economics.

Throughout the book, I will make use of what I call mechanisms of micro. A mechanism is a series of choices people, including business owners and managers, will likely make, given their incentives and disincentives. People respond to their circumstances, and the effects of their responses sometimes change the incentives for those who haven't yet responded.

Think of it like moves in a chess game. Each move is one "ply." Better chess players can think many plies ahead; they are not certain what move their opponent will make, but can figure out what they are likely to do because that would be the most attractive move, even if, unbeknownst to the weaker opponent until too late, it will place them in a poor strategic position that will lead to their defeat.

Chess is a game with opponents, while the economy is a cooperative interaction of millions of people, so the analogy is not ideal. Still, mechanisms based on micro are reliable because one doesn't have to consider the playing style of a specific chess opponent, who may favor surprise moves unlikely to be foreseen by their opponent. In micro, there are few surprises, so these mechanisms unfold in a predictable way, if not necessarily at a predictable pace.

Often a mechanism works through business strategy rather than the choices of consumers or workers. Macroeconomists tend to think of companies as being indistinguishable participants in the marketplace, but the smartest move for one company to make, depending upon micro factors, may be very different from the choices some of its direct competitors should make. An established company with a high market share will behave differently from a small, aggressive newcomer with nothing much to lose. Companies with high fixed costs and low variable costs will behave differently from those with the opposite cost structure.

I know something about this because, since my first summer job in the 1960s, my career was in the stock market. By the early 1970s, I worked as what was then called a stockbroker but now has various classier names. My specialty then and continuing long after I retired more than 20 years ago, was investment in micro-cap companies.

These are very small companies, in the lowest 5% or so of public companies in terms of revenues and earnings. They are all relatively unknown, with only their employees, people in their industry, and some locals near their headquarters knowing much about them. While they may be small, they are sometimes the dominant player in a lucrative niche business.

Their top officers aren't so busy and important that they don't have time to talk to a prospective investor, especially one with clients who, collectively, could buy a lot of stock. The officers of tiny companies often have most of their net worth tied up in the stock, so they pay attention to its price.

I've spoken with hundreds of managers, and one of my main interests was their competitive strategy. For the better-managed ones, it matched up to what one would expect from microeconomics. Companies with big market share in their niche are always more interested in maintaining high profit margins than sacrificing them to gain even more market share. Small outfits in bigger markets take the opposite approach. Other choices that made sense to them were exactly what one would expect, given their microeconomic characteristics.

When the Fed changes interest rates, it does so with certain goals in mind. Macro effects, to the extent they exist, operate through mechanisms in the micro world, i.e., decisions made because of changed incentives.

Nobody is ever required to do what a mechanism's incentive or disincentive suggests they do. People will sometimes pass on some lucrative opportunity or fail to reverse doomed choices because they are unobservant, capital constrained, short of staff, or for other reasons. If so, and the underlying conditions haven't changed, the incentive usually stays in effect until the opportunity it reveals does attract takers and disappears as a factor.

The opposite of thinking many plies ahead characterizes many popular viewpoints on economic policies. One-ply thinking considers only the immediate effect of some law or policy, not subsequent effects. This limitation plagues most discussions of the effects of automation, artificial intelligence, imports, welfare, unemployment, tax rates, and other topics.

Because macro as taught generally ignores the implications of micro and its mechanisms, you'll probably come across many ideas in this book that are different from what you have read elsewhere or been taught. Some of them are:

- **Living standards**, although difficult to quantify, are a much better measure than GDP of the success of the economy in providing people with whatever it is that they want. GDP is easy to quantify but counts as positives many things that reduce living standards. The economy exists to serve people—we don't exist to maximize GDP.

- **Inflation** figures could be very different and equally valid (or not) but are nonetheless calculated with great precision by hordes of government economists, as if the figures were not mere artifacts of arbitrary definitions.

- The natural situation in free-market economies is for **prices to decline** over time due to business investments in R&D, staff training, and more efficient equipment, which reduces unit costs and leads to lower prices or gives customers more for their money through quality improvements at the same price. Nevertheless, our economics establishment consistently and adamantly favors steadily rising prices, which lower living standards for the poor and middle class, while adding to the wealth of the rich.

- Despite the widespread belief that **inequality** has never been greater, and despite the massive bubble in asset prices owned by the wealthy, the fact is, in terms of living standards, inequality has rarely been less in the US than now.

- The real **cost of government** is not just the taxes we pay, but the total cost of what it spends, however financed. Another cost of government is the higher prices we must pay for output because of government and central-bank policies. Those include deficit spending that increases demand for output more than its supply, years of artificially low interest rates and money printing that make assets very expensive, and the diversion of money to people who are well paid despite not producing output that anyone would use their own money to buy.

- In addition to what the government spends, its ill-considered **incentives** impose an immense cost on society in the form of bad investments and wasteful spending by the private sector. The housing bubble earlier this century and the "everything bubble" of the last few years are good examples.

- All efforts to **make businesses "pay their fair share,"** whatever that may be, are futile. Sooner or later, every tax or cost imposition on business is converted into some combination of higher prices and/or lower pay or benefits, so these taxes and costs are paid for entirely by customers and workers, not the businesses, except briefly. There is a mechanism in micro that ensures this, and it cannot be escaped.

- **Taxes that directly target the rich**, such as highly progressive income-tax rates, capital-gains taxes, inheritance taxes, and proposed wealth taxes, have little effect on the living standards of the wealthy, but by reducing savings and investment, especially high-risk capital for startups, they reduce productivity growth and thus diminish the future living standards of those with lower incomes.

- Many of our programs to retard **climate change**, while reducing some of the expense that will be needed in the future to mitigate the worst effects of higher temperatures, appear likely to reduce future incomes more than they reduce future expenses, leaving our descendants worse off even though their mitigation expense may be lower.

By the end of the book, I hope you'll see why **no matter who or what the government taxes, or even if it taxes nobody, nearly the entire cost of government is paid for in the form of reduced living standards for the poor.** Those who think a more powerful government, commandeering even more resources in society, will somehow lead to less inequality or higher living standards for those with lower incomes, couldn't possibly be more wrong.

That conclusion should be disturbing to progressives, whose answer for everything is more government size and power, but equally surprised and skeptical will be conservatives, who believe that the government transfers excessive amounts of money from the well-to-do to the poor, with the latter getting close to a free ride. The idea that, in terms of living standards, the rich sacrifice very little to pay for the government and it is the poor who are exploited, will upset their worldview, too.

My main thesis therefore has no natural allies on the left or the right. That's a good thing. In evaluating it, no one will be able to apply their standard talking points to counter the other side—they must instead consider a very different way of looking at the economy and how it operates.

You'll have to use your imagination occasionally, comparing the world in which we live to a counterfactual world which is identical to our world except for one thing. And you'll have to be aware of how intertwined the economy is with the government and the Fed. Disentangling them is necessary to understand cause and effect in the economy.

A convention used in this book is the word "widget" to refer to some product or service offered by competing companies. "Output" is used to mean goods and/or services—whatever it is that a business wants to sell to customers. "Equity" means ownership or shares in ownership, not anything about social or racial fairness. For simplicity, I will talk of the Fed, but other countries have their own central banks where the same principles apply. Since almost all of them, as far as I can tell, believe in the same mainstream macro theories, what I say about the Fed probably applies to them, too.

UNJUSTIFIED POWER

• • •

Written in the late 1700s, when economists were close to nonexistent, the US Constitution makes no mention of them, nor does it authorize roles for anyone to interfere with market prices for loans (aka interest rates) or do anything else to intentionally manage the economy. Of course, governments even then affected the economy, but the purpose of taxes and tariffs was to raise money so the government could pay its bills, not to change any aspects of the economy.

Starting in the late 1800s, economics developed as a field of academic study, but its intent was to understand the economy, not control it. The Fed was established as a central bank in 1913 to be a "lender of last resort," to dampen any bank runs or panics, and to enhance the efficiency of the banking system by facilitating check clearance and other prosaic tasks.

In its first decade, the Fed tiptoed cautiously. In the early 1920s, the Fed got increasingly bold in its attempts to steer the economy. It decided that its policy should be guided by what today is called inflation-rate targeting, in which rates get increased and credit is tightened when price inflation is higher than the Fed's target, and rates are cut and credit eased when it is less.

Benjamin Strong, head of the New York branch of the Fed, which made him more powerful than the Fed's Chair at the time, wrote in 1925 *"That it was my belief, and I thought it was shared by all others in the Federal Reserve System, that our whole policy in the future, as in the past, would be directed towards the stability of prices so far as it was possible for us to influence prices."*

By the mid-1920s, noticing that there was consumer price deflation, the Fed took that as an indication that the sum effect of its policies was too tight, so it loosened them accordingly.

That was the wrong interpretation because monetary policy is not the only thing that affects price levels. The 1920s were a time of mass adoption of new power and communications technologies. With newly built transmission lines, factories became increasingly electricity intensive, with efficient electrical motors replacing steam, water, and manual human power in production processes. This cut production costs, and as these advances became available to all except remotely located businesses, competition forced prices to follow costs down.

Also, the widespread adoption of telephones by businesses was a big cost saver. Managers didn't have to travel to find things out in person. If a product was not selling well, the factory had a chance to cut production before massive excess inventory was created. This reduced risk and cost, eventually pushing prices down.

The Fed's credit easing did little to make consumer prices rise but did encourage banks and brokers to lend more to speculators in real estate and the stock market. The relentless rise in stock prices made banks comfortable lending speculators a high percentage of the value of their portfolios. This financing-enhanced buying power pushed stock prices to unsustainable levels, and the resulting market crash and subsequent bank failures were a major cause of the 1930s Great Depression.

In the 1930s, the government, under both Hoover and Roosevelt, actively tried to make the economy stronger with various spending programs. The result compared poorly to rebounds that came after every prior economic setback in the nation's history, including those in which widespread bank failures were a major part of what was going wrong.

Unfortunately, there are no alternative universes we can observe that are exactly like ours except for different policy choices, so we could determine which policies worked best. The economy in our universe was not much better in 1941 than it was in 1931 despite everything the government and Fed had done. Some people interpreted that to mean that the policies failed, but economists increasingly rallied around the opposite idea that the government should have done the same things, only more intensively, and then those policies would have worked. No proof was possible.

But one thing was clear even then. If it became widely accepted that the government should always be focused on managing the economy, not just leave it to its own devices, a major beneficiary would be economists.

Macro has many different schools of thought within it, and economists regularly quibble over which policies the government and the Fed should follow. The one principle every branch, except for one minor one, enthusiastically endorses is the idea that economists such as themselves and their friends should be given the power to control and alter the economy as managers of central banks and as government officials and advisors.

As is always the case in society, great power leads to great wealth, possibly a factor in the rapid acceptance by economists of the ideas of famed British economist John Maynard Keynes. He argued that any weakness or unemployment in the economy was caused by insufficient aggregate demand, which could be remedied by the government spending more money, whether it had it or not.

Nearly all politicians strongly support that idea. Not coincidentally, the consensus of economists, at least since World War Two (WW2), is that the government, i.e., politicians, can, with the guidance of economists, make the economy better than it would be on its own by frequently stimulating it with deficit-spending programs. Politicians love getting intellectual cover from academics to do what they always want to do anyway, which is to spend the government's money in ways that will benefit constituents and help their chances of reelection.

With the Fed and other governmental bodies staffing up with vast numbers of economics PhDs, paying top dollar, colleges then had to pay them much more than professors of history, anthropology, archaeology, sociology, and other social studies, which wasn't the case pre-Keynes.

This is not to imply any evil conspiracy between economists and politicians, just mutual backscratching that helps them both. Nor are my criticisms of macro meant to question the honesty or good intentions of economists as a group or individually. They are all very smart, as they must be to advance in such a technically difficult field, and they mean well. Unfortunately, the laws of economics do not care about intentions any more than the law of gravity does.

The biggest problem isn't that powerful economists are exercising power capriciously, although they are. Even when the Fed deliberates carefully before making some choice, its decision has an excellent chance of being a bad one because its foundational assumptions are wrong. It refuses to acknowledge what the record shows, that the economy is too complex for anyone, even a group of the world's smartest economists, to understand enough to manage in a way that doesn't cause more harm than good.

In this first section of the book, **Chapter 1** will address the false claim that macro has any scientific backing. The lack of a scientific backing may not bother you, and the complexity of the economy suggests that occasional mistaken forecasts by the leading economists should be forgiven. In theory, minor errors shouldn't rule out their being approximately right often enough to deserve the power they have.

In practice, though, you'll see that economists' understanding of even current conditions, especially around major turning points in the economy, is embarrassingly awful, so bad that were they doctors, lawyers, engineers, architects, or other professionals, there would be administrative proceedings to consider suspending or revoking their licenses. Yet their jobs are never at risk.

Chapter 2 will discuss one of Keynes' key concepts, the Liquidity Trap, which is the prime justification for all the power we give economists. The concept contradicts a proven law of economics and is necessarily wrong for that reason alone.

On those rare occasions when anyone questions why economists have so much power, we will be regaled with stories about how volatile the economy used to be before they were in charge. That is partially true, but **Chapter 3** will show that the reasons for that have to do with technology that didn't yet exist in the 1800s and the inherently more volatile demand for output then compared to more recent times, not a lack of management by anyone using modern macro theories.

Also, politicians will tell us stories about bad things in the economy like child labor, excessively long work weeks, factory pollution, and unsafe working conditions that they claim ended only because of new laws. The chapter will also show why the laws were passed only after these problems were mostly ended on their own.

CHAPTER 1

SCIENCE?

• • •

THE ECONOMICS PROFESSION HAS done a masterful job of convincing the world that macroeconomics (macro), which examines the economy as a whole, is a proven science, and that highly trained economists are experts at applying that science to the particular characteristics of our economy.

Macro certainly resembles a science. An advanced degree in the field requires a level of knowledge of math, statistics, and the creation of complex models no less sophisticated than those needed for a degree in physics.

Nobody would deny that physics is a science, with a vast body of established knowledge about cause-and-effect relationships in the real world. There will always be controversy and conflicting opinions among physicists, but that is mostly on the frontiers of the field. The basic theories making up the bulk of the subject matter have been proven without any doubt. Attempts to replicate an experiment that demonstrates some known principle of physics will almost always do so. If not, it nearly always indicates some error by the researchers or equipment failure, not that some basic principle of physics is wrong and should be changed.

Economics is also very quantitative, but economics is ultimately not about numbers representing natural forces. Its true subject is human beings and the decisions we make about our spending, saving, jobs, and many other aspects of our relations with others. Those decisions generate all sorts of numbers—prices, wages, interest rates, inflation rates, GDP, production and employment levels, savings, consumption, and investment data, among others. These numbers are entirely dependent on the decisions of humans.

The concepts that economics measures do not exist by themselves in the real world. If all humans died out, gravity would still operate, light waves and cosmic rays would still be zooming around the universe, but there would be no prices, GDP, unemployment rates, and so forth on Earth, because they are generated only by human interactions.

If humans no longer existed, sufficiently advanced creatures from some other planet could still measure the elements of physics and get the same results we would have gotten. Those forces exist whether or not they are being measured, and their relationship to each other is constant. An atom never has to decide anything; it does exactly what it must do, given the forces exerted on it. Humans, however, decide things all day long. How we weigh the factors that influence our choices is complex and inconsistent.

Is there a scientific basis for the economic policies that the Fed, other central banks, and most governments have been following for many decades? The answer depends on how one defines "science."

The standard for something being a science should be simple: the ability to use the scientific method to prove or disprove claims. That means performing experiments in which the possible causes for any resulting effects can be clearly identified and tested. It means that others can perform the same experiment, multiple times if need be, and get substantially identical results.

By that standard, macro is not and can never be a science.

We can and do measure many things that happen in the economy. Having large amounts of data, as economics does, may be necessary for a field to be considered a science, but it is not sufficient. If the numbers don't have a consistent cause-and-effect relationship with each other, then all one has is a collection of numbers that needs something else, a good theory, to explain any relationship that they may have.

For example, a change in people's price-inflation expectations might affect interest rates, but only to the extent that it changes people's decisions about borrowing, lending, and saving. One can never say that if inflation goes from X% to Y%, it will make interest rates change by a certain amount. It might, but it might not. It depends entirely on the choices people make, which depend on many factors, known and unknown, about their lives and situations at the time.

In other words, economics is a study of human behavior—and nothing else. It is no different from history, sociology, psychology, anthropology, and the other social studies, or social sciences, as they also prefer to be called. The overlay of math and statistics has made economics appear more precise and scientific than these other fields, but it is not. Humans, in individuals or groups, are not molecules or quanta of energy. We are at best only somewhat predictable.

How predictable depends upon what it is we are trying to predict, and how many instances of that behavior we have available for study. With billions of individuals in the world making decisions that mainly affect themselves, there are certain repeating patterns that we see so many times that, for those things, we can say people are highly predictable.

For example, we know that people like bargains and will more likely buy something offered at a discount from its usual price. We also know that, individually or collectively, we will tend to buy a greater quantity at the lower price than at a higher price. Looking at the supply side, farmers with property on which they can grow either corn or soybeans will alter what they plant based partially upon the expected prices of the crops at harvest time, visible to them in futures markets. They will produce more of what is high in price relative to the cost of growing it and less of the crop whose price is low.

These behaviors are the consequence of an obvious component of human nature: when we buy things, we want more for our money, not less, and for a given amount of work we do, we want more pay, not less. It isn't a conjecture or an unproven theory. This seems to be true everywhere and at all times; one could say this has been verified by the observation of the behavior of billions of people, over all recorded history. How supply and demand rise and fall depending upon price is reliable enough that we call it a law, not a hypothesis.

Behavioral economics is a more recently developed branch of the field that sometimes has been able to structure experiments testing many people to see how they actually make certain decisions. These studies have revealed quirks in human thinking, emotions, and decision making which contradict the very naive assumption that people are rational, profit-maximizing calculating machines.

That is OK. Understanding economics means understanding human behavior. If we aren't always rational, then that is reality, and we must take it into account.

The study of the choices that individuals make, the purview of micro as well as behavioral economics, can be done in a scientific manner, in which the experiment can be very clearly defined, large numbers of people can be tested, and if the study is replicated by some other researchers, the results should be like the original study. Not that there aren't many poorly designed studies in those fields, but at least it is possible to assemble enough subjects to do them correctly.

Macro is very different because scientifically valid experiments are not possible. The economists who run all the central banks and advise all the governments in the world may or may not be making good decisions (this book will argue for "not"), but they can never prove that the theories they use are scientifically derived. To demonstrate this, let us compare a classic science experiment with what macroeconomists do.

In grade school, you were probably taught about Galileo's dropping two objects, identical except for weight, off the Leaning Tower of Pisa about 400 years ago, done to test Aristotle's claim that the heavier one would fall faster. There is some question whether the experiment was done as traditionally described, or even done at all, but there is no reason one couldn't replicate it today.

We'll compare that to a hypothetical macro study, which examines the economic effects of a major increase or decrease in tax rates in a country or state, with those of a similar place that did the opposite. Feel free to imagine some other study if you prefer.

Let's look at Galileo's experiment, and answer some questions:

1. When should the study start? As soon as the holder of the weights let them go. Nothing before that, such as the speed by which they were carried up the stairs to the top of the tower, will make any difference, so nothing else should count.

2. Can what is tested be isolated? Yes. Starting with two objects, same size and shape, but different weights (technically mass), the only difference between them is the very thing whose effects are being tested. Either they hit the ground at the same time, or they don't. Since there is nothing else about them that differs in a way that could affect the outcome, the experiment proves whether weight makes any difference. (It does not, proving Aristotle wrong on this point.)

3. When should the study end? That is obvious—when the two weights hit the ground, and someone observes the time of their arrival. It was either the same or different. Anything that happens after that doesn't matter.

4. What is being counted, and is that what should be counted? Nothing is being counted, just observed. Assuming both weights were dropped simultaneously, solving the problem of the non-existence of stopwatches in the late 1500s, the only thing that can and should be counted is whether they hit the ground simultaneously or not.

5. Can the study be replicated? Absolutely. People can drop weights as long as there are humans, weights, and tall buildings or cliffs on Earth, and the results will always be the same. Aliens on a planet a million light years away with stronger or weaker gravity than Earth will get consistent results every time, too.

Compare that to the typical macroeconomic study:

1. When should the study start? There are many different times when one could start collecting data. That is because tax changes and other major fiscal and monetary policy decisions rarely arrive as unexpected bolts from the blue. In the US, they are proposed and politicked for months or years before being passed. The tax bill that is finally passed and signed into law may bear little resemblance to what was originally proposed, due to the various changes made along the way to gather enough votes for passage. Moreover, there is often a gap of many months or even years between passage and when the changes take effect.

Taxpayers, who unsurprisingly prefer to keep their money for their own use rather than hand it over to the government, tend to pay attention to proposed tax changes. The greater the probability that a certain change will be approved, the more people start arranging their affairs to minimize their own tax bite, should the change pass.

For example, if a tax bill signed on September 1 of some year includes a big increase in capital-gains tax rates effective the coming January 1, those with an asset, e.g., a stock or mutual fund, in which they have a big gain, that they were considering selling anyway, will have an incentive to sell it before January while tax rates are still low. Many will do so, resulting in a big jump in capital-gains tax revenues owed to the government in the last few months of the year, and a drop-off in revenue for some period after January 1.

An economist looking at the effect of different tax rates on government revenues will miss the big impact of the change if the study starts on January 1 and ignores all the activity that occurred earlier. The problem is that the extent to which people have made moves prior to the law going into effect is unknowable.

Nor is it clear when people have or will make those moves. True, the new tax law may have been signed September 1, but what about people who followed the legislative process in the news and beat the rush to sell when it appeared obvious to them, perhaps in July or August, that a big increase in capital gains taxes was likely?

And when did it become obvious? Who knows? Some people will have figured it out in advance of others. And how much selling went on early for that reason? Unless the economists doing this study are capable of accurate mass mind reading (not likely), there is no way to know.

Some people and businesses will make changes in their operations to take new tax rates into account early in the process, some much later. That is just in the nature of human beings. We don't all respond to new circumstances at the same pace. If you are an economist looking for the effect of a change, how do you know to what extent people have already responded before you even looked?

You don't. It is all guesswork, and the start date of a macroeconomics study is always just an arbitrary choice by the researcher, which by itself undercuts any claim of "science" behind the results.

2. Can what is tested be isolated? No. Unlike two otherwise identical objects with different weights, every place on Earth and every time in history are different from every other, in ways big and small, that are likely to affect the response to the change in tax rates, or whatever else it is that a macroeconomist tries to test.

Take any two places, even two that, to people who don't live there, seem similar, like Latvia and Estonia, or Kansas and Nebraska. How do they differ?

How about: existing tax rates and what exactly is taxed, employment and welfare policies, size of populations and their ethnic and religious composition, types and cyclical characteristics of their main industries and employers, conditions in the markets to which they export, the financial condition of their banking and shadow-banking systems, the amount and term structure of government debt, and savings and debt levels on the balance sheets of the citizens and companies.

Those at least are some of the things that can be measured or counted. What about more elusive things like laws, regulations, customs, myths, public mood, social trends, political concerns, the influence of local newspapers, TV commentators, popular comedians, artists, musicians and, in the old days, poets, "the unacknowledged legislators of the world"? All these things affect people's behavior.

To the extent that their economies did this or that when tax rates changed for one but not the other, that *might* have been because of the change in tax rates, but it might have been for any of dozens of *other* reasons, or unique combinations of reasons, that easily overwhelm the tax-rate difference. There is no way to know.

The same problem exists when comparing, say, the US at present with the US in the 1950s. So much is different now. In fact, one would have trouble finding anything of importance that isn't considerably different now than it was about seventy years ago.

To some people, the 1950s were a golden age. Factories employed many millions more than they do now, imports had a small share of most markets, labor unions represented a relatively high percentage of the workforce. As may be, but one can't possibly say with a straight face that if today we adopt the tax rates or some other economic policy of the 1950s, that will give us the same outcome now that we experienced then. Too many other things have changed.

Economists are aware that what they are studying is not the only thing that is different about the two or more places or times they are comparing, and some combination of those other things might be the cause of different outcomes. To try to solve that problem, they make use of various statistical techniques, among them being "synthetic control" and "difference-in-differences," methods to try to find places that seem most fair to compare to the one in the "treatment group," e.g., whose tax rate changed, while the other(s) did not.

These techniques make sense if one were thinking of comparing New York City to Yonkers or Hoboken merely because they are nearby. Depending upon what is being studied, it is likely that Chicago or London might be a fairer comparison to New York City. But there is no escaping the fact that any two places, or any two time periods, remain so different in so many aspects, that the "control" city can never be an honest control, identical except for one policy difference that is being studied.

3. When should the study end? There is no way to know the right time for a macroeconomic study to end. People's responses to any change in the economic environment are complex, interactive, and proceed at an unknown pace. If tax rates change, some people will respond quickly, others slowly.

How people react causes changes in the economic environment to which others will then respond, and their responses in turn induce further changes. It could be years, even decades, before all the effects of one initial policy change have finally diminished to near zero. There is never an identifiably correct end point.

Tax rates in particular can take many years to play out. A state slashing income and capital-gains tax rates would likely encourage investments in innovative startup companies versus, say, tax-free municipal bonds. Any effect on business activity and employment might not show up until quite a few years later, when those companies have gotten much bigger, and even then, only if the companies that received the investments happen to be in the same state as the investors.

Economists, naturally, hate that some effects of a cause unfold only over many years. The longer the time between the change in tax rates and the possible effects, the harder it is for anyone to be sure that, say, a change in employment levels was due to a tax change five years earlier and not something else that occurred in the interim. One can guess but never know.

This is a serious flaw in nearly all macro studies, made worse by the fact that changes in economic policies often have one effect initially and the opposite effect thereafter. As we all know from life, sometimes a short-term sacrifice brings a long-term reward, or short-term pleasure brings a longer-term penalty.

Haranguing consumers to spend more, which governments often do early in recessions, might make the economy stronger in the short run, but money that consumers spend sooner is money they can't also spend later. A study that ended quickly might see great results just before the post-spending-binge slump arrives.

If there are any ecologists who are interested in macro, I wonder what they think of such research. Ecologists know that you can't declare DDT to be a great success by counting what it does only to mosquitoes—you must consider its effect on birds, plants, fish, and many other creatures where the negative effects didn't show up until many years later. The world hadn't turned pro-malaria when it banned or sharply reduced the use of DDT; it did so because DDT's short-term beneficial effects on one problem were seen as being overwhelmed by other long-term problems it created.

Economists are normal people who would like to better their positions in the world, just like anyone else. They need to publish papers to advance their academic careers. Those who wait many years, if necessary, to examine the full effects of some policy change before writing a paper, are not going to publish many papers and are therefore less likely to get tenure. Also, to the extent that the longer-term effects of whatever they are studying mitigate or reverse the short-term effects, as happens frequently, that makes the conclusions of the research more ambiguous and less likely to be cited in papers by other economists looking for support for their viewpoint.

Not surprisingly, this creates great pressure for economists to focus on short-term results and end their studies quickly. One can be sympathetic to the plight of the researcher. However, let's not pretend that this is real science, whose purpose ought to be an understanding of the workings of cause and effect in the real world, no matter how long it takes for those forces to unfold.

4. What is being counted, and is that what should be counted? This depends on the purpose of the study. Often the point is to prove that a certain economic policy—e.g., high or low taxes, or perhaps high of one kind plus low of some other kind—is the best policy to produce a strong economy, as measured by change in GDP or one of its variants.

GDP is the standard measure of the strength of an economy, and, as will be discussed ahead, a severely flawed one. Even if one accepts GDP as a legitimate measure of economic strength, it is an aggregate measure, one that produces only one reading for the entire economy and covers up underlying crosscurrents.

The "Cash for Clunkers" program in 2009 is a good example. Its purpose was to subsidize the purchase of new cars with better mileage and lower emissions, but by removing and destroying all the clunkers that got turned in, the program caused a shortage of the only kind of cars most poor people could afford, which pushed their prices higher.

The program turned out to be a flop for stimulating the economy: it succeeded in getting people to buy cars sooner, but then it caused a big slump in demand when it ended, at a great cost for useless results. Should we favor an economic policy that gives a temporary boost to GDP at the cost of making the poor even poorer? We are not talking poorer relative to the middle or upper classes; this was a reduction of standard of living in absolute terms for a significant number of people who most needed the money.

Shouldn't economists who advocate such a policy be required to justify why one measurable result, change in GDP, should count, and another measurable result, the living standards of the poor, should not? Yes, but they never do. As with DDT, to be a real science, macroeconomics must consider all the effects of a given cause, no matter how long they take to play out, and not just cherry-pick some and ignore others.

5. Can the study be replicated? In macro, no studies can ever be more than vaguely replicated. The unique characteristics of every place and time prevents an exact duplication.

The most one can say about the results of any given macro study is that whatever happened, that was what happened at that particular place and time. One can't say more than that. Maybe it would happen again in seemingly similar situations, or maybe not. Humans are not inanimate weights that always provide a predictable response to a given stimulus.

There truly aren't enough countries on Earth, and/or time periods with decent records of the local economy, to find the hundreds of samples needed to make the results statistically legitimate. We wouldn't conclude that a tossed coin will always turn heads up if that is what it does on two flips in a row, but that is exactly how macroeconomists conclude that they have "proven" that some economic policy will or will not produce a certain outcome.

In 2015, two brave Fed economists, Andrew Chang and Phillip Li, attempted to replicate the results of 67 papers published in 13 different economics journals. Even with help from the authors of the papers, less than half of them could be replicated. They weren't checking replication in the broadest sense of finding some different places or times, versus what was in the original paper, and seeing if what was supposedly proven by the original paper also applied. These papers couldn't even self-replicate, in that running the data from a paper through the very model in the same paper didn't achieve the same results.

In a real science, professors who put out such shoddy work would be in disgrace; in economics, this is just business as usual.

Fine, who cares if a certain monetary policy in Country X really worked as well or poorly as the author of the paper claims? No one should care, but economists have been given the clout to impose their preferred policies on the rest of us, and they base many of them on these studies, so we should be more than concerned—we should be astonished and alarmed.

Prof. John Ioannidis of Stanford is probably the most renowned expert on the statistics of research studies. He has long specialized in medical research, where he has shown that a large percentage of studies don't prove what they claim. That is due to a variety of errors, the most common one being that the study is "underpowered," in that the sample size is too small to be sure the results are identifying a real difference as opposed to chance. Sometimes the difference between what is studied and the control sample wasn't very large, or the statistical significance test was not strict enough.

In 2017, he examined economics studies, and co-published a paper entitled *The Power of Bias in Economics Research*. He and his team evaluated 159 meta-studies that combined the results of 6730 primary studies. Even he was shocked to discover how bad they all were. He found 89.5% of them to not prove what they claim because they were underpowered.

And that was without being tough, since Ioannidis allowed them a less-strict test of statistical significance than he felt they should have employed. There are other approaches to measuring power which he prefers that, had he used them, would have shown that only 1.9% to 6.5% of papers produced valid results. It gets even worse when one considers that the average was brought up by the inclusion of papers on micro, where it is much easier to assemble a large-enough sample size.

Keep in mind that these were 159 meta-studies, analyses which combine multiple small studies to increase their statistical power. Each of the 6730 underlying primary studies were even more underpowered and, therefore, even more likely to be worthless.

That is macro today. It resembles objective science just enough to seemingly justify the massive power in society we give economists, yet the alleged proofs they offer come from underpowered studies that are designed to produce a quickly publishable paper, while intentionally ignoring the complexities of how the economy actually operates.

If macro is not a science, then this is the reality: We are being ruled by a self-selecting group of people who may have seemingly plausible theories, but not ones that necessarily give us better results than other theories that endorse completely different policies. We shouldn't assume that these powerful economists know what they are doing, just because they say, with the greatest of sincerity, that they do.

That isn't to say that many macroeconomists may not be right about many things and may have good advice to offer. So do political science and history professors, whose advice our elected leaders may or may not take. We don't give them the right to impose their ideas on us as we allow economists to do.

In case you think this is sparring with the straw man of my hypothetical macroeconomic study, and that real economics experiments don't make all those fundamental errors, please read the *Appendix*, about one of the most famous economics studies of the last several decades, the Card-Krueger 1993 study of minimum wages that compared employment in Pennsylvania and New Jersey after one of the states raised the minimum wage, and the other didn't.

The study was not technically macro, in that it didn't cover interest rates or fiscal policy. That meant that it had a better chance to be constructed in a way that satisfies the requirements of the scientific method. With 50 US states, each with its own occasionally changing policy on minimum wages, it was conceivable that, unlike nearly all macro studies, there might be enough good data available to have a chance of statistical validity.

Nevertheless, the study fails every question asked above and demonstrates other critical flaws not yet mentioned. These errors are so endemic in economics papers that almost nobody notices them. The Card-Krueger study has been cited in more than 4000 other papers to date, and Prof. Card recently was awarded an economics Nobel Prize for this and other labor studies.

Perhaps you don't care whether economists can prove that certain policies are correct in a statistically legitimate sense. Maybe you accept that they can't be *proven* but believe they might be right *anyway*. There are things in life we strongly believe to be true but could never prove if required. Perhaps macro is one of those.

My objection to that view is that even being very generous in our evaluation of the performance of the most powerful macroeconomists, they still seem to have no idea what they are doing.

The members of the Fed Board, aided by the more than 400 PhD economists that they employ and the hundreds more to whom they offer consulting jobs, can certainly be considered at the very top of the economics profession. If the theories are even approximately correct, they should be reasonably good forecasters of economic trends. While they can't be expected to get things exactly correct, they should at least be able to predict trends in a very crude way, one would think, such as "up a little" or "up a lot" or "down a little" or "down a lot."

Unfortunately, they rarely come close except when making the default prediction that the future will be about the same as today. Here are quotes from speeches of Ben Bernanke, member of the Board of the Fed from 2002 and Chair from 2006 to 2014, and 2022 Nobel Prize winner:

"We've never had a decline in house prices on a nationwide basis. So, what I think what is more likely is that house prices will slow, maybe stabilize, might slow consumption spending a bit. I don't think it's gonna drive the economy too far from its full-employment path, though." (July 2005)

"With respect to their safety, derivatives, for the most part, are traded among very sophisticated financial institutions and individuals who have considerable incentive to understand them and to use them properly." (November 2005)

"Housing markets are cooling a bit. Our expectation is that the decline in activity or the slowing in activity will be moderate, that house prices will probably continue to rise." (February 2006)

"At this juncture, however, the impact on the broader economy and financial markets of the problems in the subprime market seems likely to be contained. In particular, mortgages to prime borrowers and fixed-rate mortgages to all classes of borrowers continue to perform well, with low rates of delinquency." (March 2007)

No hint that he noticed what any house buyer or renter of the time could have told him, that houses were way too expensive in most markets relative to the median incomes of those who might buy them for themselves, and also overpriced, based upon the rents that they were likely to fetch, for houses to be an attractive purchase to investors. Nor is there any hint that he was even slightly aware that, were house prices to decline, the result would be the insolvency of many over-leveraged banks who held mortgage paper as investments.

To generalize, one can earn a PhD in economics from the finest institution—and know nothing at all about business. Yes, elite economists, going from academia to working the revolving door between powerful political/Fed positions and overpaid consulting jobs at major Wall St. firms, are technically in the private sector half the time. But have they ever run a real business, dealing with financially stressed customers, rising labor and material costs, and a bank that could pull the plug on them at the slightest misstep? No.

Here is the next Fed Chair, Janet Yellen, in comments in late 2007, even as major banks and financial outfits were on the brink of collapse: *"One reason that risk premiums may be low is precisely because the environment is less risky . . . The Fed has long focused on ensuring that banks hold adequate capital and that they carefully monitor and manage risks. As a consequence, banks are well-positioned to weather the financial turmoil."*

More recently, even as inflation ramped up and was still at least a year and many percentage points from its peak, she said, *"I don't believe that inflation will be an issue . . . My judgment right now is that the recent inflation that we have seen will be temporary. It's not something that's endemic."* (May 2021)

As late as June 16, 2021, as inflation was starting to take off around the globe, the Fed continued to believe that there was no serious threat of inflation. The "dot plot" in the Fed's news release that day, in which the ten board-member economists on the Federal Open Market Committee made predictions of where they thought various indicators would be in the near future, wasn't remotely close to what actually happened.

It is astounding that nobody seems bothered by this. True, it isn't easy to predict the economy. The best our leading economists can do is make a guess, hoping they are right. To the extent that the economy did finally do what Fed economists wanted for many years, produce sharply higher inflation, it wasn't too long before even they realized they should not have wanted that.

Macroeconomists are such advanced scholars that they forget what is taught in the earliest weeks of any introductory micro course. Prices reflect the balance of supply and demand. When, as took place in the US, the government runs a deficit of more than $3.1 trillion in 2020, $2.7 T in 2021, $1.4T in 2022, and something very large projected for 2023, that adds an enormous amount of dollars to the economy.

Many of those dollars were stimulus debit cards given out to nearly everyone, available to be spent on goods and services. At the same time, because of the lockdowns, caution on the part of many workers, and the need of workers to stay home with their kids due to needlessly closed schools, the supply of goods and services were constrained.

When demand rises while supply shrinks, prices will rise, as anyone who takes the first couple weeks of a micro course would know. This should not have been a surprise, yet brilliant, Nobel

Prize-winning economists, whose whims affect the lives of hundreds of millions of people in the US alone, seem to have forgotten it.

While no macroeconomic theory can be proven correct, and like religion can be believed or not as each person chooses, that does not mean that they are equally valid. A correct economic theory must be consistent with human nature and recognize the constraints of reality, not based on wishful or magical thinking. Whether over time a society gets wealthier or impoverished absolutely depends on it.

CHAPTER 2

THE IMAGINARY LIQUIDITY TRAP

• • •

WHY HAVE WE GIVEN economists such immense policy-making power? And why do they place so much weight on what they suppose the public's inflation expectations to be?

The two questions are closely connected by way of Keynes and his Liquidity Trap concept. This idea is central to mainstream macro. It is the prime self-justification for the power that leading macroeconomists have achieved and the policies they favor.

The notion was spawned entirely in Keynes's imagination and thereafter taken on faith by most economists without a shred of proof or even any evidence that it might be valid. Had economists thought about it carefully, they might have noticed that it contradicts one of the most established laws of economics, the law of demand: people buy more of something at a lower price than at a higher price. In terms of the implications for economists, though, one can see the appeal.

The claim is that capitalism is not just unstable, but worse, has a natural tendency to end up in a permanent depression because it will be stuck in a trap, the Liquidity Trap, unless the government and Fed rescue it through a combination of lower interest rates and deficit spending.

The interest-rate decrease is a minor part of the rescue operation because interest rates typically drop during recessions anyway, whether the Fed does anything or not. Companies and individuals become cautious and pay down debt. Demand for new loans by those who are creditworthy fall. Interest rates being prices, the reduced demand for capital pushes them down.

The main part of the rescue operation is to be played by increased government spending to make up for allegedly insufficient aggregate demand. Keynes allowed that cutting taxes to create a government deficit might have the same effect as keeping taxes higher while spending more than came in, but he argued the latter course would be better because there was too much risk that people would save their gain from lower taxes rather than spending it immediately.

The economy's fall into a Liquidity Trap begins when, for whatever reasons, people decide that they want to save more money, i.e., they want to hold more liquid assets, hence the name. Each person cuts their spending to increase their cash balance, but by doing so, their reduction in spending hurts business conditions. Because every business has some share of costs that are fixed and can't be reduced when revenues are weak, that leads to a disproportionately large drop in profits.

Business may try to restore profits in a variety of ways that are all bad for the economy—layoffs, cutting workers' wages and overtime, and selling inventory at steep discounts to raise more cash. Weak companies that were barely profitable even in good times, or that have excessive debt, go under, creating more unemployed people and cuts in spending.

So far there is nothing objectionable about that description of the early phase of a steep recession. Recessions can start for many reasons. The specifics may vary, but what they have in common is that humans are human, and therefore make mistakes and bad predictions, which, at some point, get noticed, forcing retrenchment.

Perhaps too many businesses enter a promising market and collectively add more capacity than demand can support. Or consumers are too optimistic about their future incomes, spend too heavily, and take on too much debt; then they slash spending to pay it down. Or external changes overturn budget plans, as we saw in 2021-22 as soaring food and energy costs shrank people's ability to buy other things.

Few businesses have the cash to withstand severe losses. In a recession, excess inventory must be sold off at a big discount if need be, to raise cash, and production halted. Resources of various kinds, such as workers, factories, and equipment, must become idle for a while until consumers replenish their cash and confidence, and entrepreneurs and businesses think of new products and services that will get them spending again. Then the resources can be redeployed to produce that output.

Where Keynes parted from reality was his claim that downward trends are inherently self-reinforcing and cannot be stopped from leading to a steep and very long-lasting depression, unless there is extraordinary government action to turn things around. Not true.

The automatic mechanism that supposedly makes things get steadily worse with no reversal is an alleged characteristic of human nature that Keynes claimed is extremely powerful. In reality, this human characteristic is not only not powerful, it does not even exist.

Keynes believed that people have an intense aversion, so strong that it dominates all other considerations, to buying anything whose price they think may drop in the future, no matter how much we might want it, and no matter how trivial its potential price drop is relative to our net worth.

In Keynes' worldview, seeing prices drop makes people stop buying. That makes businesses even more desperate to unload inventory, so prices drop some more, people buy even less, and so on and so on, until presumably the last billionaires on Earth die starving in the street, rather than buying and eating a few potatoes, because they fear that potato prices a year later might be a few pennies cheaper.

Of course, the idea is utter nonsense, and it conflicts with the most proven principle of micro, the law of demand. The law states the obvious, that people prefer discounts and are more likely to buy something at a low price than a high price. The Liquidity Trap concept claims the opposite, which is why it is wrong.

Yes, sometimes people do postpone buying something in anticipation of lower prices, but primarily under only two circumstances. Very large purchases such as a house or car can have a big effect on personal finances, so we will usually wait if we believe the seller will cut the price.

Also, if a product, even an inexpensive one, is not needed immediately and will soon be on sale, e.g., right after Christmas, many will hold off buying. If there is no rush to buy a T-shirt that isn't meant to be a present, and won't be worn until the weather warms up, why not wait a week or so and save 25%?

Other than that, when prices are soft, price expectations are a very minor factor compared to the very many other things that people consider when deciding whether to buy something. Put another way, price drops are a consequence of a recession, not a cause of one.

During periods of strong inflation, the psychology is different. People see their money losing value at a rapid pace and buy whatever they can before its price gets so high that they can no longer afford it. In countries undergoing hyperinflation, people will stock up on staples they never expect to use or need themselves, but which they believe are a better store of value than the country's rapidly devaluing currency.

With the exceptions noted above, most people do not care about future prices provided they are not rising swiftly. Do you own a computer, a tablet, a cell phone, or a TV? Almost everyone in a developed country owns some or all of those. When you bought these devices, were you aware that if you waited a year, those for sale at that time would be more powerful, faster, have more features and probably sell at the current price or lower? I'll bet you were not only aware of that but also knew it with complete certainty. Yet you bought that device anyway, because you did not care about the price a year later.

What happened was that you made the same kind of decision that you do multiple times every day. You asked yourself, *Would I rather have this computer today or hold onto the money or credit that the computer would cost?* If you chose to buy the computer, you did so because you felt the benefit to you over the next year would be worth spending the money now, rather than waiting a year to get more computer per dollar spent, at the cost of not having use of a new computer until then.

For electronic devices there is no uncertainty about future prices. Unless we run into some extreme price inflation situation where costs are soaring, we can be sure that prices will keep dropping. This has been the case since they were invented more than 70 years ago. Certainly, since computers got cheap enough to become a consumer and small-business product in about 1980, the rate of decline in prices has been intense. A US Bureau of Labor Statistics (BLS) publication stated that the quality adjustment for the microprocessor segment of the Producer Price Index determined that prices for a given quality level during the 2000-09 period declined 33.66% per year. The complete computer, of which the microprocessor is the most expensive component, may not have plummeted quite so much, and it is unclear how the BLS handled things in the 20 years before 2000, or since 2009, but that is still a stupendous rate of decline.

If Keynes were correct that people won't buy something whose price looks like it might decline, nobody would ever have bought a computer, cell phone, or tablet. Yet nearly everyone has. And if people don't fear buying products whose prices are guaranteed to keep dropping, why would they hold back buying products where the future price is either unknown or, if expected to be weak, might only be a few percent lower than today's price? Would you hold off buying something you really want today because you think its price a year from now might be 2% lower? I doubt it.

What actually happens when the country goes into a recession? Why do recessions never lead to any kind of trap from which the economy cannot escape on its own? What is the self-governing mechanism in a free-market system that always turns the economy back up without either extra government spending or monetary manipulation?

The early stages of a recession are indeed scary because it isn't yet known how bad things will get and what will turn things around. Perhaps you previously thought your job was safe, but now that isn't so certain. You hear of neighbors and relatives losing their jobs. Times had been very good, and you had been spending as if that would be permanent. Now you realize you'll need more savings and less debt if you or your spouse get laid off. Even if that doesn't happen, you may want to make some loans to relatives who have lost their jobs, and you'll need money for that.

So you cut your spending, and yes, that does make the recession worse for others, but you worry about yourself and your family first. However, the free market has built-in, powerful mechanisms that always turn that around, just not instantaneously. Some things must happen first.

Despite their fears, most people do not get fired. If we take the 1930s Depression as an extreme example of bad economy, at its worst, unemployment in the US peaked at 25% for one month in 1933. That meant that even then 75% of the workforce did not lose their jobs. Yes, some of them had their pay cut, and factory workers lost lucrative overtime pay, but most people's incomes were unchanged or down slightly at most. In less dire economic downturns, unemployment is not as bad. The post-housing-bubble collapse in the US, a very severe one, saw the rate peak at only 10% in 2009, meaning 90% retained their jobs. There are also many people whose income does not depend on their current job, such as retirees collecting pensions and those with disability income.

The unemployed get benefits that are less than 100% of their working income, but still something. Yes, unemployment benefits are government-paid assistance, rather than some natural feature of a free market, but one's employer must pay federal and state taxes on payrolls to provide the money that later gets paid out to the unemployed. If the government were not in the business of insuring against unemployment, the odds are high that some insurance companies would be offering that service, and employers would sign up to help them recruit workers who want that backup.

In other words, even in the steepest part of a recession, most people have continuing income, and most of them will keep spending below that level, pay down debt, and build up savings. Meanwhile, lower prices caused by the recession makes those savings worth more, and it takes a smaller percentage of one's savings to satisfy one's desires for goods and services than before the recession, when savings were lower and prices higher.

The decision process about whether to buy something is always the same, regardless of whether the economy is in a boom, a bust, or somewhere in between. People ask themselves, *Will I be happier buying that car, computer, vacation, or whatever, or will I be happier not buying it and holding onto the cash or credit instead?* The question is always the same; the answer typically changes over the business cycle.

Early in a recession, when fear is high, "not buy" has the edge. After it becomes clearer that one's employer isn't going under, that the jobs of those not laid off by then are safe, and that the months of choosing not to buy things has built up one's cash to the point that the benefit of having even more cash seems diminished, then attitudes change. People start buying again, companies start hiring to serve the rising demand, and the economy turns up again.

This process—initial fear causing a spending reduction, followed by increases in cash balances combined with price reductions that make people feel richer, equals lower fear and a higher inclination to spend—we'll call the *Recession Reversal Mechanism*.

The factor that Keynes thinks will keep consumers frightened until their dying day, the fact that there is downward pressure on prices early in a recession, is something whose role is the exact opposite of what he claims. The lower prices go, the greater in terms of purchasing power any given amount of savings becomes. Deflation makes anyone with savings genuinely richer, and people who feel rich buy more than those who feel poor.

The imaginary Liquidity Trap is connected to Keynes's concept called the Paradox of Thrift. Each person may try to save more, but by making a recession worse, their actions cause more people to get laid off or have their wages cut. The total amount of savings in society therefore drops rather than increases.

The Keynesian solution for this is for the government to pressure people to spend more. If that doesn't work, which it rarely does early in recessions, the government's job should be to spend much more to overrule its citizens' desires to spend less. Even if this strategy made for a stronger economy, it can't be denied that, by intentionally thwarting the will of the people, it is anti-democratic.

Economists might argue that by creating a stronger economy, the result will eventually be an increase in the total of savings, so economists really are giving people what they want, only collectively, since the Paradox of Thrift prevents people from accomplishing their goals individually.

That might be plausible if the intent of economists was really to do what people want at that time, i.e., to pay down their debts and increase their total savings. But that isn't their intent. According to Keynes, more savings are never good for the economy, unless they are immediately employed in spending of some kind, any kind. Keynesians accuse savings of being "idle resources" that must be galvanized into immediate action, even if nobody can yet figure out anything sensible to do with them.

It is never entirely clear to businesses what will be a good investment even when the economy is fine. When it is weak, business managers and entrepreneurs, the ones who start projects that use saved capital, are even more uncertain about when the recession will end and what the public will want to buy when it does end. A major cause of every recession is that what had been profitable businesses and occupations are no longer so, and it takes a while for entrepreneurs to figure out some new way to deploy people, capital, and other resources that will be profitable again.

There was a severe worldwide recession soon after World War One (WW1) not long before Keynes developed his theory. The Fed and government did the opposite of what Keynesians subsequently recommended. Interest rates went up during the recession, not down, as businesses needed capital to invest in machinery to turn out civilian instead of military goods. The government slashed its spending as part of military demobilization. Nevertheless, the recession ended quickly on its own and set the stage for the strong Roaring Twenties economy. Laying off soldiers made them temporarily idle but very available to produce the consumer output that they and their fellow soldiers wanted as they resumed their civilian lives.

Had the government unwisely followed what would later become macro orthodoxy and kept all those soldiers on the payroll to maintain aggregate demand, it would have prevented the economy from turning sharply higher. Taxes would have had to stay at high wartime levels to pay their salaries. The populace would be further harmed by the continuation of the high wartime inflation since the soldiers would not be producing the consumer goods and services that they and everyone else wanted. That is exactly what we did in 2020-22, when the government sent out massive stimulus checks while output was restricted, causing higher prices.

If, in fact, there is no such a thing as a Liquidity Trap, just occasional time periods where people build up cash before later spending it, then how does that affect mainstream macro, which is still strongly rooted in Keynesian theory? Well, it destroys the justification for what the government and the Fed do to supposedly help the economy.

The leading macroeconomists are adamant on this point: when the public is not spending as much money as economists think they should, the government should spend more money to make up the shortfall. Also, the central bank should cut interest rates to reduce the incentive for people to save rather than spend. Once those alleged liquidity hoarders start spending again, then the "pump has been primed" and "the economy will reach escape velocity," to repeat some common cliches. The economy will supposedly continue up on its own without the need for further government assistance, at least until the next time it mysteriously gets stuck in the trap and needs powerful economists to rescue it.

Keynes himself felt that government deficit spending during recessions should be balanced out by lower government spending or higher taxes to create surpluses when the economy is strong. His followers today, economists and certainly the politicians, don't like the second part. They believe that there are two excellent times for the government to run surpluses—in the past, and in the future. Now, however, whenever "now" happens to be, is never the right time.

Government stimulus spending is also intended to push those who have been hoarding money into spending more. Who are these evildoers who have been messing up the economy by refusing to spend their savings? Well, everybody who gets worried that they have been spending too much for what has become changed circumstances and who try to pay off some debt and build up some cash, are the public enemies in question.

But one can narrow the list of suspects by thinking about their levels of wealth and income. Without getting too specific about where to draw the line, let's divide the country into three broad classes—the poor, the rich, and the middle class. Who is piling up savings because they supposedly fear lower prices, which makes prices spiral downward, thereby putting us in a Liquidity Trap?

We know the poor and at least some of the middle classes aren't doing so, because they spend almost every penny by their next paycheck. Surveys repeatedly show that about half the country has either no savings of any kind, or something fairly minimal.

We know the rich aren't afraid to spend if they decide they want something, deflation be damned. A wealthy Keynesian friend back during the long post-housing-bubble recession, when the official US inflation figures were hovering near 0% with occasional dips into negative territory, was planning to put on a fancy wedding for his child. I asked him whether, given figures showing slight deflation, he had tried to talk the young couple into postponing their wedding a year so that he could save 1% or so.

As one would expect, he laughed. He had more than enough money, his child wanted to get married then, and he wanted the event to happen soon so that they could move on to the important business of creating grandchildren. That was much more important to him and his family than a hypothetical savings of what to him was a trivial sum.

Just as anyone who ever bought a computer despite knowing that the price would soon drop, he did not care if the price in the future was likely to be lower. When we eliminate the rich, the poor, and much of the middle class, the only people left who supposedly are causing the entire world to be caught in a Liquidity Trap are a small minority, some part of the middle class.

This group, probably a single-digit percent of the population, includes those who don't have to spend 100% of their income to maintain a certain lifestyle. They also can't spend in a carefree manner like those with great income or wealth. This small group of culprits can choose to spend or save. Evidently, when we are in a Liquidity Trap, they are supposedly stupefied by their terror of deflation, so all they want to do is hoard their money and not spend it.

The self-assigned mission of the Fed is to push interest rates down to punish them for saving, even if that forces retirees to move their savings from insured accounts at banks to risky investments to maintain their income. The mission of the other branches of government is to borrow and spend wildly on all kinds of waste, if need be, to increase price inflation to cure these hoarders of their deflation psychology. That is supposed to be a good thing, even as the inflation lowers the standard of living of the least wealthy.

If the small amount of extra savings that this segment of the middle class has accumulated is somehow the cause of such huge damage to the world economy as to require a response that is so damaging to so many others, isn't there a better solution? One that doesn't involve the massive waste of resources and buildup of burdensome debt that Keynesian deficit spending causes?

Yes, and the free market—without any government or central-bank involvement—provides that solution. It is called "the passage of time."

Whenever this evil middle-class person who could spend but instead saves, gets their paycheck and doesn't spend all of it, their savings balance goes up. As the *Recession Reversal Mechanism* dictates, the combination of higher savings and discount prices make purchases less costly and more attractive, so their bias will switch from saving to buying. Others will follow suit, employment will rise to serve higher demand, and the problem of a weak economy is solved.

Another reason to expect free markets to right themselves naturally is that they have been around for a good 5000 years. There is evidence of extensive trading networks going back to the Bronze Age before or around 3000 B.C.E. Was the world economy really stuck in a depression for 5000 years until Keynes came along?

To summarize, the imaginary Liquidity Trap is just another part of Keynesian theory that appears very scientific looking, with competing theories of IS-LM curves (don't ask) and other theoretical folderol but is completely meaningless as a concept to explain how actual human beings make decisions in the real world.

This is far from the only thing that Keynes and his followers get wrong. It is, however, most beloved by economists because it is the concept that got them into bed with politicians, who granted them their immense power over our lives, and the path to personal wealth that power always provides. Avoiding or escaping the dreaded

Liquidity Trap is what provides politicians with the theoretical cover to take other people's money and spend it in ways that benefit themselves and their cronies, allegedly to help the economy.

This makes the government and the Fed devoted employers of macroeconomists and followers of their nostrums. That's great for politicians, their pals, and economists but not for anyone else.

Macroeconomists regularly claim that their theories are built upon a base of microeconomics. That is false. The Liquidity Trap concept, to which they owe their power and wealth, directly contradicts the proven laws of supply and demand and of diminishing returns. Without the Liquidity Trap concept, the case for economists having power any greater than the right to write occasional op-eds, collapses.

CHAPTER 3

THE BAD OLD DAYS

· · ·

IT IS AMAZING HOW many educated people believe that active management of the free market by economists and self-serving government administrators and politicians is the safe way for an economy to operate, and that letting the self-regulating forces in free markets that keep everything in balance and moving forward is some kind of crazy thing, never tried, on which it is too dangerous to take a chance.

Perhaps it reflects the poor job the biased public-school systems do teaching history in general, let alone economic history. In their effort to maintain their power over society, politicians, administrators, economists, and teachers are happy to spread fairy tales about the bad old days before they had so much power.

Their story starts out with evil capitalists exploiting workers by giving them bad jobs at low pay while the capitalists got rich. Fortunately, the workers were saved by dedicated union organizers and the kindly politicians of the Progressive Era through the New Deal, who took control of the government and made things right.

Our politicians today claim they continue in that tradition. If it weren't for a government that cared deeply for the little guy, starting from childhood, they maintain we would all be working long hours per week in dirty, dangerous factories, with no weekends off, and we would live in tenements with a woman working a spinning wheel in the kitchen so we could afford scraps of bread to eat, while breathing polluted air and drinking filthy water.

In fact, any society's standard of living, working conditions, and incomes are all a function of the society's economic productivity. Being able to produce output that others want to buy is what creates income. If the managers and workforce of a society cannot produce much of value to others, the standard of living will necessarily be low.

The value of any individual's output depends on a variety of factors, such as whether their skills allow them to produce output that others want, but a major factor is how much capital is available to magnify those skills.

When cars started replacing horses, an old-time, highly skilled blacksmith may have been able to make parts by hand that could possibly have gone into an early automobile, but at such a slow pace and with such inconsistent quality that few cars would ever have been made, would not have worked well, and would have been astronomically expensive. Workers in a car factory today, although lacking the artisanal skills of blacksmiths of yore, work with numerically controlled machine tools, robots that can lift thousands of pounds, conveyors, and other equipment that allows each one to produce output worth many times more, even adjusting for inflation, than what the blacksmiths could have produced. As a result, they get paid much more, and, because the price of everything made with heavy capital input is so much lower than if they were handmade by artisans, their living standard dwarfs that of the old blacksmiths.

Before the industrial revolution, productivity and therefore pay was extremely low because capital intensity was minimal. Most income went toward maintaining subsistence, leaving people with very little to save and invest in tools that would make them more productive.

Politicians and unions can ask or demand whatever they want, but what a business can afford is limited by the value of its output. In the 1800s, when all these horrible conditions that the forward-thinking politicians supposedly fixed were universal, factory productivity in the US was very low. Machinery was slow and unreliable, and even the richest customers were very poor by today's standards and not able to pay much for output.

Nevertheless, factories were more automated than the typical farm. When job applicants flocked to the early New England factories that used fast-moving rivers for power, it was because the capital invested in the factory and its machinery made each worker more productive. That allowed them to be paid more than the value they could add at their struggling subsistence farms, where, speaking of child labor, even toddlers had tasks.

If some kindly politicians in the 1840s had proposed a law that would make child labor or more than 40-hour workweeks illegal and required that all companies provide two weeks' paid vacation, sick pay, a pension contribution, and other now-common benefits for their workers, the politicians would have been laughed out of office.

No business then could possibly have provided those things without going under. Their costs would have mandated prices so high that nobody could afford to buy their output. Most consumers at the time had low incomes and were extremely frugal. If the cost of providing better pay, benefits, and working conditions 200 years ago made a company's output even a tiny amount more expensive than the competition's, it would lose most of its customers.

Something similar would be the response today if a politician decided that it was time for the government to end poverty by requiring all workers be paid at least $1000 per hour. It would be insane; people cannot be paid more than the value of their output, or their employers would go broke.

Once there was enough capital invested, making worker productivity higher, workers could be paid more. Better-paid parents then were no more likely to need the trivial additional income from sending their kids to a factory to do low-paid, unskilled labor than they do today.

It was only **after** child labor nearly disappeared that laws were passed to forbid it. It was **after** factories could make good money by attracting skilled workers with a promise of no more than a 40-hour week with weekends off, that such a workweek became common. Labor laws protecting the worker against this or that alleged exploitation are never passed until after the practice has mostly disappeared due to rising productivity, with workers compensated accordingly;

otherwise, the workers themselves would be against it because their employers would go under, and they'd lose their jobs.

Once a labor practice that exists only because of low productivity diminishes sharply in the marketplace, then productive and successful businesses themselves want the practice banned. Companies are always in favor of marginal competitors being forced out of business. That's the sort of help from politicians they expect for their campaign contributions.

CEOs of big companies could get in trouble if they burned down smaller competitors' factories, but by encouraging the government to impose costs on all employers that make the marginal ones unviable, well, that is not only good business for big companies, but their CEOs can signal their personal virtue to the community for protecting competitors' workers out of their jobs.

We see the same thing today with producers of "green" energy all in favor of shutting down their fossil-fuel competition, only because they want to save the planet, naturally.

Tough labor conditions, as well as companies that pollute air and water, are characteristic of poor countries. Most of the poorest countries in the world still have child labor, unsafe factories, and rampant pollution. Productivity is so low that there is no way for a family to have food on the table unless the kids also work.

It isn't that their business owners or politicians are especially greedy and don't care about anything except their bank accounts, any more than anyone else in the world. No government of a poor country is going to cause all the employers to go bankrupt, which is what would happen if they tried to operate with US environmental and labor standards.

Instead of the US demanding they behave like we do without the money to afford it, we should encourage the kind of free-market-oriented policies that have made dozens of other countries rise from poverty elsewhere in the world. In every case, as their society gains wealth due to business investment, workers get higher pay and benefits because their higher productivity allows their employer to pay them more and still profit. In fact, higher productivity **forces** employers to pay more to retain workers, because, otherwise, competitors who can pay more and still profit will pirate them. Similarly, people in a wealthy country can demand stricter pollution laws and get them without wiping out employers.

The problem with fairy-tale thinking is that it makes people believe that the government is a force for good, run by benevolent, wise people who have their interests at heart. In reality, the government is run for and populated by normal people, no more or less self-interested than anyone else. Being in the government puts them in a different position than people in the private sector, who need to find volunteers to be their customers, employers, and employees, and who compete with others to offer those potential volunteers more attractive deals to get them to sign up for those roles. Volunteers isn't a word used to describe taxpayers.

No doubt, politicians at least start out intending to be public servants, but needing funds to win elections to keep their jobs, their focus over time turns toward serving friendly entities and groups instead. Businesses, their owners, and managers are a regular source of campaign contributions. Politicians are not going to enact any laws that will turn donors against them or force out of business the companies that employ many voters.

Another fairy tale told by politicians and economists: we are much better off with major decisions about the economy in their hands, because now the economy is so much more stable, without the booms and busts that existed before the creation of the Fed in 1913. How can one blame the Fed for mismanagement when there were plenty of financial crises and depressions before it took over?

There were indeed plenty of recessions in the 1800s and the pre-Fed 1900s, but, in general, they were short, localized, and far less intense than one would think, given what we have experienced since the Fed, starting in the late 1920s, created very large-scale bubbles and consequent busts.

One period, the five years after the Panic of 1873, was called "a depression" by economists who assume that steep price deflation must equal a depression. It was actually a period of decent growth, as the price inflation from the Civil War and its aftermath got reversed, and the explosion of new railroads slashed transportation costs. People who previously could never hope to visit relatives who moved away could now get there quickly on the trains, reducing demand for some of what they bought previously, causing unemployment the way every major shift in demand does.

Factories could be much bigger and more efficient, since the trains let them serve distant markets. The resulting economies of scale cut costs and created price wars, making deflation "worse" in terms of the statistics, which really means better for the living standards of consumers, who could then buy what they wanted more cheaply, leaving them more money for other purchases or savings.

There are good reasons why business cycles pre-Fed ought to have been much more volatile than those of the 20th century and beyond. The non-agriculture part of the economy in the 1800s was overwhelmingly oriented toward manufacturing. A person in the 1800s would have trouble imagining how we live today, where even many poor people in the US have more stuff than they can fit into their homes, which themselves are huge by past standards. We currently have a self-storage industry offering about two billion square feet of space to deal with the overflow, not to mention the vast amounts of reasonably good stuff that gets tossed into landfills rather than refurbished or repaired.

In the 1800s, most people desperately needed the same stuff of which we have too much—furniture, lamps, beds, books, dishes, etc. Someone living back then, with a bit of savings, might use that money to buy a soup bowl or a pen, or, if they saved a lot, a second bed so the kids could share the bed and not sleep on the floor. Everyone needed manufactured goods. Compare that to today, where people spend on services like yoga lessons, video streaming, destination weddings, and other service purchases that make up such a large part of modern budgets.

The pre-1900s economy dominated by manufacturing was necessarily far more volatile than the service-based economy we have today. The main reason is that inventories were held at multiple levels between the factory and the retailer, which is how products were distributed in a world of primitive communications and slow transportation. Production had to be high for there to be sufficient inventory at all steps between the manufacturer and the end customer, and often that production turned out to be too high.

If a textile manufacturer in 1870 guessed wrong about what would be the most popular colors or fabrics, it could take months in the pre-telephone era before the company even began to realize that the mistake had been made. The error might require a lengthy factory closure to reduce the excess inventories at the retailers, wholesalers, master distributors, and the factory itself before production could start again. That assumes the mistake wasn't fatal to the business, which it often was.

Moreover, demand in the 1800s could fluctuate based upon agricultural conditions. Unpredictable bad weather could hurt all manufacturers at once, because that led to high food prices, which was bad news for sales of manufactured products in an era when food was such a large part of the average consumer's budget. Too much good weather could cause the opposite problem, a glut of farm products, and prices so low that farmers defaulted on loans, and little country banks went under, dragging down the bigger banks that lent to them. The sources of volatility were many and powerful, so it would be odd if the 1800s economy didn't have steep booms and busts.

Some of the booms and crashes we had pre-Fed came from the same errors the Fed still makes, only made by different entities. Until the Civil War, there were a multitude of state banks in bed with local politicians, who encouraged excessive lending, especially to the home state itself. Whenever local bubbles were starting to burst, the states regularly gave legal permission for their pals in the banks to break promises that the bank would repay their note holders (i.e., depositors) with specie (i.e., gold and silver) upon demand. This caused cascading bank runs at the slightest rumor of difficulties.

Increasing the risk of failure were laws in most states that prevented branch banking, forcing a bank to have complete reliance upon conditions in a narrow geographic area. By contrast, Canada always allowed national banking, so the banks were bigger, less dependent upon the financial health of just one or two industries, and rarely ran into any trouble despite having a less-diversified economy than that of the US.

After the Civil War, a national bank system was set up in the US to replace the state-chartered banks, and this also allowed banks to lend out liberally with limited reserves. Interstate banking was not allowed, so a severe local recession would still find the local banks with no diversification into more profitable towns, so they often failed.

In today's economy, manufacturing companies have eliminated the sources of many errors. In clothing, for example, a sophisticated manufacturer, even one overseas, knows almost minute by minute which colors, styles, and sizes are being bought by consumers and which aren't, and can instantly adjust production so as not to be stuck with bad inventory. Many manufacturers sell direct to customers, and some produce to order—possible today but not in the 1800s—eliminating inventory risk.

Service industries now dominate the economy and have no inventory whatsoever. That doesn't mean they can't fall upon hard times, but errors in predicting demand no longer force a business to close until the pile of unsold goods is reduced.

Business cycles will always exist, because humans work with incomplete knowledge, and nobody is perfect at predicting what others might buy. People will always make mistakes. Given our computers and communications, and the replacement of manufacturing with services as the biggest part of the economy, the down phases nowadays *should* be mild, as demand changes, errors are discovered, and resources are temporarily idle pending redeployment.

Yet cycles have been more extreme in the last 100 years, when the Fed has supposedly been taking care of us. There was nothing in the 1800s that was comparable to the Great Depression of the 1930s, the creation of the Rust Belt in the 1980s, or the worldwide Great Financial Crisis (GFC) that occurred in roughly 2007-2010 due to the collapse of our housing bubble and the loss of confidence in sovereign debt in Europe. These unsustainable booms followed by busts have caused significant damage to our standard of living.

A major reason why business cycles have become so extreme is artificially low interest rates set by the Fed and other central banks for most of the last four decades. Excessively easy money is an incentive for businesses and consumers to take on too much debt when times are good, with an asset-speculation boom fueling a temporary consumption boom that encourages even more debt, much of which can't be serviced when the tide turns.

In addition, the US tax policy of making interest payments on the debt, but not dividends to stockholders, tax deductible, is an incentive for businesses to finance themselves with a greater amount of debt and less equity. Dividends on equity are optional, but interest on debt must be paid—otherwise, creditors can put the company into bankruptcy—so our tax policy deepens most downturns.

There is no reason to think the risks of these financial collapses have been reduced. If anything, the explosion of governmental debt, and the debts accumulated on real estate and other speculative assets during the Covid stimulus-check bubble, are going to amplify the damage from any downturns to come.

MACRO'S FLAWED TOOLS AND CONCEPTS

• • •

BESIDES HAVING NO SCIENTIFIC justification for its theories, and its direct contradiction of what we know about human behavior that is the basis of the proven laws of micro, mainstream macro has many other fundamental flaws. Economists hold dear certain concepts that distort their understanding of how the economy works and what its purpose is. As a result, they advocate policies that are harmful to the entire economy, but especially to those with lower levels of incomes and wealth.

Chapter 4 will discuss GDP, macro's main scorecard of an economy's performance, which counts as pluses many things that actually make us poorer. Not understanding that fact, most economists favor programs that consume resources to produce little or nothing anyone wants but which increase GDP. Then they wonder why the public isn't as appreciative of the state of the economy as the rise in GDP says they should be.

Chapter 5 discusses inflation figures, which macro takes very seriously even though the numbers are highly arbitrary, with guesses and adjustments that are irrelevant to many people. Economists take government-issued inflation numbers as gospel and were in near-panic mode in the mid-2010s, when the monthly numbers almost went negative. Most consumers neither know nor care what the official numbers are and react instead to prices in their market baskets of expected purchases.

In **Chapter 6**, you'll see why economists should focus more on living standards, the measure of people's ability to buy whatever it is that they want. Completely overlooked is that those who need to spend all their income to maintain what they consider acceptable living standards are much more affected by changes in prices than those with more financial room to spare.

This has important implications because, through several mechanisms, the cost of government spending and many of its policies raise consumer prices. That directly reduces the living standards of lower-income people but not of others, whose financial resources allow them to still buy as much of what they want as before, despite the higher prices. Bigger government is favored by those who think its programs tend to reduce inequality, when, in fact, paying for them fosters inequality.

• CHAPTER 4 •

GDP—AN UNWORTHY GOAL

• • •

To macroeconomists and the public, GDP (Gross Domestic Product) is the economy, and the economy is GDP. If we want to know how the economy is doing, just check the recent growth rate of GDP, and there is the answer. Anything we do to make GDP go up supposedly makes the economy better, while anything that reduces GDP supposedly makes the economy worse.

GDP is a good, rough measure of overall activity or spending, but an awful one for understanding the economy. The universal acceptance of GDP (and its variants) as the standard with which to measure an economy's performance forces us to misunderstand true cause and effect in economics and results in economic policies that don't work as intended.

A country's GDP can be calculated in several different ways, all of which come up with approximately the same number. The easiest method to understand, and supposedly the most accurate, adds three typically large sums—consumption, investment, and government spending—plus what is usually a much smaller sum, net exports (total exports minus total imports). In a country like the US, which regularly imports more than it exports, that last term subtracts from GDP but isn't a major factor. One usually sees the formula as GDP=C+I+G+(X-M).

Note that the term "investment" in the formula means primarily business investment in plant and equipment, and consumer purchases of newly built houses. In today's economy, spending for R&D, software acquisition, and employee training have the same economic characteristics as business investment, and will be treated as such in this book. Purchases of existing assets or financial products, such as when one invests in stocks or bonds, or any other colloquial use of the term ("I'm buying these vintage Beanie Babies as an investment") do not count in GDP.

GDP—and its similar predecessor GNP (Gross National Product)—were invented in the 1930s. They became very popular among economists after WW2. The big edge was that GDP allowed them to reduce the immense complexity of the economy to a single number.

When economists compare two or more countries with different monetary, government spending, or tax policies, the winning country is "proven" to be best based on which one had the fastest growth in GDP or one of its derivatives, such as Real GDP (GDP adjusted for inflation), or Real GDP per capita.

There are many things other than GDP that one might reasonably consider in evaluating the consequences of some fiscal or monetary policy. Looking at multiple effects would create the inevitable problem of discovering that, say, a certain economic policy helped business revenues but hurt consumers' balance sheets, in that they spent more than they earned and had to go into debt to do so. Or a policy may have helped median incomes, but hurt the living standards of the poorest 10%, while also producing some other positive and negative effects.

Nobody would know what to make of such results, and there would be long, inconclusive arguments over which measures should count more than others. Without GDP and other seemingly scientific measurements, economics would appear to be what it truly is—no different from history or any other social study, where academics try to understand society in all its intricacy.

Fortunately for economists, using GDP as the standard measure of a policy's success or failure turns macro into a game like baseball, where the only thing that counts is which team got the most runs, regardless of who had the most hits, errors, strikeouts, homers, or anything else that happened in the game. That is certainly convenient for the researcher. However, the point of research in any field should be to understand the real world as it exists, i.e., to observe all the effects of a given cause, not just one of them.

There are quite a few known flaws in GDP, mostly related to arbitrary choices of what to count or not. The goal of most GDP critics is to make the GDP figure more inclusive of various measures not traditionally in the domain of economics, such as the health of the natural environment and the happiness levels of a country's citizens, along with estimates of unpaid work that goes on in society, mostly provided by women at home. No objection here—those are all worth considering as an adjustment to GDP or an adjunct measure of countries' progress on various fronts.

However, there are **three serious flaws in the use of GDP**, the first two of which have always gone unnoticed, and the third was well-known eighty years ago but is now forgotten. These flaws are fatal to using GDP to understand an economy's performance. All three create bias toward bad policy choices that destroy wealth and living standards even as they raise GDP.

Fundamental Flaw #1: GDP counts aggregate spending and fails to make the critical distinction between consumption spending and investment spending.

Consumption is necessary for us to live, and our ability to consume is a good definition for standard of living. True, we can be very happy with simple lives, perhaps much happier than if we owned multiple houses, sailboats, classic autos, etc., that require constant maintenance and attention. Having a high standard of living just means we can consume if we *choose* to—it doesn't *oblige* us to do so.

But consumption does nothing to increase our income in the future. Investments are the opposite, in that they usually require refraining from current consumption to create savings to make the investments. If invested wisely, however, they will increase our future income.

Let us imagine two 18-year-old twins, F and W (for Foolish and Wise), with equal skill sets, who each receive a substantial inheritance. Twin F spends all of it on parties and travel, while W uses the money to pay for education.

We've all read stories about students who spent a fortune on college and discovered their job prospects have not improved. Investment always entails risk. If you prefer for this example, instead of college, assume that W went to a trade school to learn some specific skills that let W become a welder, electrician, software engineer, or some other trade that usually provides a higher income than unskilled labor. Or assume that both twins were immigrants to the USA from a place with a very different language, and W's education was to become proficient in English and qualify for more jobs, whereas F still lacks that skill.

F has had fun. W may or may not have enjoyed the studying, but if the course of study was one that provided marketable skills, W can now earn more than would otherwise have been the case. What F did with the inheritance was *consumption*. What W did was *investment*.

When the money inherited by both F and W is gone, who is the wealthier? If you just looked at their balance sheets, they are both equal in having no money. In fact, W is much better off. F has nothing to show for the consumption spending other than the memories. W has lived a more ascetic life so far but, with the extra education, has a greater chance to have a more financially rewarding career than F.

Let's extend the example one more step, and assume that, in addition to their inheritance, both F and W managed to borrow additional money, which F spent on even more parties and travel, and W spent on even more advanced job qualifications. Now for sure W is in better economic shape than F. While they both have an equally negative net worth, in that they have no savings and are still in debt, W has even better job prospects than before and over time can pay back that debt and come out far ahead.

After the most recent spending spree, F is not only broke and in debt but also lacks skills that can fetch higher income. Some portion of what F does earn, in a job with lower pay than what W will likely have, must now be used to repay creditors instead of being used for F's needs and desires. If we say the ability to consume is a rough measure of standard of living, then until the debt has been repaid, F's standard of living will be lower than ever.

Just as with our twins, whether a country's GDP includes a low or high amount of investment has very significant implications for what its income is likely to be in the future. The GDP as expenditures calculation, by counting consumption and investment as the same, obscures that important distinction and encourages bad government policies intended to create a higher GDP by increasing consumption at the expense of savings and investment.

Economists use a term, "marginal propensity to consume," that measures what percent of the marginal dollar of income a person will spend on additional consumption. The higher it is, the greater the increase in GDP that can be gained in the short run by taxing money from those who will save and invest it and giving that money to those who will spend all of it. Good for GDP, bad for future productivity and incomes.

There is also a time gap between when money is saved and when it gets into the hands of businesses who use it to make the kind of investments whose results will eventually show up in GDP. That often won't happen until after the next election, hence politicians' preference for immediate consumption over investment, despite the longer-term consequences.

Beware of politicians using the term "investment," since they know it always sounds much better to voters to say that the government is going to "*invest more in education and national defense*," rather than say "*More taxpayer money will be showered upon teachers' unions and military contractors, and politicians who voted in favor expect reelection campaign donations from the beneficiaries, or it won't happen again.*"

Here is a tricky angle: capital invested in businesses also funds consumption. Money invested in a start-up company, for example, will go primarily to salaries and fees as its initial products are designed. The engineers, support staff, the lawyers and accountants all get paid for helping the company set up shop and develop their initial offerings. Those people use their pay to buy food, clothing, plane tickets, and other consumption items, just like anyone else.

When there is a lot of such investment going on, as during the late 1990s NASDAQ bubble, the conversion of savings to investment to salaries to consumption, combined with the usual multiplier effect as that spending bounces around the economy, can have a strong positive impact on the country's GDP.

Well, if consumption is consumption, and savings become investments which become paychecks which are largely consumed, what is so special about investment? Is everything just consumption, either visible or in disguise?

No. If you spend your money on wild parties, you may have had fun, but you get nothing that will increase your future income or reduce your future expenses, and your diminished net worth suggests a lower living standard ahead. Savings and wise investment add to one's ability to consume much more in the future.

Put another way, the most important thing to know about a country's economy is **not** the level of spending, which is what GDP measures, but **what people actually do** to earn a living.

Most people in every country are involved in providing goods and services for others' consumption. But to the extent that savings have funded many people working on R&D, creating new products, developing more efficient processes, learning valuable skills, or anything else that involves investment, the basis is being created for a higher standard of living to come. That is what wise investment does, even while those working on investment projects spend their paychecks on consumption. Keynes worried that savings would be hoarded, thereby weakening the economy by being removed from it, but nearly all savings ends up in the economy being lent out or invested.

Let's avoid delving into the controversy about whether banks lend out previously saved money, or whether they just make loans, and in the process of so doing, effectively create deposits to back those very loans. Either way, the more deposits a bank has, the more inclined it will be to lend them, if creditworthy borrowers exist.

Even genuinely idle resources, like unemployed people and closed factories, are useful to society, in that their potential availability is what inspires entrepreneurs to think of new ways to deploy them. If everyone were given an income from the government just for being alive, as some propose (Universal Basic Income, or UBI), how could innovative new companies get started without requiring much more capital investment to lure potential employees away from their free money? Government-guaranteed jobs programs, by making innovation more costly and riskier, are a recipe for long-term economic stagnation.

Perhaps because of Keynes's hatred of savings, macro misunderstands what makes for a successful economy. More consumption spending and higher GDP per se do not make us rich; rich countries do spend more and, therefore, have a higher GDP. That is a reward they can give themselves from what actually made them rich, including sacrificing consumption in the past to have the savings to fund wise investment which produced higher earnings now.

Fundamental Flaw #2: The GDP calculation doesn't concern itself about the source of the money that is paying for the spending that comprises GDP. Was that money earned, or was it borrowed?

We saw in our twins example how F's borrowing money for consumption allowed F an extravagant lifestyle, but the debt combined with no increase in earnings power guaranteed F a lower living standard when the debt had to be repaid. Borrowing to consume makes a person or a country poorer, despite the boost to GDP when the money is initially spent. This is an increasingly critical issue in a world where most governments spend more on their own consumption and to fund more consumption by the public than they receive in taxes.

Greece earlier this century was a perfect example. For years its government ran large deficits, which it was able to finance by borrowing at very low rates, helped by European bank regulators decreeing that all sovereign debts of EU members would be valued as AAA (ultra safe) paper. What the Greek government did with the borrowed money was add a large chunk of the Greek populace to the government's payroll, with little concern for whether what they did while at work, assuming they bothered to show up, had any value to anyone.

That was great for Greece's GDP. All the workers got their paychecks and spent most of the money, boosting consumption spending in the GDP formula. That spending provided a multiplier effect, since their spending supported car dealers, restaurants, and other businesses, which all hired workers, who then could spend more. It also caused an increase in investment spending, as businesses seeing strong growth in demand from the free-spending government workers expanded their capacity, without thinking about whether that rising demand was sustainable.

But unlike, say, Germany, which had decent GDP growth because its businesses made high-quality cars, machine tools, instruments, chemicals, and other products in great demand throughout the world, Greece after ancient times has never had much to offer the world economically other than tourism and agricultural products, like many other poor countries. Yes, there are some very wealthy Greek shipowners, but they keep their money far from the clutches of the Greek tax authorities, as do many of their fellow citizens.

In other words, Germany's GDP growth was sustainable because it made unique products that people want to buy, whereas Greece's GDP growth was unsustainable because it came from what was essentially a Ponzi scheme. Borrowing money and recycling it into salaries, consumption, and waste could continue only as long as Greece's debt could grow exponentially, since a rising portion of the debt was needed to repay older debt when due.

Anyone looking just at GDP figures would have been completely misled as to the very different situations of Germany and Greece. In the decade leading up to 2009, the point when banks finally realized that "lending" to Greece was going to mean not getting paid back, Greece was seemingly growing twice as fast as Germany. Its GDP growth averaged close to 4% per year, with three years exceeding 5%, while Germany's GDP grew only at a 1.9% rate. Greece's debt was rising fast, but because the government's borrowing and spending served to increase the country's GDP, its ratio of debt to GDP, widely used as a check on whether a nation's debt is getting too high, increased modestly and didn't set off any alarms.

Despite slow GDP growth, Germany was becoming steadily richer with the earnings of its thriving industries. Meanwhile Greece, while supposedly growing fast, was actually becoming steadily poorer, just like twin F, as it kept taking on more debt, but not using the borrowed money for anything that increased its ability to service the debt.

Fast growth is not unknown in smaller, less-developed countries, when infrastructure investments eliminate transportation bottlenecks that held back potential growth, or when industries that are capable of underpricing those in developed countries get the capital they need to expand and enter new markets. Since those are investments with potentially high returns, there would be nothing wrong with borrowing money to fund them since they should generate more than enough income to pay off the debt over time and come out ahead.

That isn't what was happening in Greece. The country was just living it up on borrowed money.

To most macroeconomists, Greece's GDP growth showed it was gaining on Germany and getting stronger every year. In reality it was getting poorer by the day. Greece was borrowing and spending itself into a modern-day version of debtors' prison.

For comparison, although private industry in the US is much more like that of Germany than Greece, our GDP, like that of Greece, has been goosed for many years by continuous deficit spending by the government, very little of which can be considered investment at all, let alone wise investment that will increase our future net incomes to let us pay down the debt without having to slash living standards.

There is something dreadfully, horribly wrong with the GDP concept, if it causes blindness to the difference between a Germany and a Greece. Its use invariably corrupts one's understanding of how economies operate. Despite this fiasco, GDP's exalted position in macro remains completely unchallenged.

One could defend GDP by saying it is only doing what it is supposed to be doing, which is to measure spending. Fair enough, but why would macroeconomists or anyone else want to measure spending and economic activity without caring whether it was making us richer or poorer? Shouldn't the purpose of economic indices be to help us notice important differences, not to obscure them?

Fundamental Flaw #3: Economists today count government spending in GDP. If one thinks that it is very important to measure total spending, regardless of the source of the money and the nature of what is being bought, then sure, add in government spending and ignore the implications.

The biggest change in the composition of GDP over the last 100 years has been the rise in government spending. Not counting temporary spikes during major wars, the total of US federal, state, and local spending stayed below 10% of GDP through 1930. Since the mid-1970s, the percentage of GDP consisting of government spending has never been less than 30% and lately has been more than 40%. In many countries, such as France, government spending accounts for more than 50% of GDP.

Those percentages underestimate the growth of government spending, since much of it is counted in GDP, thereby increasing the denominator of the fraction as well as the numerator.

Government spending, however, is not the same thing as private spending. When we buy something as individuals or businesspeople, we are spending our own money and want to get the best value for the money, however we define that. In every case, when we make a purchase, we are doing so because the value to us of what we are buying exceeds what we spend on it.

Let's say you paid $4 for a cup of coffee because you prefer the coffee to the $4. As much as you may want the caffeine, you wouldn't have paid $14 for it, and with numerous other sources of coffee at around $4 or less, there is no reason why you should. We can fairly say that $4 was the right amount that GDP should rise to reflect your purchase.

Governments however, when buying various things, often gladly pay the equivalent of that $14 cup of coffee. There might be a sole-source contract with the supplier, who just coincidentally is a big donor to the political party in power. The contract may have been awarded to the low bidder, but often the specifications were manipulated in advance to effectively eliminate most of the competition, so the low bid is actually high. And since the money that politicians are spending is not their own, paying more and getting reelection support is obviously a superior choice over getting a better deal for taxpayers and getting no kickbacks.

For all projects involving building and construction, the federal government is required by the Davis-Bacon Act to overpay, since non-union contractors are effectively disqualified from bidding. Technically they can bid, but being forced to pay high union wages means they would have bid higher than a union shop because their less experienced non-union staff would take more hours to do the job. So, they don't bother to bid, and the union shops can write their own ticket.

If, as it is often described, GDP represented the true value of the goods and services produced in the country, we should only count $4 toward GDP for all those $14 equivalent government purchases. But that is too complicated, and neither the government nor economists have any interest in highlighting their inefficiency and corruption.

The developers of GDP in the 1930s were reluctant to count government spending in GDP. Their thinking was that in the private sector, we know that every transaction is viewed by the participants on both sides as adding value. The buyer wants what they are buying more than they want the amount of money it costs, while the seller wants the money more than whatever is being sold. They both come out ahead. The transaction would be counted in GDP and also improve the living standard of both the buyer and the seller, because they both got something worth more to them than what they gave up getting it.

That isn't the case with government spending. The buyer is some official of the government who is not spending their own money and is not particularly motivated to get the best deal available, since the purpose of much spending is to transfer as much as legally possible to the politically connected recipient. It is just not the same as you buying a cup of coffee with your own money.

Upon the approach of WW2, which required a gigantic increase in government spending and taxes, and a shift of factories from consumer to military output, propaganda needs became the highest priority. Not counting government spending in GDP would show the collapse of the consumer economy, and might hurt morale on the home front, so they decided to make government spending count toward GDP.

The orthodox macro narrative of the 1930-1945 period is that the US was mired in the Great Depression all during the 1930s, but it was WW2 that rescued us. Once the war started, factories geared up to make war goods, men got hired as soldiers, unemployment dropped so low that factories were largely "manned" by previously "unemployed" (i.e., working hard at home but not being paid) women, and GDP, which measured all that work and activity, took off, ending the Depression. The economy was now booming, at least officially. Counting government spending in GDP did indeed make it go way up during the war.

My parents lived through the 1930s, and my father, by then married to my mother with a baby on the way, enlisted after Pearl Harbor in 1941 and was sent to the China-Burma-India Theater, not to return for four years, after the baby had died. There was no question in their minds, that whatever the GDP figures may have shown, life for them and everyone they knew was hell during WW2, compared to life in the Great Depression before the war.

Despite the high unemployment in the 1930s, most people had jobs. Wages faced downward pressure, but prices were dropping faster, so people on fixed incomes or who retained their jobs had decent purchasing power. Socially, the 1930s were a time of strong family and ethnic ties, so those with homes and jobs took in or helped less-fortunate relatives and neighbors, and there were charities, churches, and volunteer organizations that helped provide an informal, if not entirely comprehensive, social safety net.

At least in the Depression, spouses got to stay together, no one was trying to shoot, shell, or bomb either of them, and if one did have some money, as most did, there were goods and services available to buy.

With the need to supply the troops by shifting factories from consumer to war goods, WW2 brought rationing, deprivation, loss of freedom, and the inability to buy previously available consumer goods. It took millions of people from their families and chosen occupations and sent them to the military, where there was an excellent chance of their being killed or wounded. These are not the marks of a society that is doing better than before.

This is not to say it was not a worthy sacrifice, or that people then weren't willing to suffer to achieve national goals, but you can't say the economy was better off, if by economy you mean the standard of living, the kind of lives people had to actually live.

GDP as a measuring stick can't tell the difference between a car and a tank, or between mustard and mustard gas, but, in both those cases, civilians want the former and flee in panic from the latter. Mainstream macro doesn't care, since its concern is to maximize GDP regardless of what makes it go up.

One entertaining aspect of the fact that government spending counts as part of GDP is to watch Keynesian economists, who are always in favor of more government spending, make fools of themselves by forgetting that fact. The years 2010-13 were a period of "austerity" in Europe caused by the lenders' concern that governments with big deficits would default on their debt. Other than Greece, which was effectively shut off from new debt, very few governments slashed spending. Rather, most increased their spending but raised taxes considerably. The "austerity" was imposed on their citizens, not the governments, even though it was the latter whose spending got out of control to create the deficits.

Paul Krugman, the popular writer for *The New York Times*, had multiple columns and blog posts in which he "proved" that austerity was bad for a country's economy, because countries that raised government spending showed higher GDP numbers than the ones who kept spending flat or down a bit, and both did better than Greece, which really did slash spending.

Well, of course, higher government spending is good for GDP; it is counted in GDP!

Shut off from new borrowing, Greece had no choice but to cut government spending. Yes, that was bad for its GDP, but it meant that it was no longer impoverishing itself by consuming ever-greater amounts of borrowed money. As the saying goes, if you are deep in a hole, the first thing to do is stop digging.

The worship of GDP has turned mainstream macro into a cargo cult. Made famous by physicist Richard Feynman, cargo cults arose during WW2 when communities on some isolated Pacific islands, with little prior contact with modern civilization, saw planes landing and disgorging Jeeps, food, weapons, and other supplies for the Allied troops. The islanders, not understanding correctly where that stuff came from and why this was happening, concluded, not implausibly, that if one makes an accurate mock-up of an airplane, cargo might come out of that as well. They made ever more elaborate constructions, trying to replicate as best they could a plane on a runway, yet no cargo ever rolled out the back.

Non-islanders knew why. The cargo doesn't come from the plane because the plane looks like a plane, it comes because the stuff was manufactured somewhere, placed in the plane, and the plane was flown to that island, where the cargo was unloaded for a particular purpose, to aid the war effort.

Economists notice that prosperous societies have a high and growing GDP. They then make the cargo-cult mistake of concluding that if a country's GDP can be made to increase, that will make the country prosperous. That might or might not be the case. It depends on what it is that is making GDP rise.

Is the country's GDP rising because its businesses have invested in creating and producing new and better products and services which are in great demand? Have the citizens built up their balance sheets with savings, and therefore have the ability and inclination to buy more of what they want? Is the society operating with a rule of law, a reasonably efficient court system, unambiguous property rights, and a sound monetary and banking system, all of which make businesses willing to invest due to the fair and predictable environment? If so, then rising GDP is indeed a sign of an increasingly prosperous society.

Or is GDP rising because the government is spending heavily on consumption for itself and subsidizing consumption by the populace, and doing it with borrowed money? Are interest rates set by the central bank excessively low, leading businesses to borrow heavily to invest in capacity to provide things for which demand is unsustainable? Then GDP would be rising, but what it would really measure is how quickly society is becoming less wealthy and financially weaker.

Mainstream economists confuse cause and effect. A higher GDP is never a sensible goal by itself. A rising GDP is a result of the higher spending that is typical of a wealthier society, not a cause of that wealth, and certainly not when GDP is rising because of more debt-financed consumption.

This book won't be abandoning GDP entirely and will occasionally use the ratio of certain things to GDP to show their relative size. Despite its major drawbacks as a measure of economic progress, GDP is a decent-enough indicator of overall spending in an economy, with easily accessible data.

There is something much better than GDP to try to improve in a country—the living standards of its inhabitants, to be discussed ahead. First, though, we cover macro's other main statistic—its measures of price inflation, because as many people discovered with our current inflation surge, it can have a big effect on living standards.

CHAPTER 5

INFLATION AND THE PROGRESS MECHANISM

• • •

T HE OTHER MAJOR YARDSTICK of mainstream macro besides GDP is inflation. The two are closely connected because the preferred measure of economic growth is the change in real GDP (GDP adjusted for price inflation), either by itself or per capita.

But which inflation measure to use? The problem is that inflation can be almost any number at all, depending upon very arbitrary choices about how to calculate the figure. These choices, made by economists working for the US Bureau of Labor Statistics (BLS) or the Bureau of Economic Analysis (BEA) are not necessarily wrong, but have no more justification than other choices they could have made which would produce different outcomes.

The BLS calculates not just one Consumer Price Index (CPI), but also separate ones for urban consumers, for urban wage earners and clerical workers, for the elderly, and additional ones for each of

38 designated geographical areas, plus regional averages. The BLS also calculates the Producer Price Index (PPI), which has more than 600 sub-indices for various commodities and products. The BEA has its own staff calculating the Personal Consumption Expenditure Deflator (PCE) and other inflation measures.

Each of these indices is calculated using some different raw information and/or different mathematical techniques, leading to much skirmishing by economists and statisticians about which index is best for what purpose. The problems with inflation figures go much deeper than which is best.

Most inflation indices start with an assumption of a market basket. That alone makes everything about them dubious, since each of us, including your next-door neighbor with roughly the same income and lifestyle as you, has a very different set of things we regularly buy.

For example, I'm on the Board of Music Maker Foundation, a charity in North Carolina which serves the needs of elderly and poor blues and country musicians in the US South, most of them African Americans. I'm a retired, well-off white guy living elsewhere in the country. I would guess the percentage overlap between what is in my typical market basket and that of the artists supported by this charity is probably on the order of 5%.

They and I all buy toilet paper, salt, and a few other things, but that may be it. We prefer different food and drink, and some things I buy they might also prefer if they could afford to buy them, but they can't. Depending upon whether the official market basket used to calculate price inflation is more heavily weighted to what I buy versus what they buy, the resulting inflation rate is as meaningless to the other party as would be the rate in some foreign country.

In addition, everyone's market basket can change radically over time as circumstances do, such as when you start or stop paying for kids in college. If you buy a new house and want to make some changes, you might give up expensive vacations to afford new carpet and furniture or to add a deck, and whether plane-ticket prices are up or down means nothing to you.

Even if we somehow became a nation of people with 100% equality of incomes, wealth, and identical baskets, calculation of a reasonable price-inflation rate would not be easy. If steak jumps 20% in price while chicken drops 20%, is that inflation, deflation, or neutral? If you strongly prefer steak, you experience steep inflation; if you strongly prefer chicken, you have steep deflation. Vegetarians would be unaffected.

Non-vegetarians differ in their inclination to substitute one protein for another when their prices diverge. No economist can read the minds of all those who really want steak but must cut back. How bothered are they? If greatly, in that they don't consider anything other than steak to be an acceptable dinner, then they are truly experiencing 20% inflation on that item. If they are happy to switch to chicken, then they can immediately take advantage of the 20% deflation and use their savings for something else. Maybe even a steak dinner on occasion.

Not being able to read minds, economists never know what hardship, if any, there is in substituting chicken for steak, or other substitutions that people regularly make because of changing prices.

But without knowing that information, the inflation figures they produce will be very different from what many people perceive. That is a big problem for the theory behind mainstream macro, because the Liquidity Trap concept considers that perception a critical component of people's willingness to spend.

The agencies that calculate inflation recognize that some prices are much more volatile than others and create "core" price indices that exclude them. Unfortunately for common sense and the English language, the most volatile prices are those of food and energy, which constitute a very core part of the budgets of the poor, and a noticeable percentage of middle-class budgets as well. We have the absurdity of economists obsessed with an index they call "core" that actually means little to millions of Americans, while disregarding any "non-core" index, comprising costs that truly are significant.

Moreover, when food and energy prices are both rising sharply, that leaves many consumers with little money left after paying for those "non-core" things. That reduces "core" inflation because sellers of what used to be a bigger part of most people's budgets can't raise prices when demand is so weak. Economists then claim that inflation isn't bad at all—the public is just needlessly upset about the increases in their non-core groceries and gasoline. The public very reasonably responds with anger and disbelief.

Another flaw in all price indices is the arbitrary adjustments that must be made to reflect quality changes over time. Cars today are more than ten times the price they were in the 1950s, when the most expensive new car around, at about $5500 then, was a top-of-the-line Cadillac. I recall that, some year in the 1950s, my parents bought a fundraiser lottery ticket for some charity and won a Chevrolet Impala, then, as now, Chevy's top-of-the-line regular sedan. They had just bought a new car and didn't need it, so they chose to receive instead its list price of $1900.

Today's cars are more expensive than the roughly $20,000 that the Impala's price would be if it went up in line with the CPI. But cars are also vastly better by any measure. Are they three times better? Ten times better? Who knows? But what number some economists pick makes a big difference when calculating price inflation. Their intentions are to make that adjustment as accurate as possible, but there is no getting around the fact that their choice is arbitrary.

Real scientists in other fields attempt to measure reality as accurately as possible, and, because they deal with objective matter and forces, they can succeed. Economists can, at best, hope for a plausible guess on a number to pin onto a fuzzy concept.

The quality adjustment seems particularly arbitrary when considering the prices of electronics such as computers, phones, and other devices that didn't exist in the past but are now an important expense for many people. Devices today are much more powerful and feature-laden than ones of five or ten years ago, but their prices are still about the same. We could say that the prices of these things are flat, and the extra speed, better display, and other features are nice but not strictly necessary for the main things the devices do. Or we could say the prices of the devices measured by speed, memory, features, etc. have plummeted.

Either choice or something in between is reasonable and justifiable. It is all arbitrary, not objective in any respect. Whatever the

BLS and the BEA decide would affect their inflation adjustments and, therefore, cost-of-living adjustments in contracts, Social Security payments, and pensions, and the choices of the Fed about which short-term interest rate to impose upon us.

Writer Andy Kessler in the *Wall St. Journal* has pointed out that some new products and services grow spectacularly because they each do something for a very low price that would have been prohibitively expensive before they existed. Only after the price has already collapsed and they have become mass-market products do they get added to the basket used to calculate an inflation index.

He writes, comparing conditions today to those decades ago, *"Your smartphone is your newspaper deliveryman, librarian, stenographer, secretary, personal shopper, DJ, newscaster, broker, weatherman, fortuneteller—shall I go on? The mythical man of 1973 certainly couldn't afford $100,000 or more for dozens of workers at his beckoning. By the time the BLS puts something new in the CPI basket, it's already cheap, so it misses the massive human-replacement price decline."*

True, but in 1973 we managed to live without having a phone, GPS, library, etc., in our pockets. A comparison in a price index of the near-infinite cost of those services decades ago, versus the negligible cost of apps on smartphone today, would show spectacular deflation. That doesn't seem right, just as it doesn't seem right to ignore the quality improvement in cars and claim inflation is very high.

The issue of varying market baskets, the guesses on what products people will substitute for others when prices change, and arbitrary adjustments for quality and changes in technology, all make a mockery of the false precision of inflation figures with even one decimal point. Government economists are delusional if they think that anyone other than fellow economists and investment managers care about their inflation figures. People respond to what they personally are experiencing, and don't care whether that matches some figure that the government reports.

Suppose the government calculated no inflation figures whatsoever and merely took surveys of what the public estimated the price-inflation rate had been over the previous year. Instead of the narrow band of what the government releases (in recent years, not much more than a 1%-or-so range in the major indices from the highest to lowest), there would probably be a good 12% range, as a guess, to cover just half the estimates of those surveyed, say from 2% to 14%, with the other half of the estimates above or below that range. The guesses would depend on what was in each person's market basket that year, versus previous years, as much as actual changes in prices.

No doubt the BLS and BEA would claim that their numbers are based on solid data, whereas people's experience of inflation are emotional responses, probably biased higher due to sticker shock on a few items.

Objectively, they are correct. But they can't have it both ways. They denigrate the general public's experience of what it costs us to buy what we want. Then, because they consider inflation expectations critical to spending levels, they base economic policies on official inflation figures whose readings the public, to the extent we even know what they are, think are nonsense or at least not applicable to ourselves.

Moreover, thinking of inflation/deflation only as the changes in the prices of goods and services means looking at only part of the true picture. Those aren't the only things money can buy. It can also buy assets—stocks, bonds, crypto, houses, art, collectible cars, etc.

Nearly every transaction in the US involves the exchange of goods, services, or assets in return for US dollars. The dollar's value has historically changed slowly over time, so we automatically assume it is a stable measure. Looked at over a longer period, it is clearly not. The purchasing power of the dollar, when used to buy almost anything, has fallen roughly 98-99% over the last 110 years since the founding of the Fed in 1913. Although there are exceptions above and below, many things that cost about $1 or $2 a century ago now sell for about $100.

Thinking of inflation as the dollar losing value will help you understand the tremendous increase in asset prices we have had in recent decades. The price of anything often depends on its abundance or scarcity. Air is incredibly valuable to a human—we can't live without it, but it is so abundant that nobody would pay a penny for a big bag of it because they can get all they want for free.

An original work of art by some famous painter, like Picasso, for example, can be worth amazing amounts of money these days—tens or even hundreds of millions of dollars. Only one original exists. Meanwhile an attractive, good-quality unframed but matted print of the same work might be offered for sale in the museum gift shop for $19.95, and you can find slightly dirty, framed used prints in yard sales for $2.00 or less. Both are so much cheaper than an original because there is no limit to the number of prints that can exist.

The Fed, through creating new money to buy bonds, other government paper, and mortgages, and its policies encouraging the creation of new credit by our banking system, makes new dollars come into existence. Its ability to create new money far exceeds the growth in supply of anything for which the money can be used, whether the goods and services that are counted in inflation indices or the investment assets that are easily exchangeable for money.

When the Fed creates more money and credit, dollars get more abundant versus what can be bought with dollars. When two things are regularly exchanged for each other, in this case, money and whatever money can buy, over time the holders of whichever is relatively scarce will demand higher amounts of whatever is abundant to do the exchange.

That mechanism of price inflation is common knowledge, but it also explains asset inflation. It is the exact same process. Produce more money and credit, and prices of something will go up. Which things, and how much, depends on who gets access to the new money first and what they want to buy with it.

When the public has more money to spend and does so without a big increase in supply of what it wants, we get conventional inflation. When the public is shut off from loans due to lack of creditworthiness, as has been the case most of the time since the 1980s until the Covid stimulus money showed up, easy money goes to rich people with assets as security, so we get asset bubbles rather than price increases in goods and services.

Stocks, bonds, art, bitcoin, real estate in places rich people prefer to live, and other real assets all share the characteristic of not being able to be conjured into existence by a central bank. The Fed and its system employ many hundreds of economists with PhDs and pays hundreds of academic economists substantial consulting fees. They are all very smart people, but the Fed could send them all to art school for the rest of their lives, and they would never be able to turn out even a single original Picasso.

Hence the rising demand in recent decades by people with substantial savings to trade in dollars for assets whose supply is more constrained than the money needed to buy them.

Those who blame rising wealth inequality on something built into capitalism ought to look instead at the Fed's imposition of easy credit at low interest rates for many years, at times when the public is neither creditworthy nor inclined to spend more. The new money went instead to those who have plenty of collateral to finance more speculation, pushing up asset prices and making the rich richer.

How macroeconomists handle inflation indices displays some of the fundamental flaws of their beliefs. There is the fake science. Hundreds of millions are spent every year on data collection and complex statistical manipulation by armies of well-paid economists, which allows inflation to be calculated with seeming precision despite nearly every factor in the calculation being based on some very arbitrary decision as to what to count, how to count it, and how much weight in the index it should have.

There is also the self-important claim that these nonsense numbers affect consumer behavior, despite ample evidence that humans don't respond the way the mainstream theory claims they do. Meanwhile, even though the inflation number could be anything within a wide range and just as legitimate or not, it is treated as if it is a measurement of something real, as opposed to a mere artifact of the assumptions made by the economists who create the index.

Then they take the poorly designed GDP index, adjust it for the inaccurate inflation indices, and treat that or changes in it over some time period as if it tells us something precise and authentic about reality.

Here is a trick question: If there were truly no price inflation or deflation, and there existed an index that somehow could measure inflation with 100% accuracy, what would it state as the inflation rate?

I'll guess your answer is 0%. If so, that is wrong. The correct answer is not exact, but probably around minus 1%-2%.

How can "no inflation" mean that prices decline? Simple. It results from this thing called "progress," which means that businesses strive, by spending on R&D and investing in better equipment and worker training to get greater output per given amount of input, which cuts unit costs. Helping the environment by saving resources is a pleasant side effect.

A company that lowers its costs may wish prices would stay the same and let its profits rise, but that happens only temporarily. The *Progress Mechanism,* one of the automatic mechanisms of the free market, will push prices down. It works like this:

Company A designs or purchases some better equipment that can turn out their widgets at a lower cost. It may or may not want to keep their methods secret, but over time competitors find out. Employees switch jobs and tell their new employer what A has been doing, or suppliers of the equipment call upon Companies B and C to get them to buy the new machines, too. Nobody wants to be the high-cost producer in an industry if they can help it, so they invest like A to get their costs down, too. After a while, everyone in the industry has lower costs, so if nobody changes prices, profit margins are higher. That sounds ideal for the companies in that business, but that never lasts long because of how business strategy plays out.

A company with a large share of market that was able to cut its costs would love to have the now-higher margins remain. But a competitor with a small share of market, or a new entrant to the industry, is much better off trying to gain market share and have high sales rather than trying to maximize their profit margin on a relatively low level of sales.

Here is an example: To keep numbers simple, suppose companies sell widgets for $1 each. They all have a 60-cent cost of goods sold and a 40-cent gross margin, after which they all have their own marketing, administration, and other expenses to pay. Let's say they collectively sell 100 million widgets per year.

Suppose first one and then the others all buy more efficient machinery that cuts unit costs by 20%, so widgets now cost 48 cents to make, giving them a gross margin of 52 cents, which is an extra 12 cents per unit profit if nothing else changes. Big Company, with a 50% market share, is happy for nothing to change. 50 million widgets sold at an extra 12 cents in gross profit each gives them an extra $6 million in gross profit before expenses.

Small Company, with only 5% market share ($5 million in sales and a $2 million gross margin before their costs dropped), looks at things differently. The extra 12-cent gross margin times 5 million units would bring in an extra $600,000 in gross margin. That isn't bad, but management likely sees an opportunity here to gain market share by going after the price-conscious segment of the widget market.

Suppose it cuts the price it charges for widgets from $1 to 88 cents, letting its customers benefit from the entire 12 cents per unit cost reduction. Suppose that discount is attractive enough that Small Company gains an extra 10% of the widget market. Instead of selling 5 million widgets per year, Small Company will sell 15 million. Its revenues at 88 cents each would be $13.2 million, and its gross margin stays at 40 cents each. Gross profits would now be $6 million, triple its previous gross margin, and more than double the $2.6 million it would have had, had it not offered discounts.

Big Company doesn't want to start a price war because it already has a big enough market share that the profits from a higher share wouldn't make up for the loss of gross margin on its existing business. That is why disruptive low-cost innovations usually start with small companies who have little or no high-margin incumbent business to protect.

Those with the biggest market share will tolerate a certain amount of market-share loss because they hate to give up their high margins to chase after what to them is a limited number of price-sensitive customers, but once increasing numbers of smaller competitors also offer discounts and gain customers as a result, then the big player has no choice but to cut prices, too, before it turns into a small player itself.

The *Progress Mechanism* works in service industries, too. There is always one step in any multi-step process that is the bottleneck, the highest-cost part of the process, and the thing that provides the tightest constraint on capacity. A priority for any sensible management is to see if that step can be automated, be given more capacity, or redesigned in some way to make it easier for less-skilled people to do that job.

Keep in mind that the *Progress Mechanism*, like all the mechanisms named in this book, are created automatically by microeconomic conditions. They state what choices a certain category of industry participant is most likely to be rewarded for making. Nobody is obliged to do so, and if they don't, the message stays in effect.

For example, there may be reasons why the Small Companies in the widget industry never find out that the Big Company has reduced its costs through business investment, so they don't make the effort to do the same or are financially or managerially constrained from doing so. If so, they won't start a price war because they don't have the extra profit margin to sacrifice to gain market share, and Big Company can keep the extra profit advantages of lower costs until they do.

The *Progress Mechanism* is an ideal example of why things change within sectors of the economy, but in real life, they sometimes unfold only after a time lag. Nevertheless, this mechanism exists everywhere throughout the economy. Business investment creates new, more attractive products or enables companies to produce existing products less expensively. Initially, they gain some extra profits, but, sooner or later, their competitors can match their innovations and lower costs. The sensible strategy of the smaller competitors of aiming for market-share gains by offering discounts ultimately puts downward pressure on the prices of all the competitors.

The default situation in the economy is for steadily decreasing prices due to business investment. We keep learning new ways to get a higher value of output for a given amount of input. This is the engine of economic progress. It creates what is known as "consumer surplus," the benefits all consumers get from innovations of others.

William Nordhaus, who was a co-winner of the 2018 Nobel prize in economics, is known for his work on the idea of a carbon tax to combat global warming. In 2004, however, he wrote a paper on a different topic, in which he calculated the benefits to the public from innovations. Because of the *Progress Mechanism*, consumers in a free-market economy receive almost all (97.8%, Nordhaus calculates) of the benefits from the original innovation or investment. The only reason it isn't 100% is likely the time lag it sometimes takes for prices to follow costs down.

The more efficient we become as a society, and the faster we develop technological improvements, the more prices should drop. Mainstream macro seems unaware of the concept of progress. Despite no attempt whatsoever to provide any theoretical or empirical justification, the major central banks, including the Fed, have all decided that price inflation of 2% per year is a worthy goal. The macro establishment considers deflation of any kind, even from greater efficiency by producers that gives consumers a boost in their buying power, to be a curse upon the economy.

Mainstream macroeconomists hate declining prices for four main reasons:

First is they think that, if prices are rising, salaries and wages will necessarily be pushed up, too. But that isn't true. Just because the prices of whatever we normally buy goes up, why should that make our employers pay us more? No reason at all. In an inflationary environment, if employers must pay more for everything they buy, that squeezes profit margins, which makes it harder to pay even existing salaries.

We saw a good example of this in 2022. There were millions of unfilled positions in companies, and we've all heard excuses that some product or service is not available currently because the supplier is short staffed.

Yet, as economist Arnold Kling has pointed out, it is easy to get all the staff a company wants if it is willing to pay people enough for them to want the jobs. Companies know this, but with all their other costs soaring, the only way they can make any money at all is to pay people the same as what they paid a year or two earlier, wages that are no longer attractive enough.

The second reason is that, because of Keynes' imaginary Liquidity Trap, economists think deflation caused the 1930s Depression. Price declines were actually an effect, not a cause of the Depression, and since lower prices make people more inclined to buy things, they are an essential component of the *Recession Reversal Mechanism*, as discussed in Chapter 2.

The third reason economists associated with the Fed prefer inflation is that the Fed wants to appear to come to society's rescue when there is a recession by cutting rates. Low or no inflation means low interest rates, so how can it cut them if they are already low?

The fourth reason economists want inflation is that it gives their politician friends an additional justification for running up big deficits to benefit their constituencies. If anyone asks, won't we have to sacrifice in the future to pay these debts back? The economists can explain to them that, because of inflation, the dollars that we pay back won't be worth much then, so no harm done. (As if the creditors are unaware of this plan and won't take it into account in the interest rates they demand to reflect the fact that the dollars they get back won't be worth much.) This is consistent with economists' goal of making GDP go up, even if it gets there by wasting lots of borrowed money.

What mainstream macro gets wrong is that normal deflation from growing productivity makes people richer, not poorer. When greater efficiency and technological advances make prices drop, people can buy the same quantity as before, only now they have money left over to buy other things, too, or strengthen their balance sheets to allow future purchases.

True, in a deflationary environment, a company that was selling widgets for $1 can now only get 88 cents for them, but its increased productivity from its prior investment in R&D or new equipment has cut its (and its competitors') costs from 60 cents to 48 cents, giving it the same 40 cent gross margin as before.

Its customers now have an extra 12 cents per widget that they didn't have before. At the lower price, they might buy more widgets, or new customers might buy widgets, spending the extra dime or so they have because what they normally buy went down in price, too. The widget company could easily sell more units and end up with higher revenues and profits despite the deflation. And if the widget company has debt, it could refinance it at lower interest rates in a deflationary economy.

It may be hard to see progress leading to deflation in the economy, since it has been overwhelmed for many decades by rising price pressures from non-market factors. The *Progress Mechanism* should be viewed as a mild, persistent slow-motion version of what has been so visible in electronic devices, where there are massive investments in R&D, computer-chip production, software to make the chips more efficient, and other advances, which have caused the rapid decline in the prices of computers, cell phones, and TVs.

Think of how fast our standard of living would have grown if we could have had that level of deflation in everything we bought. That is just a fantasy, since, unlike newer technologies, many products and services are already being produced fairly efficiently and have reached the diminishing-returns point, where even massive R&D and capital investment can't make them that much cheaper or much better as a product. But there is still room for improvement in many goods and services, and new products and services get invented that replace older, more costly alternatives.

That is why businesses aiming for the temporarily higher profits that come from successful innovation keep investing. They are on a treadmill, where the extra profits they earn from their innovations and cost improvements prove transient, as small competitors who also cut their costs choose to slash prices to get more market share. The alternative, however, of not trying to improve quality and cut costs when their competitors are doing so, will eventually drive a company under.

CHAPTER 6

LIVING STANDARDS

• • •

MACROECONOMISTS, WITH THEIR FOCUS on GDP, fail to notice what counts to most people: living standards—the extent to which we can buy the goods and services we want and, ideally, have some money left over to put away for future use.

The GDP statistic is calculated as an aggregate, without any concern for how income is distributed within society. Notoriously poorly performing economies don't usually bother the small group of rich people who live there. Genuinely successful economies, such as the US through most of its history, certainly help the rich but have the greatest positive effect on the living standards of the poor.

Your living standard depends on a combination of your financial resources, what goods and services you want, and what it costs you to buy that output. Looked at as concepts rather than strict formulas, your financial resources consist of your after-tax income plus your savings, minus any debts other than a mortgage, which gets paid down slowly. Although ability to spend borrowed money on consumption can enhance your lifestyle in the short run, in the long run, it is a net negative, because you will eventually have to use some of your income to pay back the debt plus interest.

To have a better idea of the financial resources about which you have real choice, i.e., the money at your disposal, we should subtract expenses that you must pay first. You must live someplace, so your rent or mortgage costs are in that category. If you are a tradesperson who must work at various job sites, the cost of owning and operating your vehicle is also not something that you can eliminate without endangering your income.

Your needs are the essentials—food, clothing, shelter, and protection against various threats and risks. Your wants are up to you, in theory, but, as social animals, we can't help wanting at least some of what others expect us to want. Most of your lifestyle relates to things you buy, although having a competent government adds to living standards by allowing you to live in a civilized community unworried about criminals or environmental degradation.

If you have enough income or wealth to get most of what you want, not counting unrealistic daydreams, you probably have what you consider a satisfactory lifestyle. The most financially comfortable people are those who are satisfied with how they live and wouldn't spend more even if they had more. If you can afford to buy a yacht but don't want to, then you have the same living standard as someone who has the same resources and does buy one.

Yes, higher living standards in a society result in higher consumption, and consumption has environmental costs of various kinds, but higher living standards come from more wealth and income, reaching levels beyond what many people want to spend, which means more savings. More savings means more investment, including in R&D to make more efficient products, and make them more efficiently, both of which improve the environment. Successful economies are universally associated with respect for the environment, while most poor countries feel they can't afford that luxury.

Your living standard can rise either by having a greater income or by being able to pay lower prices for what you want to buy. If there were no income taxes, you wouldn't care which of those happened, but given that higher income is taxed and discounts are not, your living standard gains more from lower prices than a higher income.

Living standards are something people understand intuitively. It is easy to see that living standards of developed Country X are much higher than that of underdeveloped Country Y. To some extent, this can be measured objectively by checking calorie intake, life expectancy, infant mortality, and other measures of people's health, along with the percentage of homes with electricity and indoor plumbing, and so forth. Even by casual observation, though, it is easy to tell that a middle-class family in a developed country has a much higher living standard than a subsistence farmer in a poor country.

But when trying to observe changes over time or among people of different income levels within a society, living standards are harder to quantify. Unless you can read the minds of great masses of people, which nobody can do, you'll never know what other people want, especially since what people want keeps changing. We could take surveys to see how they feel about their living standard and its recent trend, but such surveys have many flaws. How people answer questions is strongly affected by the exact wording of the questions asked and by changes in public moods, which can be volatile.

This is why economists would much rather do the very straightforward GDP calculation, apply their arbitrarily defined adjustments for inflation, and pretend that they have told us something very useful about how people are doing. The craving to make macro look like a real science makes economists want to quantify everything, and ignore more important things, like living standards, that they can't easily quantify.

As British industrialist Sir John Banham said, *"We are in danger of valuing most highly those things we can measure most accurately, which means that we are often precisely wrong rather than approximately right."*

Everyone wants higher living standards, but economists interpret that as meaning everyone wants GDP to be higher. Ask around, and you'll see that absolutely nobody cares what the GDP is, if our own living standards and that of family, friends, and others to whom we are connected are in good condition.

The biggest difference between GDP and living standards is that GDP is always helped by higher spending in society, even if living standards are being reduced by that very spending. That can happen for the reasons discussed previously, the worst offender being the spending of borrowed money on consumption. That boosts GDP and may temporarily boost living standards but lowers a country's net worth and future living standards, since the debt will have to be repaid, while consumption, unlike investment, does not increase a borrower's ability to do so. Most government spending is for consumption, and much of it is borrowed.

We've seen this disparity between living standards and GDP in the three years since Covid arrived in the US in early 2020. We had trillions in government stimulus programs, so after an initial dip, GDP soared. That happened despite a decreased supply of goods and services as people were locked down, at home tending kids whose schools were shut, or otherwise not producing much except what could be done from home. That imbalance of strongly subsidized demand and limited supply led to the greatest price inflation in decades, lowering living standards for anyone whose income didn't keep up, i.e., most people, and who lacked the financial reserves to make up the difference in prices.

That shouldn't have come as a surprise to anyone. If we and the rest of the world are producing less of what people want, how can our living standards collectively be anything but lower, no matter how many stimmy checks are handed out?

The best things about focusing on living standards rather than GDP is that it allows one to see how economic inequality really plays out in society. Let's oversimplify for this explanation and imagine that society is divided into two classes, the "rich" and the "poor." The quotation marks are there because the definition is non-standard.

The "rich" are people who have either high income, a large amount of liquid savings, or both. They are people who can afford to buy what they want to maintain an acceptable living standard, and still have money left over. If the prices they must pay go up, they may not like it, but they can still buy just as much output as before.

The "poor" are all those of any income level who need to use their entire income to maintain what they consider to be an acceptable lifestyle. They are already at their credit limits and have no extra reserves. Their living standard is directly harmed by any inflation in their market basket because they literally can't pay higher prices. They have no choice but to reduce or eliminate some of what used to be regular purchases.

A high-income person can effectively be one of "the poor" if they spend extravagantly and consider that necessary for their self-image. Price increases force them to give up something. A low-income person can effectively be one of "the rich" if they lead a frugal life and manage to build up substantial savings by spending less than their income. Prices have some room to rise without it requiring them to give up anything.

If prices drop for any reason, however, the "poor" get all the benefit, because they can now upgrade their living standards if they so choose. Lower prices let the "rich" save more but have little effect on their living standards because they were not financially constrained before prices dropped. That is the *opposite* of what leftists constantly state: that free markets help the rich and not the poor. The *Progress Mechanism*, a major engine of free markets, by constantly pressuring prices lower, helps the living standards of the poor, not the rich.

Leftists claim that profits at any level are exploitation of the employees of an organization. So, are we, in our role as consumers, exploiting owners and employees of every company who effectively give us raises in our living standards when they invest and risk their own money to produce output at a lower cost, which we soon thereafter can buy from them at a cheaper price?

No, we aren't exploiting anybody. This is parallel to what, in theology, is considered divine grace, a gift one receives from God because God is merciful and loves us, not because we have done anything to deserve it.

The free market bestows rising living standards upon everyone in society, whether we work hard and sacrifice some of our current consumption to save and invest, or are pure consumers, saving nothing and sitting on our couches watching TV, who benefit from others' hard work, sacrifice, and investments. This mechanism is the *Grace of the Market,* given to us by a "god" that doesn't care whether we thank it, curse it, or ignore it. The market is one of the very few gods who is never jealous.

This use of the term "Grace" is ironic. There is no reason to believe that God is lurking about the free market, making it behave, or that one must have a religious belief in the market to be in favor of it. Quite the contrary, *Grace of the Market* shows up because of businesses doing what makes sense for them to do in their competition with others in their industry. This is what Adam Smith meant by "the invisible hand."

As economist Joseph Schumpeter wrote in 1942, "*Queen Elizabeth [the first] owned silk stockings. The capitalist achievement does not typically consist in providing more silk stockings for queens but in bringing them within the reach of factory girls in return for steadily decreasing amounts of effort."*

Grace of the Market is not unidirectional from the rich countries, who can afford to invest, to the poor ones who can't, but whose living standards rise when being able to afford newly invented technology. Rich countries also benefit from international trade, wherein labor-intensive production moves to countries with low wages, freeing more people in developed countries to work at jobs where they can add more value and be paid accordingly.

One-ply thinkers see the closing of clothing factories in the US when production moved to China as something that should have been prevented with high tariffs. But they forget that US consumers' living standards rose when they could get a shirt for their child for $10 rather than $25. What do they think the buyers did with their $15 savings? Turned it into dollar bills, set them on fire, and roasted marshmallows?

No, they used those dollars for something else, whatever that may have been. Providing that output requires employees, too. Because we can't know what people did and continue to do with those savings, we can't point out who exactly got hired doing what because consumers can get clothing cheaper, but they must exist.

When our needs for goods are satisfied, we spend more on services, which generate jobs that are usually better paid and have better working conditions than a dusty, noisy textile factory. Providing services tends to be more labor intensive than producing products, so by importing products inexpensively, it may help to increase total employment, not destroy jobs, as protectionists claim.

It is likely not a coincidence that the entrance of China into international trade starting in the 1980s, combined with the rise of Walmart, which specializes in distributing low-cost goods manufactured abroad, coincided with the rise of yoga studios, health clubs, spas, Pilates classes, personal trainers, massage therapy, and the like. Saving on clothing and other items gave consumers the money to afford those things, and it created service jobs which few of those who have them would want to give up for a job in a shirt factory.

This argument is also useful against Luddites, who are against technology because, allegedly, people lose their jobs. In the year 1800, more than 90% of the population had to work on farms so people would have enough to eat. If you could go back in a time machine and tell somebody living then that, in 200 years, only 2% of the population would work on farms and they would produce so much food that a billion people here and abroad could be fed very well with their output, that person from 1800 would predict that there would be massive unemployment of farm workers. Obviously, we have figured out other things for people to get well paid to do, with easier work than farming.

This has always been true and always will be true of any new technology, artificial intelligence included. New technology gets adopted when it cuts unit costs or adds quality and features at the same cost. That cuts prices for consumers, thereby raising their standard of living and giving them more to spend or save and invest. When they do, that creates new jobs that weren't needed before. This is just the normal working of the *Progress Mechanism*.

Of course, the older, laid-off textile worker from the closed factory is unlikely to move to another city and become a yoga instructor. Society should always be looking for better ways to ameliorate their loss of income. But there is no point keeping alive businesses whose output isn't wanted just to keep people working there.

One characteristic of living standards is "stickiness." Most people place a lot of importance on their social standing. Should they suffer financial reverses, whether due to reduced income or inflation in the prices of their market basket, they often take steps to keep that unknown in their social set. They may immediately cut their spending on things that are not detectable to outsiders, such as switching from expensive wine to beer, but still attempt to maintain their previous lifestyle as much as possible. The stickiness of their living standards means they keep buying as before and save less or run up credit-card debt. Collectively, lower savings means lower business investment, which means reduced growth in productivity and incomes.

This is significant because, as you'll see ahead, the cost of paying for the government itself and its programs adds to everyone's cost of living. People respond by maintaining their living standards while shrinking how much they save. Reduced savings equals reduced business investment equals a slowdown of the *Progress Mechanism* and diminished growth of living standards.

WHAT RAISES LIVING STANDARDS?

• • •

THE CLASSIC WORK ON economics, Adam Smith's *The Wealth of Nations*, published in 1776, pointed out that economic output is greatly enhanced by the division of labor. That means you specialize in producing something others want and get efficient at it. Then you sell what you have produced and use the proceeds to buy food, clothing, shelter, and anything else that others specialize in, rather than try to produce everything yourself.

There are only a few things you can do with your income. You can spend it on consumption items, donate it to charity, or you can save and invest it. Without savings, there can be no investment, and without investment, there can be very little growth in living standards in a country. Even very poor countries with little ability to save can still experience a rise in living standards through the *Grace of the Market* mechanism, as investment elsewhere makes newer products and technologies available, and rising efficiencies elsewhere makes products and services available at lower costs.

Still, the biggest increases in living standards come from higher incomes, which are highly correlated to the value to others one adds by one's work. There is a great range of models. Some people add a lot of value to a few customers, such as trendy painters who can sell each of their artworks for enormous sums to rich collectors. Or one can add a small amount of value to many customers at once, such as sports or movie stars. Those with high incomes and some self-discipline can save enough to invest in higher-risk opportunities that, should they work out well, can add to their future incomes.

In talking about economic history, people correctly emphasize advances in technology that have increased living standards, but incorrectly believe that technological advances show up on their own without us having to do anything. For most of us that is true, but first somebody had to innovate, and companies had to raise and spend money to turn the new ideas into a sellable product or service. A successful technology also requires continued savings and investment to turn what starts out as an expensive niche item into something with widespread usage.

Business investment involves using money that could have been used by a company or its investors for consumption, risking its loss. If we want future generations to have higher living standards than we do ourselves, some of us must be willing to forego consuming all our income, and instead invest it in people with the knowledge and incentives to use the money wisely, in the hopes of achieving future income much greater than what had been sacrificed earlier.

This section of the book covers how people get good ideas on where to invest, and how capital flows around the economy, constantly moving toward where it will do the most good. These are natural developments in free markets, since they are self-regulating ecosystems like many others, with a built-in communications system and forces that keep things in balance. You'll see incentives that are generated to direct capital toward where there is the greatest need for more capacity—and away from where supply is more than ample already. We'll examine a couple examples of investment spending by governments that were great successes, find out what made them so, and discuss why they are so rare.

When you start reading **Chapter 7**, *The Marsh and the Market*, you may think a chapter from a memoir by some tree-hugger got placed in this book by mistake. Not so. When I say the laws of economics that control micro and its mechanisms are based on innate human nature, that underestimates its source. Humans are just one life form among many, and the behavior of all have much more in common than you might think. The self-regulating ecosystems into which all life finds its roles have a lot in common with free markets.

Chapter 8 discusses two other mechanisms that keep free markets organized in a way that gives consumers more of what they want. **Chapter 9** covers the communications system that alerts those with money where others think capital will be most rewarded, and where it will be lost. **Chapter 10** compares the motivations of people in private and public sector and uses the Erie Canal and the Interstate Highway System as examples of two government-funded and -managed projects that more than paid their own way.

CHAPTER 7

THE MARSH AND THE MARKET

• • •

M Y FAMILY SPENT MANY summers at a house in New England next to a large tidal salt marsh, home to a variety of wildlife. Besides the fish, frogs, turtles, and shellfish in the water and the birds and raccoons that eat them, there are many other creatures there, such as insects, mice, squirrels, chipmunks, snakes, deer, foxes, and coyotes. Unlike us, they were not on their summer vacation. They were there to eat, reproduce, and try not to get eaten themselves.

We noticed that the populations of some of these creatures fluctuated considerably over time. The coyotes and foxes in particular seem to come and go. Some years, we heard what appeared to be several packs of coyotes yipping and howling at night. The next several years there might not be any of them around, and then they would come back, almost as if they decided to leave our marsh fallow for a while to let the population of their favorite prey—mice and other small rodents—build back up, while they worked some other marshes along the coast. Their occasional disappearance never guaranteed a complete revival of the prey population, because there are hawks and snakes around who eat the same prey, and those populations also vary from year to year.

The combined forces of the predators never wipe out their prey. Even if they did, it would be temporary, because without much food left in the marsh, the predators would have to go elsewhere to survive. Eventually some hungry rodents would happen upon our marsh again, and not knowing of the recent slaughter of their distant relatives, would find it to be an attractive place to build a home and raise a family, at least until their predators chance upon the marsh again.

Nothing about that story should surprise you. We've all learned that the natural world is very complex, but also has various forces that keep things in balance without requiring any human intervention. Nobody would suggest the government keep track of how many rodents are in the marsh and either import or export foxes and coyotes if the mouse count seems too high or low. We know nature will take care of that without us doing anything, other than perhaps correcting problems we humans caused, like permitting the hunting of deer overpopulations that exist due to our elimination of the wolves, who were their main predators.

We know there are complicated relationships between different types of ocean fish, such that when humans overfish one species, that can lead to an overpopulation of its prey and a consequent population plunge in the prey's prey. Nobody doubts though, that if humans stopped all fishing, all that would come back into balance, although a different balance, given that some species might have been overfished to extinction.

That is the way nature works. It self-regulates perfectly well without requiring management by humans. Over long periods of time, the climate and geography can change, altering the mix of species in various areas. Occasionally, after tens or hundreds of millions of years, something drastic happens to the world, like an asteroid strike or a massive volcano eruption, that lead to mass extinctions and the ultimate rise of newly evolved creatures. Outside of that, things usually stay in balance.

The marsh is an ecosystem that has been in existence in many places on the planet for hundreds of millions of years. It has been self-regulating its animal and plant populations all that time in much the same way. The principle is simple—if predators become too successful against their prey, they over-reproduce, shrinking the prey population further. Then they starve, shrinking their own numbers back down. Their prey disappears or diminishes and later, when the predators have died or wandered off, the prey can come back and do well for a while. If the ratio of predators to prey seems out of balance, just wait—the passage of time will cure that.

Besides having natural governing forces, the marsh has three communications/mapping systems to alert creatures to the presence or absence of others that they either view as food or fear as predators. Probably the most important part of the system is smell; many creatures use scent to mark their territories, scare off rivals, and attract mates. That has the unintended side effect of alerting both prey and predators to their presence, making their lives a little tougher in both directions. Sounds are also important, with mating calls letting other creatures, whose interest in the caller is in eating it or trying to avoid being eaten by it, know they are there. And hawks, owls, and other sharp-eyed creatures get visual messages to help them get their next meal.

Humans regularly demonstrate that, if ever we think we know enough about a natural ecosystem to change it, we actually don't know enough. Early in the 20th century, experts recommended that the town restrict tidal flows to a different marsh several miles away to reduce or eliminate a mosquito problem. Bad idea. That made the mosquito problem worse, because it prevented all but a few of the fish who love to eat mosquito larvae from gaining access to them, and had other negative effects. Noted ecologist Frank Egler put it best: *Ecosystems are not only more complex than we think, they are more complex than we can think.*

A marsh isn't all that special. Nature consists of nothing but self-regulating ecosystems on land, in the sea, in forest canopies, inside digestive tracts, and everywhere else where there is life. They all have communications systems and mechanisms that have emerged to keep things in balance.

The human economy is also a natural ecosystem, much like all the others, that emerged in prehistoric times in the form of markets and trade. We know this because of the presence in many of the earliest archaeological sites of jewelry, beads, and other goods which originated in places far from where locals could have traveled. The economy's purpose is different in that we humans are not trying to eat each other, but rather interact with each other to take advantage of the higher productivity that comes from the division of labor when everyone does what they do best and trades their excess output to others.

Within a family or in a small village or tribe, where everyone knows and is at least somewhat related to everyone else, no special economic system is needed since people naturally try to help those with whom they are close. What the free market provides is the system by which millions of strangers who may not even like each other can trade to get what they want as cooperatively as if they were related. That allows vastly higher income and wealth.

What keeps the economy providing these benefits are the same two things as in every other ecosystem. One is a communications/mapping system that reports on what exists and where, what other people want, what they will offer in return, and on what terms. The other is a collection of powerful self-governing mechanisms that keeps resources moving toward where they can be most productive and output moving toward where it is most highly valued.

Worth noticing about natural ecosystems is how differently real scientists look upon them versus how macroeconomists look at the economy. Natural ecosystems are studied by many types of scientists, whose focus is to understand them in all their complexity. In only a few of them, such as the bacterial biome in the digestive tract of people with certain illnesses, are scientists trying to make changes in the ecosystem. Most scientists studying ecosystems are just "trying one's utmost to understand the real workings of the world" as one of this book's two epigraphs states.

What they would never do is invent a poorly designed number, like macroeconomists did with GDP, to try to characterize an intricate ecosystem, as if only that one number tells us all we need to know. It requires a combination of simplemindedness and hubris to assert control over a spontaneously ordered ecosystem to maximize one defective measurement.

The parallels between any natural ecosystem and the economy are many and deep. For example, every living thing, from humans to the tiniest, single-cell creature to bacteria and viruses, are all in business, whether they know it or not. That business is generating enough energy to live, reproduce, and prosper as much as possible within the constraints of their nature and their environment.

Energy is to all living things what money is to the economy. Humans perform jobs, get paid money, and use it to buy food and other things, some of which indirectly result in reproduction. In most societies, we no longer directly purchase a spouse, but we need money to have the right wardrobe and other lifestyle signals to attract potential mates. Yes, humans are vastly more complicated in what goals we choose (which might include not reproducing) than creatures whose diets are limited to one favorite food, and who follow a set format for reproduction. But the principle is the same.

The amount of energy a creature expends in obtaining food relative to the calories (energy) derived from the food is critical to its survival. Just as a business that keeps losing money will eventually go broke, a creature who consumes more energy than the calorie content of what they eat will die. As a result, there is a premium throughout nature for creatures to use whatever brainpower they have to be shrewd cost accountants, looking for an energy profit.

The lioness must ask herself, *Is it worth the energy expense to chase after that group of gazelles, with the risk that they might outrun me?* A lion who is good at assessing costs, benefits, and probabilities of success will likely outlive another who is faster and stronger but wastes too much precious energy in futile chases.

The classic book *Bumblebee Economics* by biologist Bernd Heinrich showed that nearly identical assessments govern the behavior of insects. Bumblebees consume a lot of energy in flying. They cannot consider going after flowers that are too far from the hive, because the nectar and pollen they gather won't cover the energy expense of getting there and back.

Perhaps you've been offered, but turned down, a higher paying job at a location that would require a much longer commute. Your evaluation may have been a bit more sophisticated than an insect's, because you counted as negative your subjective cost of being stuck in traffic for more hours per week or you considered the greater cost of fuel and wear and tear on your car. Still, the analysis is the same.

Bumblebee behavior is dictated by their nature. They are in constant competition with foragers from other hives trying to harvest the same field of flowers, but they never attack each other. Because bumblebees evolved more than 25 million years ago in northern latitudes where there were many small flowers, each with limited supplies of food, it has never been worth their while to fight to capture or defend any given flower or tell other hive members where they found whatever they found.

By contrast, honeybees evolved in the tropics, where there are banana trees and other plants with huge loads of nectar and pollen, too much for any one bee to fully exploit. Thus, they developed elaborate methods to communicate the location of a big find to other members of the hive, along with aggression against other colonies to monopolize the rich resource.

It was not by random chance that honeybees behave differently than bumblebees. Their behavior is an effective response to the environment in which they evolved. Neither an aggressive bumblebee nor a placid, inarticulate honeybee is doing their hives any favors, given the economics of how they acquire food, so those traits died out long ago.

This difference in behavior matches the different corporate cultures one finds in human industries, where what it takes to be successful, and the background and nature of the people who regularly work in the field, can vary considerably. Insurance sales, steel manufacturing, software development, farming, clothing manufacturing, etc., all have different characteristics in terms of capital needs, volatility of demand, fixed versus variable costs, the degree of government regulation, and many other factors. Those affect how many companies are in those industries, how they compete and cooperate, and the personality characteristics of people who typically do well or poorly in them.

The desire for profits isn't limited to the animal world. Underground fungi interact with the roots of various plants, hand over nitrate and phosphate raw materials that the plants need and the fungi gather easily, and receive from the plants nutrients they need, namely sugars and fats that plants make through photosynthesis.

A 2019 article in *The Economist* discussed a study published in *Current Biology* by a Dutch scientist, Dr. Toby Kiers, that suggests that *"like cunning merchants who know how to make a profit, fungi exploit resource scarcity by marking up their prices. They demand more nutrients from plants in return for their valuable mineral commodities."* This study showed that, when, on occasion, there is a shortage of minerals, plants get into a bidding war and pay the fungi more nutrients to get those scarce resources.

In other words, it isn't an easily erased cultural trait in humans to look out for our own welfare first before sacrificing for the benefit of relative strangers. Fungi, which have been around for more than a billion years, behave like that, and all of life on Earth acts similarly.

An overlooked but fascinating book from 1990, *Bionomics*, by Michael Rothschild, focused on the great number of parallels between the economy and the natural world. He pointed out that there are efficiency gains from specialization both within companies and between companies, but that, beyond some size, a big organization ends up bloated and bureaucratic, as the cost of coordination and maintaining focus between all its components more than eats up any further efficiency gains from growth. As a result, there are vast numbers of single proprietorships in the economy, not quite as many small companies, even fewer big companies, and just a handful of giant ones.

Similarly, in the natural world, there are huge numbers of different viruses, bacteria, and single-celled creatures, with the number of species diminishing as their size increases. At the largest size, there are blue whales, giant sequoia, and some strange fungi with thin mycelia that stretch for acres underground, and that is as big as they get. One would think that in the billions of years of evolution even bigger things would have evolved, and there were a few very large dinosaurs, but the larger it is, the harder it is for an organism to operate at an energy profit.

That is as true for organizations as it is for organisms and is why the claim that free markets tend toward monopolies is false. It does explain, though, why governments are so incompetent at so much that they try to do. Lacking competitors and maintaining a monopoly on the use of force in the territory they control, they survive anyway.

If there is a profitable niche somewhere, whether in the natural world or the economy, it will get filled. Maybe not right away, but as long as an opportunity keeps growing without a living thing or company exploiting it, the payoff for doing so keeps rising.

We often see this in the economy, where a company or group of companies dominate some industry. If their strategy is to maximize short-term profits by charging high prices, they become extremely attractive targets for other companies who will invade their markets and do well by offering customers a better deal.

Just as we can see the economy in terms of the natural world, the comparison works in the other direction as well. When the marsh has a shortage of mice, the predators must think of it as if the price of mice has soared in terms of the energy cost to find and catch the few that remain, which induces predator migration to lower-cost locations.

Ideological leftists, along with others of varied political opinions, support the idea that the best thing humans can do with the natural environment is leave it as pristine and untouched as possible, because our efforts to manage or change it have so often caused more harm than good. They recognize that the natural world is teeming with living things whose interrelationship is beyond our ability to fully understand and who act as checks and balances on one another.

Yet many of those who feel that way are the very ones who advocate more government control of the economy, as if it were not also an intricate self-balancing natural order, just like any ecosystem. They may believe in evolution in the natural world but are creationists when it comes to the economy.

As economist Don Boudreaux put it, "*Statists, simply unable to grasp the reality of emergent, spontaneous, complex order, trust that all that is good in human society is traceable ultimately to the wise and wonderful conscious designs of the state . . . Despite most statists' pride in their unusual smarts and learning—many boast BAs, BSs, MAs, MSs, MBAs, MDs, PhDs, or JDs from elite universities!—they are as ignorant and as unreflective about society and the economy as the most cartoonish opponent of Darwin is ignorant of the origins of opposable thumbs and the migration of geese.*"

If you are a Progressive, you may deny that you and your friends have any thoughts of profit. Sorry to inform you, you think of little else most of the time—you just don't call it *profit*. Most people of all political views fail to notice that they personally are as hungry for profits as the "greediest" corporation.

A way of looking at day-to-day living as a human is that we are making thousands of decisions every day. Most decisions are very inconsequential, such as what to say or not say to people we meet or work with, and what facial expressions and body language to use in response to what they say.

Few choices, though, are cost-free. Shall we eat another slice of that delicious cake, or sacrifice short-term pleasure to not gain weight for health or appearance reasons? Every decision involves advancing toward one goal we have, with a cost of retreating from some other goal that another option might have provided.

We all want the benefit to exceed the cost. In other words, we want profit.

Consider your job. You have out-of-pocket costs on clothing, transportation, and meals outside the home. You also have the opportunity cost of giving up whatever else you might be doing if you did not have the job. If you don't enjoy the job, you also have the emotional expense of having to deal with whatever it is about your job that makes it annoying.

Those are your costs. If you feel that the total cost is too high relative to the value of your paycheck, the social interaction with friendly coworkers, and other benefits, you demand a raise and/or look for some other job that meets more of your wants, a place where your services are valued more highly. Your goal is always the largest profit differential between your financial and psychological revenue and what you feel are your costs.

Nobody who thinks profits are somehow bad would ever hesitate to get a better job at higher pay if one were offered. They are hypocrites to favor profiting personally, while thinking there is something morally wrong when others, such as those who run businesses, do the same thing.

It is part of human nature that we are all looking for profit all the time, whatever people care to call it. We share that characteristic with every living thing on Earth. To expect us to act differently than all the natural world is to assert that humans are not part of nature.

To Karl Marx and vast numbers of even non-Marxists, value comes only from labor, and profit is something that capitalists steal from the working person. In fact, the value of any product has little or no relationship to the amount of labor that went into making it. Its value to you depends on how much you want it, period, regardless of the work that went into it.

Workers' wages and employers' profits differ in two critical ways. The worker gets paid first for doing the job; only much later, after the product has been completed, distributed, sold, and the employer has been paid by the customers, does the company perhaps make a profit. Moreover, workers get paid even if the company does not make a profit. When that happens, one could just as easily say that the workers are exploiting the capitalist, who puts up money and loses it, yet the workers get paid just the same.

In fact, nobody is exploiting anybody—they have just signed up for different deals, with different potential payoffs and risks. Some people would rather have a steady paycheck and no risk of their hard work giving them zero or negative pay, while others are willing to work for long periods with little or no pay to have a chance to earn much more than a regular paycheck. People often switch sides, with workers quitting to set up a business in competition with their old employer, or owners closing or selling a business to take a salaried job in management.

Work that produces nothing anyone wants has no value. Only by transforming resources to make them worth more than they cost is any value created, the differential being the profit that is the ultimate source of wages to both workers and management, and any return to investors.

The process of trying to maximize profits has important implications. Striving for greater efficiency, increased productivity, and conservation of resources, is the essence of progress. The steady growth in the value of output relative to the cost of inputs is what has produced the explosion of wealth in every capitalist country for many centuries. The *Progress Mechanism* has that name because it is about companies trying to reduce unit costs, and what happens as a result.

What is the alternative? Those who think that the world would be better if business profits were lower or non-existent are essentially suggesting that people should acquire resources and then use them to produce output that is not worth more than the inputs. Those who hold that opinion may call themselves Progressives, but what they want would end all economic progress.

Socialism is based on the idea that people will work hard despite getting little or no reward for themselves for doing so, other than the dubious pleasure of knowing they have helped their collective group increase its output.

In the early 1920s, less than five years after the Bolshevik revolution that put them in charge, the USSR's communists recognized that they weren't getting the economic output they expected. They correctly diagnosed the problem as a contradiction between socialism and human nature. There were no incentives for hard work since bonuses for some would make workers unequal. Consequently, nobody worked hard unless threatened by the management thugs who were needed to get much output at all.

Those thugs were under pressure from the more violent thugs above them, all the way up to the national leadership. That process gave the world leaders such as Lenin, Stalin, Mao, Hitler, Pol Pot, Castro, Chavez, and numerous dictatorial socialist leaders of African countries.

The obvious conclusion, that socialism is certain to be a failure and free markets should be reintroduced, was not one that the USSR's early leaders would accept. They had worked hard and risked their lives to seize power in the name of socialism, and, like most politicians, they weren't inclined to give up their power merely to let the population have better lives.

Rather than admit that they had been wrong, they preferred that socialism would stay, but human nature would have to change. What they needed to do, they said, to make socialism work right, was to create the "New Soviet Man."

From the current Wikipedia article: *"The Soviet man was to be selfless, learned, healthy, muscular, and enthusiastic in spreading the communist Revolution. Adherence to Marxism–Leninism, and individual behavior consistent with that philosophy's prescriptions, were among the crucial traits expected of the New Soviet man, which required intellectualism and hard discipline. He was not driven by crude impulses of nature but by conscious self-mastery, a belief that required the rejection of both innate personality and the unconscious . . . He treated public property with respect, as if it were his own. His work required exertion and austerity, to show the new man triumphing over his base instincts."*

And so on, and a new Soviet Woman was needed as well. Have you ever met anyone like that? Not just pretending to deceive their boss, but actually like that? No? Didn't think so.

It doesn't sound like they really wanted humans at all; they wanted bees or ants in human form, allowing the top leaders to remain the pampered queens. If such workers existed, or could be created over time, then socialist governments wouldn't need the brutal coercion they all eventually use to get the populace to do their bidding. And no, starting out as "democratic socialism" cannot prevent that outcome.

The USSR's attempts to create such hypothetical humans, using education, inspiring art and movies, and everything else it could think of, all flopped. Human nature, formed over hundreds of thousands of years of human evolution, thousands of years of civilization, and derived from all of evolution since life began, cannot be changed with inspiring wall posters, no matter how cute and kitschy they might now be as apartment decorations.

Altering human nature, if it could be done, is necessary for socialism to produce anything other than poverty and oppression. Necessary, but not sufficient. If through genetic alteration someone in the future could turn out a country's worth of Socialist Man and Woman clones, socialism would still be a flop.

The free-market economy has market prices for everything, and they, along with the commentary and opinions that usually accompany them, convey information to participants. Market prices, based upon people and businesses spending their own money, reveal what people really value and are the free market's automatically generated communication/mapping system.

That allows people to produce the greatest value of output while minimizing as much as possible the cost of inputs, thereby adding value and raising living standards by doing so. Socialism doesn't have prices, except nominal and arbitrary ones at best, and flies blind as a result, constantly wasting resources because it lacks the information needed to use them most efficiently, impoverishing their populace.

Vile tyranny though it was, the USSR shouldn't be singled out for trying to contradict human nature. Politicians everywhere will do the same to promote their agenda. As mentioned previously, 2020-22 featured government-restricted supply combined with government-stimulated demand. Why that resulted in sharply higher price inflation should have been clear to anyone.

Nevertheless, senator Liz Warren and ex-cabinet member from the Clinton administration Robert Reich claim that the cause of the inflation was corporate greed. Supposedly businesses were greedy for more money, so they all raised prices.

Not counting people suffering from a personality change due to Alzheimer's or some other disorder, have you ever known even a single person who was not self-interested at all for more than ten years (inflation rates were near 0% for more than a decade after the housing collapse) and who then, suddenly, with no warning, became wildly greedy? No? Not surprised. But if you have met such a person or know of one, have you met a second one? That would be extremely rare.

Yet Warren and Reich claim that millions of businesses who raised their prices in 2022 are managed by CEOs who are exactly like that, kind and generous to their customers for more than a decade, and then instantly, and simultaneously with a million other insane CEOs, becoming greedy. It is a strange world they think we live in.

CHAPTER 8

TWO IMPORTANT ORGANIZING MECHANISMS

• • •

IN THE MARSH OR any natural ecosystem, if the prey population has diminished to the point where the cost of catching them has risen close to their calorie value, the predators will head off to where the living is easier, allowing the prey population to recover until it has expanded enough that it pays for the predators to return.

There is a similar process working all the time in free markets that causes the output of various goods and services to rise and fall as anticipated demand relative to supply changes. Businesses invest money where they expect there will be a high return relative to the risk they are willing to take. A high return is likely if, when the investment creates an expanded supply of widgets, there is still an excess of demand, keeping prices and profits high.

Being human, businesspeople sometimes err, either overestimating future demand or underestimating the supply in addition to their own that will show up. With an excess of supply over demand, profits are low or below zero.

Misdirected capital produces too much of what people don't want and not enough of what they do want, which hurts living standards. Losses mount up for those who aren't good at assessing future supply/demand imbalances. Reducing their bank accounts is the free-market ecosystem's Darwinian way to punish poor predictions, limiting the ability of those who make them to misallocate savings in the future, while profits give good predictors more money to deploy.

Capital moves to where the best opportunities are. This is no different from anyone moving to a better job with more pay and other benefits, financial and psychological. Everyone does that for themselves, if possible, and they do it with their money, too. Since it is their own, their business's, or their employer's money at risk, people assess it carefully.

I call this the *Capital Cycle Mechanism*. It is a cousin of the *Progress Mechanism*, discussed earlier, which had to do with companies' investments in their own business, trying to lower unit costs, innovate, and raise quality, eventually leading to lower prices which raise living standards. The *Capital Cycle Mechanism* describes the flow of capital from companies into promising opportunities outside their current operations where their existing technology, distribution connections, or other advantages make them believe they can succeed.

The *Capital Cycle Mechanism* also goes in the opposite direction, when companies withdraw capital from businesses with poor results and prospects, extracting as much cash as they can to use where the outlook is better. Nobody likes to see a factory or a chain of stores close and lay off all employees, but keeping around zombie companies that aren't adding value to anyone prevents other businesses from using those people (workers and management) and other resources (machinery, buildings, and capital) to satisfy other needs where demand is rising faster than supply.

Smart capital allocation is important because we don't have infinite capital. Investments can come only from savings, and we save only a small part of our incomes. From the 1950s through the first half of the 1980s, in the US, savings were always at least 10% of disposable income. In the current century, except temporarily during Covid when the government was issuing stimulus checks faster than people could spend them, the number has always been under 10%, recently under 5%.

Those personal and business savings have been more than counteracted by government deficit spending, the overwhelming bulk of which goes to consumption or waste, including much, if not most, of what politicians call "investment."

Fortunately, businesses save and invest a lot, at around $600 billion per year in the US in recent years. The capital they invest comes from earnings not paid to shareholders in the form of dividends or stock buybacks, which is an example of the sacrifice of current consumption, plus non-cash charges against earnings. If opportunities look good enough to justify it, they can raise equity by selling shares and raise debt by selling bonds or getting loans.

Let's suppose that widget demand has been strong, widget prices high, and there are plausible reasons to expect demand to continue to rise sharply in the coming years. Widget companies could pay high dividends to shareholders and big bonuses to executives, and some will, but the temptation will be great for them all to invest much of their profits to expand their businesses. The producers of luxury widgets might want to put out a stripped-down line to attack the middle and low end of the market and will need new production equipment and perhaps a new factory to do that. The middle and low-end players may want to go after the higher end of the market. That will require more investment in R&D to add features and innovations to justify the higher prices, as well as more productive capacity.

Finally, some companies not yet in the widget industry but capable of winning a decent market share if they enter may do so. A big increase in supply may well be entering the market ahead, solving the problem of excess demand. The high profits were both an automatic message that the problem of expected excess demand existed and an incentive to solve it.

Even before the new widget supply shows up for sale in the marketplace, effective widget prices will likely drop. Seeing higher output on the way, including more of their own in many cases, widget makers will want to sell off excess inventory, at a big discount if need be, before competitors show up. Meanwhile, more buyers may have had the time to look for less-expensive alternatives, and some found them or figured out a different way to solve whatever it was that they needed widgets for, without having to use widgets at all. Reduced demand and extra supply are negative for prices and possibly fatal to profits.

But that is as it should be. If there will no longer be a shortage of widgets, we shouldn't want more capacity expansion. Lower prices are a loud message to all that says, *We have plenty of widgets now. We don't need more investment. Your capital, engineers, and staff would be much better off deployed elsewhere.*

No humans specifically create this very useful information. Price information, and all that it implies, is a cost-free byproduct of people buying and selling widgets, trying to get the best deal because it is their own money at stake.

Compare that to a socialist state, where central planners or workers' councils make all the plans. Even if they correctly anticipated strong widget demand, the degree to which the industry needs more investment to expand output keeps changing as supply and demand do. But planners are busy (and are fallible and sometimes corrupt) and can spend only so much time on widgets. The probability of a mismatch of supply and demand constantly getting worse over time, with nobody willing to deviate from their required course until the next new plan is adopted, is a common problem, one of the many maladies to befall socialism in the USSR and everywhere else it has been tried.

With free markets, we never have to wait for a committee of experts to investigate the widget market to form an opinion about the need for widget capacity, and order a certain amount of new investment, which they hope turns out to be the right amount, but personally losing no money if wrong. The market for widgets itself, through prices, will speak the truth about the current supply/demand balance to anyone with sufficient knowledge of the industry.

When demand is rising faster than supply and prices are rising, that is a message that more supply will be rewarded with high profits. If supply grows too fast and prices start dropping, that is a message that capital should go elsewhere. That is the *Capital Cycle Mechanism*, and it acts like the governors on steam engines in the old days, mechanisms that kept speed at the appropriate level, pressuring it down if too fast and up if too slow.

If the reason why widgets are being bought heavily is one that suggests strong secular growth in demand, and there exist barriers to entry or other reasons to expect a modest investment response to the high profits, then prices and profits can stay high for a long time, continuing to broadcast the message that providing more supply will be rewarded.

If investment takes the form of companies purchasing a new generation of equipment that can make widgets much cheaper, *The Progress Mechanism* kicks in and reduces prices, and if demand turns out to be very elastic (small decreases in price cause a big jump in demand), then supply from business investment won't necessarily exceed demand.

The fact that prices and profits are simultaneously a message and an incentive seems obvious, but this seems unknown to most politicians and many economists. One current example involves the recent energy shortage worldwide, with many causes, including the Russia-Ukraine war and active governmental discouragement for climate reasons of companies drilling, putting up pipelines or refineries, or getting financing. This is the policy of many developed countries, intended to make the use of fossil fuel less attractive than renewable resources.

As the *Capital Cycle Mechanism* commands, this reduced business investment resulted in a shortage of supply relative to demand, consequently high prices, and profits. Ordinarily this would attract a lot of investment and, after a lag for drilling to produce oil and gas, and refinery expansions to convert crude and gas to usable products, much more supply would show up and push prices back down. If we wanted to eliminate the shortage and high prices, that is all we need to do—nothing at all—and let the profits attract investment.

Instead, there is talk in many political capitals of imposing a windfall profits tax on energy companies, and such a law has gone into effect in the UK. The concept is that the jump in energy prices was an unexpected windfall to the energy companies, not something they deserved, so the government should grab any extra money they earned. That takes away capital from the only people who know how to use it to solve the problem of shortages and high prices and discourages the investment that will be needed to create the supply that will reduce prices.

Energy prices make big swings in both directions because, in the short run, both supply and demand are inelastic (the quantities participants desire to buy or sell are not greatly affected by changes in prices.) During the collapse of demand in 2020 due to government ordered Covid lockdowns, oil prices went below $0.00 per barrel for a while, because production was coming in faster than there were places to store the stuff.

What is the opposite of a windfall—apples flying up off the ground and reattaching themselves to trees? That is what happened then. One didn't see any politicians saying the government should write big checks to energy companies because of a price collapse that the government itself caused, to make up for losses that the oil companies didn't do anything to deserve.

Fairness doesn't matter when businesses are concerned, but the risk assessments of businesses do matter to their investments. Would you put money into a business that will have periods of big losses and big gains, in which the gains get heavily taxed, while the losses are tough luck to the business? Increasing the chances of a poor return over time under those circumstances is a strong discouragement to investment.

The idea of taxing companies because of windfall profits makes one wonder about government-operated lotteries. They have been described as a tax on people who aren't good at calculating probability. If you bet $5 per day for 25 years, you will have spent almost $46,000, not counting interest you might have earned having left that money in the bank. The odds are high that the total of any winnings over those years will be less than that.

Lotteries are a great deal for the government, which nets a nice profit without annoying people by raising taxes. But it isn't necessarily a bad deal for the bettors. Most are perfectly aware that betting on lotteries is not a rational strategy to invest for retirement, but they bet anyway because that isn't why they buy the tickets.

If they place their bet in the morning for a lottery whose winning number is revealed at the end of that evening, then they have all day to daydream about what they might do if that is the day their number comes in and they win a million dollars or whatever the payout is. A weekly lottery is even a better deal, when, for one small purchase, they are buying the right to daydream for up to seven days about a payoff likely far bigger than all they would earn over their entire working life.

Now suppose the government said that winning a lottery is a windfall profit that was generated randomly, not something you earned or deserved. Those who win will be subject to a special windfall profit tax of 95% of the lottery payoff, so even if you win, you won't get much money after taxes.

How many would still buy lottery tickets? Nobody who knows about the tax, and government revenues from the lottery would plummet. This seems obvious, which is why no government ever proposes such a tax, but they do exactly that with companies that provide oil, which we need a lot more than the government needs lottery proceeds. For a government in recent years, lack of money is no longer a constraint on spending.

The government, through taxes, regulations, cost impositions, and other methods, can suck profits out of an industry, but it can't prevent people from moving their capital elsewhere when that happens, reducing output or output growth, and setting the stage for higher prices and profits in the industry on any increase in demand.

A plausible question about the *Capital Cycle*: does its existence mean that all industries trend toward having the same ROI? One might think that capital would flow from low-ROI industries toward higher ones, subtracting capacity growth from the former and adding it to the latter, pressuring prices and profits up in the first and down in the second, eventually equalizing expected returns.

No, that doesn't happen, for a couple reasons: One is that industries are very different, and while a copper-mining company could move into zinc mining easily enough, it isn't going to enter high-fashion clothing no matter how high the ROI might be there.

The other reason is that different industries have different risk profiles. A copper miner in a third-world country must earn a high return to make up for the political risk of a revolution that nationalizes the property or a new regime that tears up the old contract and doubles taxes. Companies, as well as investors, want the highest ROI only after they adjust for what they perceive to be the risk. Money keeps moving around to more attractive opportunities as assessments of risk and reward change.

Some people are frightened of change and want things to be as stable as possible. But economic reality, which reflects people's changing wants and the changing ways to meet those desires, is not stable. In free markets, the reward goes to those who best anticipate change and respond ahead of others. The result is a system that quickly gives people what they want because businesses are rewarded with profits for doing so and penalized with losses for not, as opposed to the stability of a system that has long since stopped serving people's needs, but never changes.

One way in which the *Capital Cycle Mechanism* differs from the *Progress Mechanism* is that the latter operates in only one direction, toward greater efficiency, lower unit costs, and eventually lower prices because of business investment of various kinds. The *Capital*

Cycle Mechanism operates in both directions. Governments often impose on businesses various obligations that raise their costs, such as higher taxes, mandatory employee benefits, the hiring of extra administrative staff to submit reports to government bureaucracies, and other things that require increased legal expenses.

As costs rise, some companies can restore profits by raising prices or cutting other costs, but those that can't foist the higher costs on others will suffer reduced profits. That makes the business less attractive for investment and less attractive to banks or other lenders. The reduced availability of capital will slow or end any further investment, which will reduce the growth of supply. That will pressure prices higher in the future should demand rise. In other words, if companies can't recover higher costs and taxes from their customers or employees sooner, they will be able to do so later.

There is another mechanism that does the same thing as the *Capital Cycle Mechanism* for staff—where people work, where they form businesses to work together, and what they do when working. This mechanism is called *Patterns of Sustainable Specialization and Trade*, or *PSST*, named by economist and writer Arnold S. Kling. One might call him the inventor of the concept, but he would probably claim to be no more than the person who noticed its existence in the economy and pointed out its importance.

The division-of-labor concept says we should each just do one job and get good at it. The job for most of us has nothing to do with creating the food, clothing, and shelter that are everyone's basic needs, but that is not a problem because what we do is valuable enough to our employer or, if we own a business, to our customers, that they pay us money we can use to buy those things from others.

As standards of living have risen over the years, we all can be more demanding and specific about what we want, e.g., bread and water are no longer good enough by themselves for our whole diet. Some of the output we want requires many steps before it exists and is delivered into our hands. An excellent example is Leonard Read's *I, Pencil*, the classic essay from 1958 that showed all the steps needed to get a finished pencil into the hands of a consumer. There are eight components needed to make a standard pencil, and each one has its own supply chain.

Whatever our specialty, we probably work with thousands of others whom we have never met or ever will, who have done some jobs before or after we have done ours to create the final product. Even in a service industry, some large number of people built the building you are in, made your chair, provided the electricity for the lights, and so forth.

We don't get together with thousands of others in advance to plan all this out. Rather our connection with others doesn't extend very far into the earlier or later phases of the complete chain of specialization beyond our own position. We need a desk to work, so we buy the one that most fits our needs, including our financial constraints. We don't concern ourselves about the cost, quality, or origin of the metal and wood in the desk—it's the desk maker's problem to come up with something we want to buy, just as we can't get too involved in what users do with our output other than making it good enough for them to buy it from us.

These cooperative chains form spontaneously and can fall apart easily as customers change what they want. After the housing bubble collapsed in 2007-2010, there were many unemployed people in the building trades. But the pattern of companies making building supplies, architects designing buildings, developers putting up projects, contractors and tradespeople building them, and customers getting financing to buy them had disintegrated.

A skilled but unemployed carpenter probably would have wanted their old job back because the pay was great and nothing else the carpenter could do would pay as much, but the pattern that needed the carpenter no longer existed. There was a glut of empty houses everywhere. Nobody could make any money building more for a long while after. If carpenters wanted to earn more than what unemployment checks followed by welfare would provide, they would have to find some other chain to participate in, either using their carpentry skills or trying to monetize some other talents or connections they might have.

Macroeconomists, who think in aggregates rather than specifics, i.e., that everyone works in a giant GDP factory (as Kling puts it), seem unaware of the need for new patterns to be formed, which can take a while, when a recession wipes out previously successful PSST chains. Macro tools involving monetary and/or fiscal policies will not be very effective at causing that to happen.

By rights PSST deserves a much larger place in this book than this, but Kling's *Specialization and Trade: A Re-introduction to Economics* is an easily understood book that explores it in much more depth than can be offered here.

CHAPTER 9

MESSAGES CROWD-SOURCED
FROM SPECULATORS

• • •

So far, we have seen the benefits of business investment in new products, processes, and other innovations that cut prices and therefore raise living standards. We have ignored as mere asset-price speculation people buying already-existing stocks and other assets.

Now we will remedy that slight by showing how asset speculators, through the prices they are willing to pay for securities, create valuable messages that help businesses throughout the economy decide where to allocate their capital. The stock and bond markets, which do that, are powerful causes of the long-term success of capitalism. This seems unknown to most economists, even the few who are principled advocates of free markets.

An article in *The Economist* gave the conventional explanation for the role of stock markets in the economy:

Stock markets still fulfill two vital functions, says Professor Paul Marsh of the London Business School. First, on the so-called "primary market," they match investors with entrepreneurs to finance successive waves of innovation. Then, by providing a forum for trading shares, known as the secondary market, they let investors "diversify risk and uncouple time horizons from those of the companies they invest in", he explains.

The professor is correct, though there is more to it than that. But first, a mystery: The ratio of the value of shares traded in the secondary market on various stock exchanges to the amount of money raised by companies from stock and bond offerings is extremely high. What could be the purpose or benefit of all that activity?

In fact, there is tremendous value to society in that trading, and it is one of the secret weapons of economic growth. Why that is, takes a little explaining.

A few of the reasons are generally known. People's lifetimes are shorter than those of many successful companies, so nobody would put money into a company if the only time they could cash out was when the company was sold or liquidated. The market for shares and bonds lets one sell much sooner than that, and one can diversify one's holdings to reduce risk by buying small pieces of many companies, directly or through a mutual fund or equivalent.

Another conceivable purpose of the stock market is entertainment, a gambling casino for the upper classes who wouldn't want to be seen buying scratch cards at a convenience store or, in the old days, ripping up losing tickets along the rail at the racetrack. This is closer to the truth, but there are two fundamental differences between gambling and investing.

When you bet on a number in the lottery, a horse in a race, or a sports team in a game, there is a set time or some other event, like finishing the ninth inning in baseball when the score is not tied, in which a winner is determined and bets are settled. In investing, there is no set time. Somebody can stick with a stock for only a few seconds, minutes, hours, days, or hold it for years or decades, as they please.

The other difference is more important. Assuming there is no cheating or other corruption, the outcome of a gambling bet is not affected by the odds. Horses probably don't know what betting even is. The more bets there are on a horse, the smaller the payoff if the horse does win, but unless the odds somehow affect a non-corrupt jockey's strategy for trying to win, and it normally shouldn't, either the horse will win, or it won't, regardless of the odds. Similarly, a number in a lottery, or a non-corrupt sports team in a game, will win or not, independent of the sentiment of the gamblers.

That isn't the case in the stock market, where bets, in the form of people pushing one stock price higher with their aggressive buying and another price down with their determined selling, can have an impact not only on the underlying companies themselves but on many other investment decisions throughout the economy.

I used the phrases "aggressive buying" and "determined selling" to clear up possible confusion, since every transaction in the stock market involves both one or more buyers and one or more sellers, such that the number of shares bought and sold are always equal. Prices change not because of inequality of shares, but because of inequality of desire to buy or sell at a given price.

Although no money flows into or out of a company because of its stock-price fluctuations, its stock price can have a big impact on a company's future. To expand its business and take advantage of opportunities, it must first invest, which requires capital, often more than a company can provide from internal funds. To raise money, it must borrow some or sell shares in itself by offering equity.

The more highly investors and lenders think of a company, the lower its cost of capital. One deemed to have poor prospects will have to pay much higher interest rates to borrow or must give out many shares at a low price to raise equity money.

Unlike gambling, the bets that investors place on securities affect the real world by making one stock go up and another down, creating the conditions where the first company is better able to access capital to expand, and the other is not. The impact that investors' valuation decisions have on companies throughout the economy, even ones that are not raising new capital at the time, is far greater than is generally understood. Which stocks are hot or not affects the decisions of private companies, venture-capital firms that finance start-ups and early-stage companies, and wealthy public companies with piles of cash that can fund anything they care to do on their own.

All those parties desire the same thing—they want to know what the future will be like. If there were high valuations on widget-industry stocks persisting over a long time, that is a message from investors that widgets are viewed to have great growth prospects. These aren't idle predictions; they are crowd-sourced opinions coming from people with skin in the game, using their own or clients' money to buy widget stocks. There will be consequences to their net worth and reputations depending on how these stocks do.

If there are a lot of people very optimistic or pessimistic about the outlook for a particular technology or industry, demonstrated by where they are betting their own money, you have to assume they have what to them are good reasons; make sure you are confident you know what those reasons are—and *why* they are wrong—before betting in the opposite direction.

The stories about why a given company or industry should have a great future have a paradoxical element to them. In the short run, a bullish story about widget-maker Company X will drive the stock to high levels and make it easy for X to raise more capital to expand.

But stories are heard not only by those interested in buying a stock and who are then sworn to secrecy and never reveal what they learn. Quite the contrary. Stories spread easily to any interested parties, and few are more interested in a company's story than its competitors, current and potential. What a company needs to say to convince investors to buy their stock could hurt them as competitors hear of their ambitions and plans and prepare their strategies to counter them.

That seems unfair, but it is no more unfair than patent laws that give an inventor some protection from copycats in return for revealing in the patent application how the invention operates and why it is a good solution to some problem. In both cases, innovators get a benefit in return for information that others can use, often against them.

The winner of this paradox is the public. We want people and companies to innovate, whether in specific inventions, new products, or in new business strategies that better respond to customers' desires. We provide them with rewards for doing so, including, for those who tell their stories to potential investors and convince them on the merits, access to new capital. At the same time, we want competitors to learn from the innovators, which will help them produce their own innovations and give customers alternatives.

The stock market, by demanding information that inevitably spreads, spurs innovation and sharpens competitive responses. That isn't investors' conscious goal; all they are trying to do is find out things from reliable sources that will help their investment performance. They are like bees who aren't intentionally trying to help flowers reproduce—they are just trying to gather pollen and nectar to feed their colony, but in so doing, they do help the flowers multiply, thereby unintentionally helping the bees' offspring the following year.

The beneficiaries of innovation derived from the spread of information about these companies start with the buyers of widgets. To the extent that the more-intense competitive battle helps them satisfy their widget needs for less money, those savings don't disappear. Widget buyers now have more money to spend on other things. The savings are used somewhere in the economy by themselves or are invested or lent out and used by someone else.

A company not currently in the widget industry but with the ability to enter it might notice the high multiples that widget stocks have and enter that business, in the hopes that the high multiples will rub off on its own stock. Venture-capital people will be more enthusiastic about funding a recent start-up that operates in a field that the stock market believes will have a great future. That raises the chances that the start-up could be acquired at a high price by one of the bigger industry leaders or go public someday at a high valuation.

As far back as the 1950s, the stocks of US companies in electronics and computers sold at much higher valuations relative to sales, earnings, book value, etc., than most other companies in the US stock market. If you happen to come across an old book about investments dating from the 1950s-1970s in a yard sale or used-bookstore, you'll see mentions about "growth stocks" or "electronics/defense stocks" or similar names, usually warning the investor away from them because they weren't good values. Ben Graham, the "father of value investing," was particularly adamant about avoiding such stocks because their price reflected hopes about future earnings rather than strong actual performance to date and solid balance sheets.

Although there was a regular turnover of companies, with many of them going broke as new ones out-innovated them, only to be replaced by even newer ones, technology stocks always sold at a premium to more prosaic companies like General Motors and Campbell Soup. This kept venture-capital investors betting on new tech start-ups. Established non-tech companies had an incentive to create divisions to develop or make use of new technologies so that they, too, could be one of the cool kids with a high earnings multiple.

And it wasn't just tech companies that got access to capital. Any business with enough loyal and enthusiastic customers to make large and growing profits could attract more capital to expand, as would other companies trying to compete directly but do it even better, or who were attempting to apply what they learned from the first company's innovations to other industries entirely.

Looked at in terms of economic systems, it was the USSR not having a stock market while the US did, that was likely a major cause of its collapse. While investors in the US, egged on by stock speculators who never lost their faith in the potential of technology and gave high valuations to successful innovators in other industries, kept investing where the crowd-sourced outlook was the most positive, the USSR allocated its capital toward whichever ministries were most politically connected, to produce even more stuff that nobody wanted.

If the Commissar of Shoes was an old drinking buddy of the top Kremlin leadership, and the Commissar of Computers and Electronics was a not very personable teetotal engineer, more of the country's capital went into putting up more shoe factories, not into developing computer technology.

The unfortunate Soviet citizens saved so much and endured poor housing and bad or nonexistent consumer products. Their government invested those savings terribly because socialism has no built-in mechanism like the stock market to crowd-source the best ideas on where capital should be deployed. When, after being exposed to Western music, blue jeans, and consumer electronics, the Soviet public realized that all their sacrifices had gone to waste, that was the end of the USSR.

This is another example of why macro errs by focusing on aggregate measures when what people want are specific goods and services. The dominant economics textbook for many decades after WW2 was that of Paul Samuelson, a leading Keynesian economist. Until just before the USSR collapsed, Samuelson predicted in every new edition of his textbook that its GDP per capita would eventually exceed the US's because their savings rate was so much higher, which allowed greater investment. Arithmetically correct, but lacking an information source like the stock market to suggest which areas for investment would add output of the most value, the Soviets sacrificed their current living standards to save for the future and then invested their savings so poorly that their future was little improvement on their past.

The messages from the stock market about where best to invest will change as opinions about prospects change. Investors predict where demand will be strong and therefore new capacity will be needed. Companies investing in that area find it easy to raise capital at high prices. An excess of demand over supply for widgets will initially allow vendors to charge top dollar and attract additional investment. There will be some lag time as new facilities and equipment are built or ordered, but the result will be an increase in supply of widgets. As supply catches up to demand, profits and stock prices will drop back to something more normal.

Sometimes multiple companies in a particular field make expansion plans without realizing how many others are doing the same. Or it turns out that everyone was too optimistic about the growth in widget demand. Either of those can lead to an excess of supply, collapsing prices, profits turning into losses, and bankruptcies of the weakest players. People are fallible because the future is always uncertain.

No economic system can ever prevent normal human errors like those, but with free markets, there are continuous reports in the form of changing stock prices of how perceptions are changing about the future supply/demand balance. We don't have to wait for the last new factory to open to see conditions changing for the worse, as a bear market in widget stocks while the new plants are still under construction will be a fair warning to widget makers or would-be entrants to the industry not to waste capital by investing any more in new capacity.

Living standards in capitalist systems keep rising partially because of this magnificent communications mechanism. Compare that to socialism, in which out-of-touch and in-over-their-heads central planners with none of their own money at stake decide that the widget industry should get X dollars of expansion capital and that some other industry should get Y dollars.

Knowledge about a given company's prospects or that of its industry or technology, good or bad, is widely dispersed. The prices investors are willing to pay to own various stocks reveal their opinions about where capital should be allocated. Only countries with functioning stock markets can take advantage of that diverse knowledge; socialist economies must hope that their central planners are omniscient, but none ever are, and plans and prospects need constant changing as new information and opinions arise.

The same is true for ostensibly capitalist countries that engage in industrial policy, in which the government decides that this or that company or industry should get major public support to make it successful. Government officials have no special ability to pick winners, nor do they have the right incentives. They personally lose no money if they are wrong, and they are invariably influenced by politicians who sell access to government money. As British writer and scientist Matt Ridley put it, *"Governments are bad at picking winners. But losers are good at picking governments."*

Investors' and speculators' usefulness to the economy depends on their ability to accurately forecast the future. We have no idea who exactly was paying such high prices for tech stocks starting in the 1950s. There must have been millions of them, because a stock's price is determined anew every day by only those people who bought and sold that day. Yet for decades they showed up nearly every day willing to pay high prices, sending a constant, and as it turned out, correct message to American businesspeople that electronics, computers, software, and other high-tech areas were great places to allocate their capital.

Ben Graham and his disciple Warren Buffett may not have agreed with their opinions, but it was the willingness of so many to ignore those favoring value investing and risk their own money on their prescient vision of where capital should be allocated that helped bring down the USSR.

If investors bid up the prices of widget makers to high levels in anticipation of great growth in widget demand but turn out to be wrong, there would be serious consequences. They will lose a lot of money, as will any companies that were induced to expand widget-production capacity. The overall economy will suffer, at least a little bit, to the extent that capital, and, therefore, also labor, management, and physical resources were misallocated to projects where they just weren't needed.

It is important to an economy that people be good at predicting what will be most needed in the future and invest accordingly, sending a message to everyone about their opinion, and that those who are good at it make decisions for more of our collective savings than those who are bad at it. The profit or loss that one gets from investing is the automatic mechanism in capitalism which does exactly that. The process is one that Darwin would have appreciated.

The popular French economist Thomas Piketty asserts that those with wealth will automatically get richer, but he hasn't the slightest idea of what generates positive returns on investment. Regardless of how good your investment performance has been, that gives you no dispensation from losses if, in your next investment, you buy at prices that implicitly predict a future more positive than what unfolds.

In free markets, over time, money keeps moving out of the hands of those who are bad at predicting the future, to those who are good at it and invest accordingly. Our rising living standards are a result of this process.

Is anyone any good at predicting an industry's or company's future? If so, can they also consistently recognize when the current stock price for a company is, therefore, too low or high?

If you have taken any finance courses in the last fifty years, you have been taught the Efficient Market Hypothesis (EMH), which claims that the answers to those questions are "No" and "No." Successful predictions of future stock prices reflect mere luck, willingness to take risks, and randomness, rather than skill, according to EMH.

A thorough discussion of the EMH is beyond the scope of this book. For now, the best one can say about it is that if one has money to invest but doesn't know much about business, then assuming that the EMH is correct is a good strategy. That viewpoint also makes sense for someone trying to manage such a huge portfolio that it must own more stocks than anyone can reasonably follow in depth. Passive investing in low-cost index funds and exchange-traded funds makes more sense than trying to do something that is impossible, given one's skills and knowledge.

Many people, however, especially those who have experience working in a particular industry, can spot situations where stock valuations are too high or low compared to their own assessment of a company's prospects. By buying stocks that are undervalued and selling short those that are overpriced, one can make good returns, provided one's understanding of the industry is correct. In addition, one is helping rectify valuation mistakes and thus, in one's own small way, helping allocate the country's available capital to where it is needed, and away from where it is not.

Once you understand that the stock market is a communications system that gathers and transmits opinions of where capital should be allocated, you may start to appreciate the role of short sellers, those widely despised bears who bet against stocks they feel are overpriced relative to their prospects.

Just as it is important for society to be alerted to which companies and industries have the best prospects, we also need to know which have been overhyped and are not deserving of more capital. Short sellers identify those situations. Like all other investors, short sellers are wrong a lot, but, without their skepticism, too much of our scarce capital would end up in the hands of promoters and con artists.

This is why we would be better off if many more private companies went public, so there would be incentives for these freelance devil's advocates to do their job on them. The trend has been the other way, with increasing government demands on public companies, ostensibly for shareholder protection and various non-economic goals, making it too costly for many companies to go or stay public. Private-equity firms own many large previously public companies that might perform better if they had a larger audience of public shareholders to crowd-source opinions on their prospects.

One delightful irony about EMH: Although invented by finance professors, it is widely supported by mainstream economists. They accept as proven the idea that what price people will choose to pay for a given stock in the future is so immensely complex, such a "random walk," as to be inherently unpredictable by anyone on a consistent basis.

Yet if humans are inherently unpredictable when buying or selling securities, why are we assumed to be perfectly predictable automatons when inside macro models, responding to changes in government spending, taxes, monetary policy, and inflation statistics in formulaic ways? Could that be why, when the Fed's and other professors' models seem to work at all, it is only for short, random time periods before they go awry?

So far in this chapter, the stock market has been treated as if it fit the old saying that "It is not a stock market—it is a market of stocks." That view describes a stock market where price changes of individual stocks were not highly correlated, rather than one in which the movement of the entire market dwarfs whatever factors seem particular to individual companies.

The explosion of the money supply due to the Fed's financing the trillions of dollars the government has borrowed so far this century, combined with the artificially low interest rates the Fed and other central banks imposed on the world for decades, until the recent inflation problem arose, have created what is called "the everything bubble." House prices, stock and bond prices, art works, collectibles, crypto-currencies, and many other real and ethereal assets have all soared together. This has encouraged more output price inflation from spending by the parties owning those assets and provided an incentive to leverage assets with debt for even greater potential gains, thereby risking another crash more devastating than when it was only housing that was in a bubble.

The main problem with a booming stock market is that it encourages the misallocation of capital into companies that will waste the money. A recent example is the "meme stocks," companies with losses heavy enough to attract many short sellers who thought they would go bankrupt. Correctly anticipating that if the stocks were pushed up enough, the short sellers would likely then start buying to limit their losses, large groups of small investors bought and accomplished that end.

Fair enough—that's the risk that short sellers take. But many of the companies whose stocks zoomed, not despite but because of their terrible records and prospects, used the rallies to sell new shares that brought in billions of dollars, which they will now invest in their companies and are highly likely to lose it all. Nothing has fundamentally changed with their prospects; their new funding will just delay their death. That capital could have been used for good ideas and companies, but instead went to bad ideas and companies.

Similarly, during the recent 2020-21 bubble, about $245 billion was invested in Special Purpose Acquisition Companies (SPACs), blind pools run by hyped money managers, sports stars, and other celebrities. The SPACs would then acquire private companies that had little chance of going public on their own, because of their embryonic stage, heavy losses, years before expected profitability, heavy future capital needs, and, in many cases, their managements not wanting to risk fraud charges by putting into writing some of the exaggerated projections of future success they made informally as private companies.

By early 2023, the losses on these issues were staggering, with many bankrupt or priced as if they were. The loss to society was not just the reduction in the assets of those who invested in them, but the diversion of capital from companies that could have made good use of the money and raised living standards by so doing.

This is entirely the consequence of the Fed's keeping interest rates at near zero for so many years. With no ability to earn an adequate return from something safe, many people decided "You only live once" (YOLO) and engaged in a speculative game that resulted in money going into the hands of companies whose main qualification is that they were likely doomed, but now can waste hundreds of billions more of scarce capital before that happens.

If we lived in an alternative universe where the Fed and other central banks made no attempt to dictate interest rates or finance government deficits with newly created money, and the government was small in size relative to the private sector and ran neither large deficits nor surpluses, the stock market would still have ups and downs, but for different reasons than today.

When many consumers spend less and save more, the higher savings would pressure interest rates down, other things being equal. In addition, companies would be increasingly optimistic about their prospects, because the money people were saving then would increase their ability to buy more in the future. Higher profits would come from that, and between that and the low interest rates, stocks would be in a bull market in anticipation.

When consumers have been on a long spending spree, reducing their savings, the higher interest rates that result plus the prospects of weaker profits from reduced future demand, would create a bear market.

Both of those are different from what we have experienced since the housing-bubble collapse, a bull market in every asset that is not a currency that was created out of thin air by a central bank. The cause is that new assets can't be created as fast as central banks can print the currency in which they are denominated. People want to get rid of their dollars, euros, and any other paper currency they own, trading them in for whatever central banks can't print.

That exacerbates inequality since poor people don't own many assets. While excessive leverage has been cheap to finance and pays well to use in a bull market, the stage is set for the next large financial crisis.

CHAPTER 10

INVESTMENT AND MOTIVATION

• • •

IN ANY SOCIETY, UNDER any economic or governmental system, the main way the standard of living can rise is if the people collectively save and invest some of their income, rather than spend it all on consumption of goods and services.

Savings are necessary to increase productivity, but only if invested wisely. That is what sunk the USSR, which had hard-working people and few consumer goods other than vodka that were in much demand. That combination created a very high level of savings which only the government was allowed to invest, which it did horribly.

This concept is simple: if you don't know what your inputs cost or what your output is worth, there is no way to determine whether your efforts to convert the inputs to output are adding value or are a giant waste of time, effort, and resources. Without market prices, it is impossible for socialist planners to allocate resources rationally. Instead, capital in socialist states is allocated based on political considerations, which might keep the leaders happy but do nothing to improve living standards.

Free markets, through the prices generated by transactions and the profits that those prices imply, guide others in their decisions about where to invest. These opinions about expected returns don't come from people filling out some survey form, but from people risking their own money that they can multiply many times by being right or lose completely by being wrong. As Samuel Johnson said about knowing you are about to be hanged, taking great financial risks with your own money "concentrates the mind wonderfully."

Governments in the US and other developed countries to this day are not much better than the old USSR when it comes to making major investment decisions. They have access to market prices, so they have some sense of how much a project might cost, and they can get competitive bids which in theory could provide some efficiencies. But bids show up only after the project has already been designed, with many costly errors spec'd in well before anything is put out to bid.

Is this project worth doing? What are its benefits versus costs? What else could the government do with the money it will cost? What else can the public do with the money that the government will take from them, in taxes and higher prices, to do the project?

That last question is very important. The fact that the government might be selling bonds to finance some large project doesn't mean the project comes for free. Until the project is up and running and we get the benefit of the new rail line, highway, high school, port improvement, or whatever it is, it is all cash flow out with no benefit. Many people will be paid for working on this project. They will buy consumer output for themselves without producing any, i.e., providing demand but not supply for consumer goods, putting upward pressure on prices, thereby reducing the living standards of those on a tight budget.

You would see that clearly if you wanted to put an addition on your house or to try to build something else while there was a major municipal construction project going on in your region. You would have trouble getting contractors, tradespeople, and certain supplies, and would have to pay more to get them. And the temporary boom to the local economy would show up in house prices, rents, and other costs. As with all price increases, not a problem if you have high income or plenty of savings in reserve, but it makes things harder for others not so lucky.

The project may still be worth doing, despite the higher prices while it is underway, and the increased taxes needed to pay for it now and in the future until any bonds are retired. A worthwhile government project sometimes happens, but usually doesn't, because the nature of government spending is that a successful outcome is usually not a high priority.

Politicians won't give out taxpayers' money frivolously—they do expect some value for the money. However, being normal human beings, their definition of "value" heavily weighs the benefit to themselves personally. Bureaucrats might prefer projects that enhance their power over others. Politicians might desire the increased favors owed to them by the beneficiaries of their spending, eventually surfacing in the form of larger campaign contributions.

To think otherwise requires the assumption that government employees are not regular humans, but are angels from heaven, or perhaps aliens from some other planet where they don't behave like us. This raises the principal-agent problem, which reflects the fact that those making decisions, supposedly for our benefit, have interests that may be divergent from ours.

Principal-agent is a problem that exists in the business world every bit as much as in government. Sometimes officers and employees of a corporation do things to benefit themselves personally while hurting their employer. The difference is that the business world has incentives to limit the damage. A good board of directors, containing large shareholders with their own money at stake, should notice the bad behavior and demand that top management change the incentives or be replaced. If the board doesn't do enough, the stock price will probably fall to the point that a better-run competitor could buy the company inexpensively and replace management.

With governments, there are no built-in mechanisms to solve the principal-agent problem. The public is the principal, and all politicians and government employees are the agents. Supposedly, in a democracy, politicians compete to serve the public, knowing that poor performance will result in their losing the next election. That is fantasy. In most areas of the country, one party wins nearly all elections, no matter how incompetent and corrupt their candidates are. Even in contested districts, most voters remain loyal to one party and aren't easily persuaded to switch.

For a long time, newspapers were the external watchdogs exposing corruption in government regardless of which party was in power, but the loss of subscription and local ad revenues has sharply reduced their ability and inclination to finance detailed investigations. Newspapers' new business model is to preach to their own partisan choir, and they won't even report any news that might hurt their favored party.

The costliest government-investment fiascos are usually not technically corrupt, other than the normal, large campaign contributions from those who benefit from the spending. For example, stupendous sums get wasted in initially popular infrastructure projects like the high-speed rail project between Los Angeles and San Francisco, or the wildly over-budget elevated rail system in Honolulu.

These projects always start off with rosy projections of ridership, speed, and speed of construction, all of which get negatively revised along the way, even as construction costs and projected operating budgets soar. Given that the projections originated from the construction and engineering outfits that hoped to participate in the project and were endorsed by politicians who were hoping to have stations or the whole line named after themselves someday, nobody had an incentive to be realistic enough to protect taxpayers from paying the cost of such huge fiascos.

As Twitter member Kevin Dalton posted:

"2008: California will have a high-speed rail from Los Angeles to San Francisco [382 miles by car] by 2020 at a cost of $30 billion.

2023: California will have a train from Bakersfield to Merced [164 miles] hopefully by 2030 at a cost of no less than $170 billion."

This type of project is typically supported by those who don't understand the basic economic concepts of scarcity and trade-offs.

We don't have infinite money. Doing one thing usually means giving up something else. An admirable goal, such as "Let's do things that will be good for the environment," which, in theory, these trains might be, must be balanced by the value of everything else of merit that we can no longer afford.

Most money-wasting government spending projects, however, don't attract attention. Much of what politicians do is intended to use the government's power or money to benefit particular constituencies in ways that are often undetectable or misunderstood by the general public.

What they do is not illegal, and probably few politicians feel even slightly guilty. Many, perhaps even most of them, start out with the intent of being honest and selfless public servants. Soon they catch on that they can provide that benefit to their constituents only if they remain in office.

That starts them down the slippery slope, since staying in office usually involves satisfying the various special interests who will help them get reelected, provided they get something in return. A few politicians are so popular for various reasons that they need not cater to donors, but for each one of them, there are many dozens of others who do nothing but work for the interests that keep them in their jobs.

That isn't their only motivation. You may find this surprising, seeing my recurrent accusations of corruption against politicians, but I believe that many are indeed as kindly and generous as they claim to be. They truly want to help people, they aren't looking for kickbacks, and by directing government money to those they feel deserving, they sleep well at night.

Unfortunately, that is because they believe in magic. They think the money they are spending or giving out rains down from heaven for free, when in fact it comes out of other, no less deserving, people's paychecks in taxes, or in their reduced living standards when deficit spending and money printing pushes up the prices that they must pay for what they want.

The odds are against any expensive government project being a wise investment. Government employees, whether elected or appointed, are not investing their own money, so they will not make or lose money no matter how the project works out. Cost/benefit analysis is there to be manipulated as a tool to help sell to the voters projects the politicians have already decided they want.

Nevertheless, wise government investments have happened. Sometimes there are projects where the potential benefits are obvious to everyone, but doing them requires much more capital than any one firm or consortium of firms can gather and risk, but which the government can supply. Or the project requires the government's coercive power to assemble all the resources needed, such as when it uses its power of eminent domain to force recalcitrant property owners to sell at a reasonable price land that is essential to the project.

Here are two such examples from American history, to show the most important thing about a wise government investment that makes it so—it lowers costs and prices, and thereby raises the country's standard of living. We'll also see why they are so rare and how easy it is to draw false conclusions from these successes.

The Erie Canal that connected the Great Lakes to the Hudson River, which flows into the Atlantic Ocean, was built from 1817 to 1825. Such a linkage had been proposed many times starting in the 1700s, and some companies formed to build it, but the capital needed to do so was well beyond the resources of any individuals or companies of the time, so it didn't get built until New York State paid for the project.

The farms of western New York State and the states around the Great Lakes were immensely productive compared to the less fertile East Coast farms, where most of the population lived. Prior to the canal, transportation costs from the west to potential markets on the East Coast were prohibitive due to the Appalachian Mountains in between, as were the costs of shipping goods manufactured in eastern factories to potential customers in the west.

It was well known that barges on a canal were vastly more efficient than were pack animals on the primitive roads of the times. One horse or mule might be able to carry 300 pounds on its back or a few times that in a cart on unpaved, muddy mountain roads, but when pulling a barge in a canal, one animal could handle up to 90,000 pounds. Equines were paid in food and needed paid human handlers. The cost savings of using one to replace hundreds to transport the same weight of goods were huge. The need was great and obvious, so the canal eventually was built, close to a century after it was first proposed.

When completed, the canal slashed the cost of food to East Coast cities and overseas markets. It is hard to overestimate the importance of this to living standards. More than half the US population were farmers, and many of them worked hard all year to produce little more than what was needed to keep their families from starving. If one were to value their output as if it were sold in the market rather than consumed, and called that their income, we could say that most of their income was spent on food, not leaving much for anything else.

When much lower-cost food from the West arrived by canal, eastern residents effectively became immensely and sustainably wealthier, and could buy more goods and services, creating demand for non-farm labor. That was a good thing because farming in much of the East no longer made sense. The now ex-farmers could get jobs in factories or elsewhere that paid more money than they ever made from farming, and by spending less on food they now had money for other things.

The same was true in the other direction. Farmers in the Midwest went from being subsistence farmers to producers of crops for market, bringing in much more income, making them wealthier, too. They now could afford to buy many more manufactured goods from eastern factories, both because of their higher incomes and the lower prices that came from products being manufactured in bigger, more efficient factories that served geographically wider and wealthier markets, as well as the lower transportation costs. Like all forms of great progress, the Erie Canal caused some turmoil, as neither unproductive eastern farms nor small-scale western manufacturers could compete.

Had today's macroeconomists existed then, they would have forecast dire consequences from so much deflation in the prices that city people paid for food and Midwest farmers paid for manufactured goods from the East. Thank our lucky stars that in the

1800s there were no macroeconomists, nor was there a Fed. Had it existed then with its current powers, it would have slashed interest rates to 0% and ramped up money printing to fight the supposedly inevitable depression from the "devastating deflation," as they would call it now, that the Erie Canal caused in the prices of both food and manufactured goods.

In fact, it was the rise in living standards that the canal created because of lower prices that allowed both Eastern consumers and Western farmers to buy much more than ever before, thereby creating more and higher-paying jobs, which helped attract increasing numbers of immigrants.

The Erie Canal was a wise investment as defined earlier: it involved the sacrifice of current consumption by taxpayers to pay for it, but increased incomes and cut costs. The explosion in wealth that came from the canal was more than enough to pay off its entire cost and continue to generate more wealth for years thereafter.

Another government investment success: after some occasional attempts at road construction in preceding decades, the US federal government in 1956 started constructing the **Interstate Highway System** (IHS).

There were many existing paved roads throughout the country at the time, but they were designed to take people from one town to the next, and traffic was regularly and intentionally slowed down by Main Street shopping districts, traffic lights, and school zones. With cars and trucks after WW2 more powerful and reliable than prewar vehicles, the narrow and congested roads were increasingly seen as a bottleneck to commerce, like the Appalachian Mountains before the Erie Canal.

By allowing vehicles to go long distances much faster on multi-lane limited access highways, the IHS had effects similar to the Erie Canal's. Transportation costs dropped significantly, in effect shortening distances within the country. This allowed much more competition, because instead of most markets consisting of local brands with quasi-monopolies protected by distance, companies found themselves competing with outsiders in their own markets, while having a newfound ability to go after what had been protected markets controlled by others. This forced them all to be more efficient, cut their unit costs by expansion, and provide a better deal for their customers, or lose them all to competitors.

Our standard of living rose because of the government's roughly half-trillion-dollar investment in today's money in the IHS. Since consumers could now buy better products at a lower price, they had more money to spend on other things, or to save and invest, both of which were sustainable stimulants to the economy. Using the definition of a wise investment as something that either increases incomes or cut expenses, or both, in a significant way relative to the cost, the IHS was certainly a wise investment.

Unfortunately, people regularly draw the wrong conclusions from the Erie Canal, IHS, and a few other large and successful infrastructure projects that the government undertook in the last century or two.

One mis-learned lesson is to assume transportation infrastructure is inherently a good investment. That is true only if there are costly transportation bottlenecks that need to be overcome. In trying to fight the recession initiated by the collapse of its real-estate bubble after 1989, the Japanese government followed the bad advice of its macro experts and spent more than $2 trillion in borrowed money on road building. But with limited exceptions, roads had not been a big bottleneck to commerce in Japan. Instead of having mostly empty roads with two lanes in each direction to places few people go, they now have even emptier roads with three lanes in each direction to those same places.

Economists who think that even wasteful spending stimulates the economy claim that it was primarily the money spent on building the IHS that helped the economy. Wrong—the spending of the road workers made little difference except in the very short run. It was the encouragement of higher-volume, lower-cost businesses that could serve a much wider geographical area, as well as lower transportation costs, that reduced prices for consumers.

The IHS was not flawless. Some of the components, in retrospect, should have been routed differently, some cities were bypassed and declined in prosperity, some inner-city neighborhoods were shut off from the rest of the city, and some poor neighborhoods were destroyed while the rich ones benefited. The highways were, in effect, a subsidy to the auto industry, and perhaps new cars and gasoline refineries should have been taxed extra to pay for it. But the benefits to the country's living standards, especially for the lower-income groups, far exceeded these costs.

When thinking about these projects, a fatal error for understanding is mistaking costs for benefits. Imagine that instead of the US taxpayer spending what it spent to build the IHS, President Eisenhower in 1956 rubbed an old oil lamp and conjured up a genie, whom he commanded to build the IHS for free, including supplying all the materials from some other universe.

Had that happened, we would have been even better off. We would have gotten the IHS, with all its permanent advantages, and still have in our pockets the money we would have had to spend to build it. The construction workers whose jobs the genie replaced at no cost to us would instead have been building houses and other things people also wanted in addition to a better road system, using materials whose prices would have been lower because the genie didn't need any earthly materials for the IHS.

In other words, the money spent to build a large project is always a cost of the project, not a benefit. The only benefits are those the project actually provides: removing bottlenecks and cutting costs, leading to the lower prices that make our living standards rise.

The way we generate wealth is to create the most output from a given amount of input. The benefits of a project are the output, the costs are the inputs. To say a project has lots of costs is not a point in its favor, yet that is what macroeconomists keep whispering in the ears of politicians, who brag about, rather than apologize, to the taxpayers, for all the high-paying jobs that will be created to build a certain project.

If a large project is worth doing because of its potential benefits relative to its costs, it is best to do it when the economy is weak, because labor and materials will be in more plentiful supply and therefore less expensive than in good times. But if it isn't worth doing or is some barely useful project thought up quickly just to have a place to spend money, then it is a waste of money and not worth doing no matter what the unemployment level is. If we want to increase the dole, then let's do that, rather than pay people to do something useless, wasting resources that could be better used by others elsewhere.

As an example of how out of touch with reality Keynesian (and therefore most) economists can be, consider this admittedly far-fetched example to get to an important point. Had we been given a choice in the 1950s between borrowing money to build the IHS or borrowing the same amount of money to instead throw giant drunken parties, economists would have asked about the "propensity to consume" of highway workers versus party workers.

If a survey showed that highway workers and those who supplied the raw materials to them tended to be frugal, spending only 70% of their income and saving the other 30%, while bartenders, waitstaff, and booze suppliers were profligate and spent 99% of their income, saving only a tiny amount, the Keynesians would have concluded that throwing parties would be better for the economy. Because of the low savings rate, there would be a greater multiplier effect from the higher spending of the party employees, and GDP would go up much more by throwing drunken parties than it would by building the IHS.

That would have been the wrong choice. Debt-financed consumption doesn't generate the higher income that allows the debt to be repaid. Only wise investment can do that. The fun parties would have caused a short-term, unsustainable boost to GDP, followed by a collapse when the party project was over, leaving a debt hangover. Building the IHS instead, while not as much fun or as stimulating to short-term GDP, raised living standards permanently, long after the cost was paid off.

Because of successful projects like the Erie Canal and the IHS, there is an undeserved halo effect about infrastructure spending in the minds of politicians and newspaper editorial writers. Yes, some improvements in our infrastructure appear to be good investments, but just because something is an infrastructure project doesn't automatically mean that it is necessary and useful.

For example, it is amazing how gullible people are about the "studies" put out by self-interested organizations like the American Society of Civil Engineers (ASCE). Designing and managing infrastructure projects are what they do for a living, so naturally, they believe the US should spend hundreds of billions more annually on such projects.

And guess what? My barber thinks I need another haircut, and my bartender thinks I could use another drink.

ASCE's most ridiculous claims concern the number of vehicular bridges which are allegedly "structurally deficient" and should be replaced or at least undergo major overhauling. Its most recent study, from 2021, says that of the more than 617,000 bridges in the US, a total of 46,154, or 7.5% of them, are structurally deficient, their most dangerous category. It alerts us that every single day there are 178 million trips across those bad bridges. Sounds awful, right?

Well, if they are really all that bad, then presumably some decent percentage of the really bad ones, at least 1% anyway, should collapse every year. Did 461 US bridges, 1% of the worst ones, fall down in any recent year? Not quite. For the last ten years, through early 2023, a grand total of eleven failed, averaging 1 per year, injuring a few people and killing one person, who was working on a bridge that was being demolished, not one that collapsed in normal use.

And every one of those collapses had something about them that indicates that the problem wasn't structural deficiency at all, although some might have had that designation, but just random bad choices or bad luck. An oversize truck rammed into a bridge span, a truck which was well over the allowable weight drove over a small rural bridge, a runaway barge crashed into a bridge support, a massive flood undercut the support, and so forth. All eleven could well have been in any category of structural strength and still gone down, such as the most recent, the bridge part of the causeway to Sanibel Island, Florida, which took a direct hit from Category 4 Hurricane Ian.

Should we rebuild all 46,154 deficient bridges just to be safe, or maybe all 617,000 US bridges just to be even safer? ASCE certainly wouldn't object. Of course, there are some genuinely dangerous bridges, but we seem to be handling them in a timely fashion within our existing budgets, which is why actual collapses due to structural failure are close to non-existent.

The point is that, yes, there have been some large infrastructure projects that were excellent investments, because they solved a big problem, slashed costs and prices by so doing, raised living standards by giving everyone, especially lower-income groups, more money left over from their market-basket purchases to buy more or save.

At the same time, there are always many projects whose returns must be low. Repaving roads that are reasonably good as is, building high-speed rail projects that will never have enough riders to even pay their operating costs, let alone construction debt, and other projects that cost a lot to make minor improvements, don't turn into wise investments solely because they are infrastructure investments. They provide a nice boost to GDP from all that wasteful spending, making politicians and economists happy to think, mistakenly, that they have helped the public, when, in fact, they have lowered living standards in several ways.

Taxes paid to cover the project costs leaves people less to spend on what they want for themselves. To the extent the government borrows money instead of taxing, then that debt plus interest will be repaid by future taxpayers, with the same result. In addition, the concrete, steel, labor, capital, management, and all the resources devoted to a low- or no-return infrastructure project are resources no longer available for better uses. If developers want to build apartment buildings in places with soaring rents to meet an obvious social need, they will have to pay much more to get the materials and staff to do so if they are competing with the government for the same resources, and they will have to charge higher rents to cover those higher costs.

A wise investment makes society wealthier and our standard of living rise. Consumption spending provides various benefits but brings no return, and an unwise investment is worse than consumption because it doesn't even provide the enjoyment or utility that is the point of consumption. That is true regardless of who does the investing, whether individuals, businesses, or government. There are reasons why individuals and businesses tend to be much better investors than the government, but a good investment by anyone makes us richer.

I say "us" rather than "the investor," because everyone benefits from others' good ideas. I personally invested a total of zero dollars plus zero hours of work toward inventing and advancing computer technology, yet my standard of living is much higher now because others invested and worked hard on that. That is what *The Grace of the Market* is about. I didn't invent or invest in cars, music reproduction, medical advances, or millions of other things that makes the standard of living of even relatively poor people today better in most ways than the richest person on Earth not that far into the past.

But for our standard of living to keep rising, we need to keep making wise investments. If we spend more on consumption and save and invest less, or the politicians interfere with the free-market process that tends to produce good investments, and instead grab resources to use for more bad investments, economic progress can and will slow or even reverse.

We must avoid a Cargo Cult mentality that mimics things that worked in the past without understanding why they worked. When roads were the bottleneck preventing more robust growth, the IHS was a great investment. It was the benefits we received for our money, not what we spent, that helped the economy. If roads are not a bottleneck, as in the US they no longer are, then building more of them is a bad investment that will lower our standard of living.

One more thing to note about the rare cases of wise government investment: they are much more common in underdeveloped countries and get increasingly rare as a country becomes wealthier. That is because the needs of poor countries are usually obvious. There are some glaring problems that everybody knows need to be solved, that would provide great benefit from doing so.

In the early days of the US, when we were still a relatively poor ex-colony of England, the immense productivity of western New York State and Midwest farms, combined with the very high prices for food in Eastern cities, was obvious to all. The lack of any efficient mechanism to transfer food East and manufactured goods West was a problem that cried out for a solution.

With some delay, it would have been solved by the free market, as train lines were built. Commercial service in the form of the precursor to the New York Central Railroad, began running on a similar route to the Erie Canal less than 20 years after it opened. But, by then, the canal had already repaid its cost many times over in the soaring living standards due to lower prices that resulted from the elimination of the Appalachian Mountains as a barrier to trade.

The tremendous growth of China in the last four decades came not only from injecting a lot of capitalism into its previously all-socialist, impoverished economy, but also from the fact that there were large numbers of obvious problems just waiting to be overcome. Improved infrastructure very often has a big positive impact on people's earnings in poor countries. Such countries lack the businesses with capital and power to solve them, so that might be a job for governments, which have a better chance of marshaling the necessary resources.

The wealthier and more developed a country gets, partially from eliminating large infrastructure bottlenecks, the lower the benefits of removing the next worst infrastructure impediments to commerce and wealth. Once a country becomes relatively developed, as the US certainly is today, there are usually very few major projects whose benefits will cover their costs. At that point, the emphasis should be on maintenance and small-but-effective upgrades of existing infrastructure.

That said, sometimes there is a change in technology that increases potential benefits of such projects. The US road system was fine for the underpowered early autos, which were also inefficient and unreliable, with tires that frequently flatted, so nearby access to repair and fuel stops made sense. The more powerful cars and trucks available in the 1950s could handle the higher speeds and avoidance of towns that the IHS allowed.

One can imagine the possibility of AI-controlled, self-driving vehicles in another decade or two that could cruise efficiently and safely at speeds of more than 120 MPH, were there dedicated roads they could use. Perhaps building them might be a wise investment then, but if so, that would only be if the benefits clearly exceed the costs.

THE BURDEN OF GOVERNMENT

• • •

Y OU'VE SEEN HOW THE free market has built-in mechanisms
that push people into doing what we should want them to do.
That includes working hard at providing the goods and services
that other people most want. It includes businesses investing their
money where they think there should be a high return on their
investment, thereby adding to the supply of whatever output is in
the greatest demand. By increasing the productivity of workers,
business investment increases the value that they add, and that leads
to paying them more, since companies know that if they don't, their
competitors will.

You've also seen some of the mechanisms that keep the economy pushing toward higher living standards, such as those that
end recessions with no need of government action, those that push
costs and then prices down, and those that move capital—and,

subsequently the resources that capital buys—away from places where the resources aren't needed to places where they are, to bring out more supply to meet strong demand.

To summarize, free markets are engines for increasing living standards, especially those of the less-well-off. Anything that lifts their wages or, even better, cuts the prices they must pay, has a positive effect on their living standards, more so than on those of the already more wealthy. Thus, contrary to the widely accepted but mistaken view, free markets help the poor more than the rich and are a source of reduced inequality, not more.

As you saw in the last chapter, governments on rare occasions make great investments that eliminate bottlenecks to commerce and, therefore, enhance living standards throughout the country. Even when not actively making any investments, governments can make a huge difference in living standards when they do what they are supposed to do and do a competent job of it. Things in that category include establishing the rule of law, well-functioning court systems and police departments to discourage and punish crime, and maintaining a strong military so people don't fear invasion.

However, as we've seen, governments operate under some severe handicaps that cause their spending and policies that purport to be for the public good to result in more harm than good. Motivation is a big problem, in that neither politicians nor government administrators have any personal skin in the game.

A second problem is that the information the government has available for many decisions is inferior to what people in the private sector work with. Businesses have a definable goal—earning a high return on any investment they make relative to the risk they take. They make estimates, and if things don't turn out as well as planned, they suffer the financial consequences.

Most government spending goes to things that have a large component of the unmeasurable. How much safer does more defense spending make us? There is no way to know.

A new school building might result in a quantifiable reduction in maintenance and HVAC costs, but those savings by themselves rarely justify the investment. The real benefit would come from a better educational experience for the students, but how can that even be measured? And, since local governments don't have a money-printing press as the federal government has in the Fed, building the school means often means not building a new public-safety building for the police and fire departments, or doing some necessary road repairs. How are those competing interests to be weighed and compared? Whose opinion should count more than others'? There is just no way to know.

At least at the local level, those who favor or oppose some of the various possible projects can speak their mind and usually get some audience. At the federal level, the politicians don't even think in terms of trade-offs. The two parties conspire against the public. They each think the other side is wasting public money, but they regularly reach bipartisan compromises, not by forcing each side to give up the worst of its bad ideas, but for both parties to hand over money to their friends, provided they split the largesse 50/50.

All fun and games for the politicians, and they make sure that no significant campaign donor walks away without at least some money taken from taxpayers. But the assumption that if both sides get all their spending priorities adopted, that things will even out and everyone will be happy, is incorrect. Every dollar the government spends on itself or gives to its friends must be paid for by somebody, in some combination of taxes now, taxes in the future, and/or price or asset inflation from a reduced value of the dollar.

Politicians, and most people because they hear it from the politicians, believe that, if we don't pay for things with taxes, but either run deficits and borrow the money, or have the Fed print up some new money, or tax businesses or rich people who have so much money that they won't notice any missing, we are getting them for free. This section will show why that isn't true and that the people who end up paying the most to support the government in all its extravagance are not necessarily those who are supposedly taxed, but those whose living standards are decreased by the greatest percentage to pay the taxes levied on others. That would be poor people.

Chapter 11 shows just how enormous the government has grown in almost a century, how that is ignored by all and never considered as a possible cause of any of the economic problems we have. **Chapter 12** is about what in economics is referred to as tax incidence, not who writes the tax checks to the government, but who really pays the tax. You'll see why in the end any taxes, fees, or cost impositions on businesses get paid for mostly by their customers, and somewhat by their employees, but not at all by the business. **Chapter 13** shows why stripping the rich of their wealth to aid the poor ultimately hurts the poor much more than they are helped.

CHAPTER 11

ENORMOUS, BUT UNSEEN

•   •   •

O NE CAN'T REALLY MAKE a ratio of two concepts when there is no way to measure either of them with any precision. But if one were to do so anyway, to name one of the most consequential ratios in all of macro, it would be this: **GGSP/OYSW**

GGSP stands for **Growth of Government Size & Power**, the stupendous growth of government at all levels in every developed country in the last 90 years or so, and its increasing dominance over the private sector, in three respects:

1) the explosion of government spending as a percentage of overall economic activity

2) the increased control that the government has over how businesses must operate, such as recent rules to cripple the gig economy, the pressure put on banks to not lend to oil companies, and, of course, the lockdowns and the mandatory halt of much economic activity in response to Covid

3) the distortions of business activity caused by the Fed's usual bias toward low short-term interest rates, creating multiple bubbles going back to the late 1920s, followed by belated reversals that cause financial crises and bank failures.

OYSW measures the amount of interest that economists, historians, political analysts, and the public have in GGSP. It stands for **"Oh, Yeah? So What?"**

The ratio of the two concepts points out that despite the astounding growth of the power and cost of governments over the years, one almost never sees that trend proposed as a possible cause for inequality, secular stagnation, rising debts, rising crime, inflation, unemployment, and various other economic and social ills, even though a very plausible case exists that it is a major cause of *all* those problems.

Since so few are aware of the effects of metastasizing government on the economy and society, the tendency is to blame free markets for all social and economic problems and demand that the government become more dominant as a remedy.

Macroeconomists seem especially prone to ignore massive government growth, despite their working all the time with data in which they could see it easily, if they would only look. This isn't just an elephant in the room, it is one that is infected with elephantiasis, and they still don't see it.

This blindness to the possible negative effects on society might relate to the fact that the government and Fed are just about the only employers of macroeconomists outside of academia, which itself flourishes on government support. Politicians, of course, always want the government to be more powerful, because selling access to government power is what they do for a living. Contemplating the damage that they may be doing to the living standards of lower-income people for their personal benefit is not a high priority for either politicians or macroeconomists.

This doesn't mean that economists and politicians are bad people, just that they are normal people, trying to make their way in the world. As Sinclair Lewis put it, in writing about his failed campaign for governor of California in 1934, *"It is difficult to get a man to understand something, when his salary depends on his not understanding it."*

There are several reasons why the public seems little bothered by GGSP. One is that instead of openly taxing people enough to cover all government spending, the federal government runs large deficits and borrows to pay bills, in effect taxing those living in the future, many of whom don't exist yet and certainly can't vote, hiding the costs from us current voters.

State and local governments have budgets that are closer to being balanced, although the income of many of them fluctuate widely because they rely upon taxing capital gains and other unstable sources. However, since the federal government transfers large sums to the states, about $750 billion in 2019 and much more thereafter during Covid, the federal deficits partially reflect state and local spending. If we had balanced federal and state budgets due to higher taxes, people would certainly notice the government's size.

A second reason for OYSW will be explained later in this section of the book: the way the cost of government spending and power transmutes into higher prices for what we buy. Not realizing this, we commonly blame businesses for the price increases.

Also, the government's own consumption appetite and its taxes reduce the savings required for business investment, the engine of the *Progress Mechanism*. We notice the weaker growth, but since economics as taught never covers how the government's cost and bad policies are the cause, free markets get the blame.

How did GGSP happen? From the foundation of the United States in the late 1700s until the 1930s, federal government spending levels were roughly 3% of GDP every year, not counting when we were engaged in major wars. US federal spending is currently (2023) about $6 trillion, or about 26% of GDP, one of the highest ever outside WW2.

Trends were similar in our two other levels of government. At the start of the 20th century, state and local spending was about 5% of GDP and is now around 20%. All three levels together went from slightly under 10% of GDP for more than a century to more than 40% now.

Recall that our GDP number (but usually not our living standards) is increased with higher government spending. That comes from how GDP is calculated. No matter how useless and/or overpriced whatever it is that the government buys, its spending for goods and services gets added directly into GDP. Transfer payments, such as Social Security and other safety-net programs are not directly included in the GDP calculation, but if we assume that close to 100% of that money gets spent by the recipients, then that also adds to GDP.

GDP gets further increased by the multiplier effect, as all that government spending works its way around the economy. By adding rising government spending to both the numerator and denominator, the ratio of that spending to GDP makes the increase look smaller than it really has been.

Something else objectionable about calculating government spending as a percentage of GDP is that doing so creates the illusion that just because the economy grows, the government should spend more. But why? Where is the operating leverage we should be getting?

The way businesses succeed is when their revenues grow and their fixed costs stay relatively stable, allowing much greater profits. Our living standards would do the same if the government kept its appetite stable even in good economic times, since it generally increases its spending in bad times.

Another way to look at GGSP is the ratio of total government spending to non-government spending. Not counting major wars, until about 1930, that ratio was very roughly 0.1111 (10% of GDP to 90%). Since about 2000, it has averaged about 0.6667 (40% of GDP to 60%), a ratio *six times* greater. And considering so much of the private sector gets its income directly or indirectly from the government, GGSP is much bigger than even these numbers indicate. Is that a large enough increase to have a substantial impact on society? It seems at least possible.

At the same time, there has been a large growth in government control over the private sector in terms of regulations that raise business costs. There are mandatory benefits that businesses are required to provide employees, increased reporting obligations, regulations on the design of home appliances and how much water can come out of your shower, and so forth. The only changes in a positive direction in government power was the reduction of oppressive regulations on the trucking and airline industries in the late 1970s that considerably reduced the cost of distribution and travel.

One doesn't have to be an anarchist to point out the damage done by GGSP. When they are small and focused on being competent at what they do, governments can be useful and add tremendously to living standards. In ancient times, when conquest, looting, and enslavement of neighboring societies was often a more profitable strategy for a group of people than hard work, production, and honest trade, it made sense for a society to have a government that developed solid military prowess. Yes, each person could and would try to defend themselves and their families, but there were significant benefits to a division of labor, to have the toughest and bravest citizens train in the militia, under a unified command.

Also, economically successful communities that had the most to lose from being invaded were also large enough that people engaged in trade with strangers, or at least non-family members. Nobody could count on family pressure to make others behave themselves. Therefore, government-provided rule of law, some form of police or magistrates, and something resembling a court system, together allowed a peaceable settlement of disputes.

When people feel safe from internal and external threats, their perceived risk is reduced, and they are more willing to sacrifice current consumption to make business investments that increased their own productivity. In ancient times, that might have meant buying a stronger ox or a more solid workbench. In current times, investments are larger in scale, but whatever they are, people won't make them without having the feeling that the future is benign and predictable enough that they can safely sacrifice current consumption to invest.

A small, competent government that focuses on doing necessary tasks encourages investment, which expands economic output, and therefore very easily pays its own way. This is effectively what the US had from the 1700s through about 1930, although starting in the 1890s, the growth of government control over the economy caused the end of steady declines in prices from the *Progress Mechanism,* which had boosted living standards so much prior to that. The *Progress Mechanism* is still a powerful influence, but its positive effect on living standards is now dwarfed and counteracted by the conversion of much of GGSP into higher prices.

A problem with governments is that, with their exclusive control of legitimate force within a geographic area, the temptation for those in the government to use that power for their own personal benefit is very strong. That is true regardless of whether those controlling the government's power obtained it through inheritance as royalty, being anointed by religious authorities, through democratic elections, or any other method.

The late political economist Mancur Olson argued that governments are descended from the thugs who, in ancient times, would let their neighbors work and then invade and take the output for themselves. He called them "roving bandits," who, according to the Wikipedia summary of his ideas, have only *"the incentive to steal and destroy, whilst a 'stationary bandit'—a tyrant—has an incentive to encourage some degree of economic success as he expects to remain in power long enough to benefit from that success. A stationary bandit thereby begins to take on the governmental function of protecting citizens and their property against roving bandits."*

That states it well. Governments are stationary bandits. They do provide protection from outside predators and protect inhabitants from bad behavior on the part of other residents. However, people in governments have little reason to protect the populace from the government's own predation.

We should keep reminding ourselves that politicians and powerful bureaucrats are not inherently bad people. In fact, like economists and everyone else, they are perfectly normal people, interested in helping themselves, their families, friends, and supporters ahead of strangers.

In the private sector, to achieve your goals, you must help others attain *their* goals as your customers, employer, or employees, because they are *volunteers*. You can't force them to buy your products, hire you, or work for you. Taxes, on the other hand, are not voluntary, which gives politicians and bureaucrats entirely different incentives.

In a society like the US, which was formed in a revolution against what the people believed was a tyrannous government, the public was alert for more than a century thereafter against the risks of excessive government power. Their attitude was exemplified by these lines in an 1837 speech by Senator Daniel Webster, who said *"There are men, in all ages, who mean to exercise power usefully; but who mean to exercise it. They mean to govern well; but they mean to govern. They promise to be kind masters; but they mean to be masters."*

Other parts of the world have had much more tyrannous governments than that of King George III, against whom we revolted, but they never developed the focus on individual freedom and the suspicion of government power that were widely shared beliefs in the US for more than a century after our revolution. Dictatorships, official or not, are still accepted in many countries, and there are developed, nominally free-market societies, many in Europe, where the governments are even more dominant internally than the combination of the three levels of government in the US.

When government spending as a percentage of private spending rises from 11% to 67%, as it has in the US, one can't help but suspect that a large chunk of the increase goes for things most people don't want at all and would not voluntarily support financially. These things are, however, intensely desired by specific groups of people who will benefit financially from that spending. These groups aren't producing many goods or services that people want in return, because if they were, they wouldn't need the government to grab money for them.

The ethanol industry, which enriches farmers, is a classic example, in existence only because the government forces motorists and boat owners to use a product that is bad for the environment in multiple ways, damaging to engines, and being made from corn, raises food prices, thereby lowering the living standards of poor people.

Not all government spending or use of its power is bad. Of course, the elderly, children, the disabled, and those caring for them can't be expected to generate any or much income in a competitive marketplace and might need some help beyond what is provided from family and friends. Other social mechanisms are needed and have arisen over the years to help the less fortunate. Government has assumed that role, too, with some of its spending intended to take care of various problems previously handled privately.

Similarly, much spending at the state and local level is a substitute for what people would have to spend on their own for schools and social work, because people do want their kids educated and social issues addressed.

Still, governments in the US misspend hundreds of billions every year in useless projects and *intentionally* overspend even on useful ones to benefit favored groups like construction companies and unions. We spend more on defense than the next seven countries combined, and at least some of our weapon systems are known to be costly and ineffective—but they still have the support of powerful politicians. US governments collectively employ about 22 million. Most are paid more than they would earn in business jobs and have greater job security and better retirement benefits as well.

When total government spending at all three levels was only 11% of private spending, the country was younger and much less wealthy than it is today. Bad choices and inefficiency on the part of the government had to be watched carefully, and it was. Now, hundreds of billions are spent based on whims and political calculations, with insincere complaints by whichever party is out of power, knowing that they will do the same thing when they are in power.

Someone must pay for all that spending. You personally don't pay for anything the government gives you, so you may think of it as being free, but it isn't. Someone other than you is paying for it, with "paying" usually meaning their living standards are reduced so you can benefit. Progressives often push for what they call free college, but nothing is free. The teachers aren't working for free. Nobody donates free buildings or free utilities. If the students don't pay, someone else who won't be handed a diploma will be stuck with the bill.

Borrowing or printing money rather than imposing taxes is no solution. Despite our wishful thinking, the government is not a rich parent with a secret stash of money that it can use to buy us treats. It has no income of its own, other than what it takes from us.

When the government borrows money, it gives us only a temporary relief from taxes. In the future, the debt will have to be paid as will the interest expense. The fact that the US has been able to refinance its debt at interest rates that were low for much of this century has given many people the mistaken impression that there will never be a problem refinancing and that interest rates will always be low. The latter is already in question, with more than $800 billion likely in interest expense in 2023, a significant piece relative to the discretionary part of the budget. With no end to big deficits in sight and high global inflation leading to higher interest rates, that could grow considerably.

And keep in mind, our actual deficits are larger than the government claims, since we have arbitrarily declared the deficits that we have every year now in Social Security as being "off-budget." I can imagine a gambler trying to get a loan from a bank and telling the banker, *"Don't worry about all that money I owe my bookie. I've declared that to be off-budget."*

If we continue our present course, we either must raise taxes enormously, or the interest rate we pay on the debt will start rising faster to reflect the possibility that we will pay our bills with so much new money conjured into existence by the Fed that each dollar won't be worth much. That is the problem with Modern Monetary Theory (MMT), which, to slightly oversimplify, claims that the government can spend whatever it wants and just have the Fed print up the money to pay for it without causing any harm. The surge of inflation from the spending of Covid stimulus checks was a taste of what could come, as critics of MMT predicted all along.

Inflation is a plausible outcome when we deal with the massive unfunded obligations that all levels of governments have taken on in the US. By definition, unfunded liabilities don't show up in the budget, because they are promises made to various parties for the government to provide or pay for various things in the future, for which no money has been set aside yet.

Total unfunded obligations cannot be calculated with any precision, since there are so many unknowns, such as how we will define acceptable medical care in future decades and what such care might cost then. Changes in life expectancy may affect how much Social Security must pay out. To the extent that there are assets at least partially backing up some pension funds, their change in value over time will affect how much more would be needed to meet obligations.

The estimate by www.usdebtclock.org is that unfunded liabilities are currently (June 2023) about $190 trillion, or more than $500,000 per capita, including babies and little kids whose allowance may be only a few dollars per week. That seems too high, because it hasn't been discounted back to reflect the fact that a dollar owed years from now wouldn't be worth as much as a current dollar, which can earn interest between now and then. But how many years, and at what interest rate? What one picks for those two items could produce very different results. But even if that number is ten times overstated, $50,000 per person is a big sum over and above what we already must pay to operate the government and still buy what we want.

Assuming our federal, state, and local governments renege on neither their debts nor promises, we will struggle to meet those commitments through some combination of higher borrowing and higher taxes. There are limits to the total of savings here and abroad available to lend to us, and limits on how much tax rates can be raised without damaging the economy so much that tax revenues decline. The temptation will be intense for the government to print money by having the Fed make fake loans to the government with no expectation of ever being repaid, which is essentially MMT.

The good news from MMT is that the government will have no problem meeting every obligation, debt, or unfunded obligations, by handing out dollars whose ink is, in effect, still wet. The bad news is that one will need staggering numbers of them to buy a cup of coffee.

There is a generational issue to consider. Voters today like getting the money from stimulus checks and all the other goodies which a growing welfare state gives out, but the combination of soaring debts and rising interest rates means that an increasingly large percentage of the federal budget is now going to paying interest on the debt. Young people today, long before they retire, are going to have a choice of crushing taxes, expectations of drastically lower Social Security and Medicare benefits, and/or soaring inflation if the Fed keeps printing new money to give to the government to pay its bills.

The only way that outcome can be avoided is a major shrinkage of the size and power of government, allowing resources to stay in the private sector, where investment raises productivity and incomes. The fact that so many young people are leftists who favor big government shows just how bad economics education is these days. It'll be interesting to see if their opinion changes not too many years from now when their taxes soar, their paychecks become worth much less due to high inflation, or both happen at once.

Any mainstream macroeconomist since Keynes' ideas took over would dismiss any concern about GGSP on the grounds that government keeps the money flowing. Paul Krugman's mantra is *"Your spending is my income, my spending is your income."* The more the government spends, the more income people have, so what is the problem? The problem is that GGSP means that a much bigger percentage of our economy generates GDP and creates future tax obligations without any increase in the supply of what people actually want, thereby reducing our living standards and wealth.

Were we living in a hypothetical other universe where everything is the same as here, except that the government there shrunk to its previous small size after WW2 the way it did after all prior major wars, we would have had more than 75 years in which a much larger percentage of our population worked to satisfy the needs of other people, as expressed in our voluntary purchases, instead of in jobs doing the bidding of politicians. Every year an extra ten to thirty percent of GDP would have consisted of people spending their money as they chose, instead of having the government tax or inflate it away from them. That would add up over time. Living standards in that imaginary universe would be substantially higher than the one we live in, especially those of the poorest, whose living standards bear the greatest burden of the cost of government.

When governments are small and handle the basics properly, they enable the free market to do what it does best: allow people to self-organize into Arnold Kling's *Patterns of Sustainable Specialization and Trade* chains that increase wealth throughout society on a broad scale. As government gets bigger, the costs it imposes on society increase, and the wealth-creating machine stagnates, losing its ability to work well for any except the wealthy and politically connected.

This is not the fault of free markets. The left-wing-proposed solution of giving the government even more money and power would, without any doubt, make matters far worse.

CHAPTER 12

HOW BUSINESS TAXES MORPH INTO HIGHER PRICES

• • •

A QUESTION NOT YET ADDRESSED concerns the *Progress Mechanism*, which states that businesses invest to reduce unit costs, and prices follow costs down, such that the ultimate beneficiaries of that investment are not the widget companies doing all the investing, but their customers, who pay lower prices. Also benefiting are other companies selling whatever it is widget buyers do with the money they no longer have to spend to get the widgets they want. The companies must keep investing, like it or not, to fend off competition. The alternative, having competitors cut their costs while their own unit costs remain high, is a sure path to the business graveyard.

The bigger question is, since businesses invest enormous amounts most years, currently in the $600 billion range, why don't we have constant price deflation?

Well, we did, not counting during major wars, from the founding of the country to the 1890s, and in occasional years early in the 20th century. Since then, prices have at best been flat in any given year and usually rise, depending on which of the various arbitrary inflation indices you use. What changed?

Mainstream economists aren't interested in this question. They look at the world through the lens of GDP, where inflation makes GDP higher, and they think higher is always better. Instead, they should look through the lens of living standards, which are increased by lower prices, not higher.

Mainstream macro, however, is staunchly pro-inflation, at least up to the 2% per year target that all the central banks have settled upon, with some preferring more than that. If macroeconomists think about it at all, they probably think the end of declining prices to be a good thing, something that prevented their feared, albeit imaginary, liquidity traps from happening.

They claim to care about the less-well-off, but why were they so determined to push inflation up to 2% all through the 2010s, when the official figures had it barely above 0%? Their ignorance of the effect of higher prices on the living standards of anyone already needing to spend all their income is a serious flaw in mainstream macro thinking.

A major reason that prices overall nearly always defy the *Progress Mechanism* is that, even as businesses strive to reduce costs, the government has worked even harder to push them up, through taxes and cost impositions of various kinds that force businesses to raise prices to recover the higher costs from their customers.

Until the late 1800s, there were only the most limited taxes upon businesses, and few attempts to force businesses to alter their practices in any respect: What they priced their products. How they made them. Who they hired. What they paid workers. How many hours in the workweek. What benefits they provided employees besides a salary. All were all considered none of the government's business.

With the rise of the Progressive Movement in the late 1800s, that changed. Progressives felt that well-intentioned government officials and experts from an academic background had the ability to restructure whole industries to solve what they felt were imbalances of power between businesses and their customers and workers.

Progressives succeeded in getting the government to increase taxes upon businesses and set up regulatory divisions within the government to control the terms of how companies competed in various industries. This was immensely attractive to politicians since that gave them more government jobs to allocate and an expanded ability to extract campaign donations from companies to keep the regulations reasonable.

Anti-trust laws, which we think of as an attempt to prevent companies with a big market share from gouging customers with high prices, were used with the opposite purpose, against the big companies like Rockefeller's Standard Oil, who were gaining market share by underpricing competitors. Over time, regulations, and increased demands by the government for mandatory benefits and data collection, add to businesses' costs, but the biggest cost increases have come from taxes.

Politicians frequently argue about the appropriate income-tax rate for businesses, but the largest business taxes have nothing to do with their income, if any. They are based upon their payroll. Social Security (FICA) and Medicare taxes come to 7.65% of payroll, while unemployment taxes, both federal and state, can come to as much as another 8%-11% of payroll, depending upon the state and other factors.

If a business's payroll is about one third of its revenues, and its combination of FICA, Medicare, and unemployment taxes amount to 16% of payroll, then that works out to taxes of 5.3% of revenues. Most companies' pretax profits are not that high as a percentage of revenues, so if companies were not able to raise prices and/or cut wages and benefits, i.e., foist their taxes off on customers and workers, their taxes would be more than 100% of pretax income, and they would have no income to tax, nor with which to stay in business.

The mere fact that politicians are currently pushing a worldwide agreement to increase corporate income taxes from 21% in the US (different amounts elsewhere) to 28% shows that businesses do make money despite the taxes and other cost impositions already levied upon them. The same will happen with any future taxes or cost increases.

To prove that businesses pay taxes and cost impositions only temporarily before foisting them off on others, imagine that a staunch Progressive from the early 1900s popped into a time machine and visited the present US. On arrival, the Progressive would be told just how heavy the taxes on businesses are now, how many benefits they are required to provide to employees, and all the new administrative rules and restrictions they must follow today to be allowed to operate.

The Progressive would conclude that profits must be zero, or close to it. Yet they aren't. They are probably closer to the higher than the lower end of profit-margin and ROI ranges that have existed for more than a century.

The Progressive might be baffled. But the explanation is simple. While businesses have their names on checks that are written to the tax authorities, on the salary checks of extra government-required administrators, and on the checks to law firms for advice to keep the company out of trouble with the government bureaucracy, they must have either raised prices to make their customers cover the extra cost or cut compensation to make their employees cover the cost, or some combination.

In other words, businesses never really pay taxes, nor do they pay the cost of any government impositions, except nominally and temporarily. This must happen, or they would have no profits, causing capital and bank loans to migrate away from them, and they would no longer exist.

All politicians and even most economists pretend this isn't the case. If they're not pretending, they just don't understand economics. Many of them regularly demand that taxes be raised on allegedly greedy corporations, as if they themselves are not just as greedy when their incomes are at stake. They demand new benefits for employees, whether the latter want them or not, and that staff be hired to file reports on pay and job promotions to make sure that there is no discrimination, even if no employee has any complaint.

Politicians and economists understood this well in the old days, when people spent more of their budget on services offered by regulated utilities. For nearly everyone in the US, phone service could come only from AT&T, and electricity came from the monopoly granted to the utility in your area. Companies were required to go before the state utility commission, appointed by the politicians, to get approval to change rates.

Politicians, when they wanted more money, would, instead of taxing the public directly, raise an existing tax or impose a newly named additional tax on, say, an electric utility, and allow the utility to raise its rates enough to reimburse itself 100% for the tax, provided that the bills they sent customers did not mention the tax. There might have been a local newspaper headline when the tax law was passed, but the tax didn't kick in for some time, and, so, was forgotten. People then would get angry when they got their bills and saw that the damn electric company had raised its rates again. Mad at the electric company, not the politicians.

Some politicians and economists have figured out that business taxes and higher costs are at least somewhat foisted off on customers and employees, but they fantasize that owners pay the biggest share of the total tax, which is what they want to happen. Wrong, except in the very short run, before price increases take effect.

But what if a widget company's competition is mostly from non-US companies not facing the same tax increases or government-created cost impositions? Or what if the competition consists of outfits that offer a different type of product or service that can substitute for widgets and whose cost of production is not rising? In those situations, a price increase by the widget company could make it lose too many customers and be counterproductive.

If raising prices won't work, then perhaps the company can cut costs. There may be some relatively less productive employees who can be laid off, and the company could be stingier with raises, bonuses, and employee benefits. But that has risks, too, especially in a tight labor market, where it is hard to get good employees. The loss of productive employees who can easily get a good job elsewhere hurts any company.

If a company can neither raise prices nor cut spending, then the higher taxes and cost impositions from the government will come out of profits, as the politicians intend, and the company has no recourse. But that is not the end of the story—there are more plies in the sequence.

From the point of view of the owner(s) of the company, it is now a less attractive place in which to invest any further. If there were any plans to expand, hire more people, buy more equipment, or the like, they will be reviewed and probably canceled.

If, like many companies, the widget company relies on bank financing of inventories and receivables, it is now a less creditworthy company than it was before. With lower profits, the financial risk has risen. The bank may choose to raise interest charges to reflect the higher risk, which itself lowers profits further. Or the bank may put in more restrictive loan covenants to put the widget company on a shorter leash financially. Marginal companies in the industry, who were barely getting by even before the higher taxes and costs, will leave the industry or go broke.

Lower profits guarantee that the pace of growth of industry capacity will slow, stop, or reverse. Reduced supply relative to demand will alter the supply/demand balance for widgets in a way that allows price increases to stick on any increase in demand, and allow margins to expand again. That won't be much consolation for the competitors who closed up shop during the hard times, but it was only their withdrawal from the industry that reduced the supply enough for profit margins to recover.

Only after prices have moved up enough for it to make sense for widget makers to invest and expand capacity again—only after the ROI on new investment in the industry returns to an acceptable level relative to the risk, enough to encourage investment in new capacity—will prices no longer be pressured up.

What if the higher taxes or costs are imposed on every company in every industry, and tariffs are added so foreign suppliers can't undercut domestic prices? Wouldn't that mean that business owners have nowhere better to move their capital? Wouldn't that prevent them from reducing their investment and therefore keep the supply/demand balance where it was, except with all businesses being forced to permanently eat the higher taxes and costs?

No, because business owners always have alternatives. They can close the business and sell off the real estate and equipment. If they have enough money to do so, they can retire and consume rather than invest much. Just as nobody will take a job they don't like and which doesn't pay much if they have better alternatives, owners have no desire to work hard at a business with insufficient ROI relative to the risks. Banks and investors also have alternatives to financing weak companies.

This process of businesses foisting off higher costs mainly on customers applies to both higher taxes and government mandates that require an expanded administrative staff and more costly legal advice for compliance. Between the two, the latter are worse for businesses and society.

At least income taxes will drop if profits drop, and if price increases cause demand to shrink, reduced production will reduce payroll and therefore payroll taxes.

But cost impositions by the government not only add to a business's costs, but they also make more of its costs fixed, which creates negative operating leverage should sales be weak, whereby profits drop by a much bigger percentage than do sales. Governments never accept weak sales as an excuse for not submitting the required reports. In a recession, a company still must file those reports, or it will be in trouble, and it needs just as much legal advice to stay out of trouble in bad times as in good.

Instead, it must lay off workers who help produce or sell output. Other employees then see productive people leaving and politically necessary but economically useless administrators staying, which is bad for morale and risks others jumping ship to work at financially stronger competitors. With a more fixed-cost structure, a business is riskier, in that it isn't able to reduce costs as fast if revenues drop in a recession and has a greater chance of going under.

That means that a level of profits that previously would have provided a good ROI on new investment is no longer sufficient to induce investment because of the higher risk from government-mandated fixed costs. Supply growth will be restricted until the greater demand relative to supply pushes industry prices up enough to make the ROI high enough to attract investment again. Widget buyers will have to pay higher prices first, increasing inflation and reducing living standards.

Moreover, administrative burdens make it much more costly for small start-ups to enter the industry. They are required to fill out as many forms as their large competitors, but with far fewer zeros at the end of their numbers. Hiring unproductive administrative staff hurts them much more than the big players.

Innovation is much greater from small newcomers to an industry, as is the inclination to start price wars since small competitors are helped more by gains in market share than high gross margins. A high administrative burden discouraging their formation or survival entrenches the existing competitors and, by preventing the action of the *Progress Mechanism*, makes free-market industries more like stagnant, heavily regulated ones.

A controversial topic in recent years has been a trend of increased business profits relative to labor income. Progressives mutter about some mysterious conspiracies to exploit labor, but it appears that a significant cause may be the very policies they favor. The more that governments pile economically unproductive regulatory fixed costs upon all businesses, they effectively eliminate the very companies, the small aggressive ones, whose natural strategy choices would drive down prices and profit margins. Repealing those cost impositions wouldn't give workers raises, but it would raise their living standards the untaxed way, by letting them buy more of whatever they want for less.

If those politicians who propose business taxes at any level more than zero and want to impose other costs on businesses, were both honest and understood economics, they would have to say:

"Hey voters, instead of taxing you directly, lowering your living standards, and making your jobs lower paid and less secure, we're going to do exactly that in a disguised fashion, to make you think that it is businesses that are paying the taxes and that the costs of other things we mandate are coming out of their profits. What will really happen is that you'll reimburse business as the prices of what you buy go up, and your pay won't grow as fast. We're certain you won't notice what we did to you, because nobody notices it, and even most economists are blind to it."

In other words, businesses are tax collectors for the government, but it is really their customers and their employees who pay for all the taxes and cost impositions in the form of higher prices and lower pay.

All this doesn't mean business income-tax rates don't matter. Tax rules for international businesses are complicated, but other things being equal, most companies would prefer to be based in a place with low corporate taxes. A country that chooses to humor its economically ignorant voters by imposing heavy income taxes and reporting requirements upon businesses will be dismayed to find them moving their headquarters to countries less greedy.

CHAPTER 13

HOW TAXING THE RICH
HURTS THE POOR

• • •

THE *CAPITAL CYCLE MECHANISM* ensures that we cannot tax businesses or force them to assume extra costs, without those taxes and costs sooner or later being converted into some combination of higher prices or lower employee pay and benefits. Both options hurt the living standards of lower-income people, not the wealthy.

How can government pay for its spending without forcing most of the burden onto the backs of the poor? *Preview: It can't.*

What about steeply progressive personal-income-tax rates? And while we are at it, how about also increasing taxes on capital gains, which governments like to call "unearned income" as if investors didn't do something worthwhile—encouraging the expansion of capacity to produce output that they correctly predicted would face stronger demand—to earn them? Or how about a wealth tax, to take money from rich people regardless of income, and let the government use that money to benefit the poor in some way? Or inheritance taxes, to prevent rich kids from having an edge?

The rich, at least personally, are not in the business of selling anything to poor people, so, unlike companies, they have no way to raise prices on anything to get customers to reimburse them for higher taxes. Surely that should solve the problem, allowing the government to finance itself and provide more benefits to the poor without making lower-income people pay higher prices on what they buy due to taxes on businesses. Unfortunately, not so.

While nothing about highly progressive income-tax rates, high capital-gains rates, or wealth taxes will hurt those with lower incomes in the short run, these taxes will at least retard and possibly end the improvement of their living standards.

Those with high incomes usually spend only some of it and save and invest the rest. Like everyone else, they normally try to maintain their living standards when their taxes or their cost of living goes up. What gets sacrificed is not their lifestyle but their savings. That is a problem, because the only thing that can significantly increase a society's income is higher productivity, which comes from savings invested wisely.

Most of the benefits of higher productivity go to those with lower incomes in two ways. When their employers invest in equipment or training, that makes them more productive, which makes them more valuable as a worker, and their pay rises accordingly. Once, say, a worker has learned how to use new and more advanced equipment, if an employer fails to compensate the worker more, it risks losing what is now a more-valuable employee to competition.

And because of the *Progress Mechanism*, business investment first reduces unit costs, and then prices follow unit costs down, so consumers get more for their money. Everything that reduces consumer prices raises the living standards of those with tight budgets.

What the government does with our money is primarily consumption, by its own employees or by those to whom it dishes out money, and malinvestment, i.e., projects that are supposedly investments but bring little or no return. Even on projects that might be worthwhile, the government intentionally spends much more than necessary because of laws like the Davis-Bacon Act to pay off unions and prevent lower-cost, non-union contractors from competing on projects.

Yes, consumption is what living standards are all about, and one can enjoy a night on the town, a luxury vacation, a fine bottle of wine, and other consumption spending. But consumption consumes. You eat the cake, you can't still have it. Only by not consuming all our income is there money left to invest.

The main reason that American manufacturing workers get paid so much more than those in Chinese factories is not that we work harder or are smarter. It is the much higher capital investment per worker here, and money invested in R&D to create new products and better processes, which lets the US worker turn out much more value and get paid accordingly.

High marginal tax rates, wealth taxes, or anything else that reduces savings, and thus the ability or inclination of individuals to buy or hold shares of stock, would have a negative effect on business investment. The lower the stock price, the higher the cost of equity capital, because it means that the company must give out more shares to raise a given amount of money.

A high cost of equity creates a hurdle that will result in lower business investment. Investment requires capital, so the higher the cost, the fewer investments make sense. The fewer the investments, the slower the growth rate of productivity, leading to greater price increases and lower growth of worker pay, which together harms the living standards of the poor, not the rich.

Politicians and economists who are fans of tax increases on the rich wave away concerns about disincentives to invest by invoking Keynes's assertion that business investment is induced by mysterious "animal spirits" that people either happen to have or not at the time of the decision, rather than anything involving thought and analysis. As he put it:

" . . . *the characteristic of human nature that a large proportion of our positive activities depend on spontaneous optimism rather than mathematical expectations, whether moral or hedonistic or economic. Most, probably, of our decisions to do something positive . . . can only be taken as the result of animal spirits—a spontaneous urge to action rather than inaction, and not as the outcome of a weighted average of quantitative benefits multiplied by quantitative probabilities.*"

That was typically clever of Keynes, evading challenge by declaring that people will do things that are irrational because thinking takes too much effort and isn't as exciting as being impulsive.

However, if you have ever been stuck in a long line at an ice cream stand on a hot night because people in front of you, both kids and adults, are dithering over what flavor to order, you know that people can think long and hard about even the most trivial decisions. The idea that people won't carefully contemplate the potential risk and reward from an investment they are considering, which would have a much larger effect on their lives than would a suboptimal choice of ice cream flavor, does not seem correct.

When we humans do the arithmetic and figure the odds, the greater the capital-gains tax, the less inclined we are to invest in something whose payoff may not even exist and would be taxed heavily if it does. That is especially the case with the US's asymmetric rules, in which a gain gets taxed in its entirety in the year taken, while any net losses can only be used to reduce one's taxable income at the rate of a few thousand dollars per year, for a time period that might easily exceed many investors' expected lifespans.

Should the US adopt highly progressive income-tax rates, that will shrink savings available for investing. Combine that with high tax rates on capital gains, making people reluctant to invest in something where gains are highly taxed if they happen to show up, there is no question—*that* will reduce demand for stocks. Add in the US's unfavorable demographics, with a large Baby Boom cohort reaching the stage in life where their assets must be liquidated to fund retirement, and there could be a long bear market, reducing stock prices and, therefore, increasing the cost of capital.

This is also a drawback to proposed stock-transaction taxes. Removing from the market short-term traders who are aiming for small gains which would be entirely taxed away is removing a category of potential buyers if you have something you want to sell, or sellers if you want to buy. That makes an asset less liquid, which makes it worth less, raising the cost of capital.

Keep in mind that most large pension plans are very heavily invested in the stock market. The weaker the market gets, the more shares may have to be sold by defined benefit pension funds (e.g., most public-employee funds) to meet obligations. Add to that, many people with self-managed retirement funds either will sell if the losses get too painful or they will hold on but slash personal spending, which, if enough people do it, hurts the earnings prospects of many companies and thus their shares. All in all, there is the raw material here for a severe downward spiral if certain bad tax-policy choices are made.

The place where the savings of the wealthy have the greatest positive impact on the economy is in "angel investing," the purchase of shares in companies in their very earliest days. Rich people's savings are what finance nearly all start-up companies, before they are established enough to attract venture capital, which itself is long before a company goes public. Venture capitalists and other institutional and corporate investors are interested in putting money into companies only after they have been established long enough to show that their concept appears to work. Occasionally a very successful, proven entrepreneur can get institutional backing right from the get-go, but most start-ups raise their money from family and friends or rich people with whom they are acquainted.

Start-ups are frequently much more innovative than established companies who are naturally disinclined to sacrifice what is working well to try something new which might not. Not all start-ups are great ideas, or even good ideas that nobody else has tried to do yet. Some ideas and/or their execution turn out to be bad, and we don't want to subsidize them. If we want the better ones to exist, though, we shouldn't want to scare off early-stage investors and remove a major source of economic innovation.

I have some experience with angel investing. It is extremely high-risk because most start-ups fail for many possible reasons. Even if the start-up can grow enough to secure venture-capital investors, the latter often drive such a hard bargain that the earlier investors retain much of the risk and give up a chunk of the upside. Still, when they do work out, one can make ten times one's investment or more. Such a gain often arises when a bigger company wants to acquire the company, pushing the capital gain into one tax year, and for that one year, turning one into a very-high-income person.

To the extent that proposals for high income-tax rates on large capital gains seem to have a chance of passing, that takes away the main incentive for helping finance a start-up. You might accept the fact that most of these companies will go broke and you will lose your entire investment, but if, when they work out, you will also lose most of your gains, why bother? Why not just leave the money in some safe, low-return investment, or spend the money on a more extravagant lifestyle?

The latter option would make sense if inheritance/estate taxes are increased. Why try to build up capital to leave to your heirs if the government is going to grab big chunks of it? Why not drink the finest wine, or take your family on a luxury vacation? *Better use the money while you can,* would be a widespread feeling on the matter.

My first trip to England in the 1980s showed how that played out. We went there soon after Margaret Thatcher came to power and introduced lower tax rates. The country seemed much less wealthy than the US in most ways, but I was surprised to see how many of the cars in London were Rolls Royces, Bentleys, Aston-Martins, and an occasional Ferrari or other European luxury car.

A local explained to me that these cars were all bought in the 1970s pre-Thatcher, when the Labour Party government imposed extremely high tax rates at higher income levels. The government's finances were shaky, and on the surface one could earn a high return owning government bonds, but if your income was even slightly above average, the government taxed away nearly all your income and capital gains.

Rather than take on risk for no benefit, many wealthy people used their savings to buy classic cars that would hold their value reasonably well. There would be no income from the car, and it would decline in value over time, but not at a rapid pace, and, in the meantime, one had the pleasure of riding around in it.

Savings can be invested, but if tax rates on investments are too high, people will consume the savings instead. Only investment can significantly raise productivity, pay, employment, and living standards beyond the benefits everyone gets from wise investments by others, the *Grace of the Market*. Had the UK government not penalized earnings from investments so heavily for so many years, there would have emerged many new, growing, innovative companies who would hire people to do things that paid much better than just maintaining and detailing older luxury cars.

The tax that would most discourage wise investment is probably a wealth tax. Since most assets are owned by the already-wealthy, there has been a flurry of interest in the concept of wealth taxes, ostensibly to reduce inequality, but also to provide more money for politicians to spend.

Most wealth is very hard to value. Yes, if you own 100 shares of IBM, the closing price on the valuation date is a good and easy measure of its value. But suppose you own some part of a private company, or a farm, or the local yarn shop, or other small business which has no stock trading on the market and therefore no easy way to value it. Works of art by famous artists can be worth millions, but unless recently purchased, their value is mostly guesswork.

What makes much wealth particularly hard to calculate is that some assets, particularly real estate but also many businesses, have a lot of debt connected to them. A house assessed at $1,000,000 might have a $900,000 mortgage on it, so the owner's equity could be considered $100,000. If the actual market value of the house were just 10% less, the owner's equity would be wiped out.

This issue is regularly dealt with when large estates need to be evaluated for inheritance taxes. Many appraisers are in the business of making hard-to-value assets appear to be worth as little as possible for estate purposes. That service is needed only at death, or, occasionally, in a divorce, but with a wealth tax, demand for appraisers would soar.

This would not happen in the first year a wealth tax was imposed, because those currently proposing it claim it would apply only to wealth above $50 million. There aren't too many people in that category. But that was the case with the income tax, too, when it was initiated in 1913. It started with a rate of only 7% on incomes earned above a half million dollars, equivalent to an annual income today of somewhere between $20 to $40 million, depending upon how one adjusts for inflation.

We know what happened next. Instead of taxing only a few wealthy people at low rates, income, payroll, and self-employment taxes now hit almost everyone with much higher rates. With the massive growth of government relative to the private sector, that's not surprising. The alternative minimum tax was initially aimed at a grand total of 155 US taxpayers who had been identified as having very high incomes but also high deductions that reduced their taxes to zero. Now millions of middle-income people pay that tax, and tens of millions must calculate it, even if it turns out not to apply to them in a given year.

That is certain to happen with the wealth tax, too, since the ability to game the calculation of wealth through friendly appraisals and other maneuverings will make the tax bring in much less revenue than advocates expect. Since revenue from a wealth tax is supposed to pay for costly new programs, the government would soon have to cut the wealth threshold that gets taxed and also increase the rate and do that again and again as the public gets more adept at hiding or consuming its wealth. That's when demand for appraisers will really explode.

We already have more than a million accountants and tax lawyers, and we'll find ourselves paying fees to hundreds of thousands of wealth appraisers as well. If most of them were working on serving people's genuine needs and wants, instead of artificially created ones, the supply of what people want to buy would be greater and prices lower.

The distortions that a wealth tax will create in how savings are invested will impose an even larger cost on society. For example, senators from the farm states will certainly see to it that farmland gets exempted, for good reason, since farmers may have a lot of wealth in land but often have little cash to pay taxes. Other lobbyists will get solar farms, windmills, woodlands, and who knows what all else exempted, too.

The response of those taxed will be obvious. All someone with wealth above the tax threshold would need to do to get out of that obligation is borrow money and use it to buy exempted property. The asset wouldn't count toward their taxable wealth, but the debt would be subtracted from it, either putting them below the taxable wealth threshold or sharply reducing what they owe.

The prices of exempted properties would soar, since so many rich people would be buying them, and anyone with a family farm would cash out and leave the business. The Midwest would further depopulate, food production would drop, and food prices would rise, as usual hurting low-income people.

Misdirecting savings into tax-exempt assets and diverting smart people from useful careers into wealth valuation and tax consulting, bad as those things are, cause minuscule damage compared to the impact of a wealth tax on stock and bond prices, and what that does to the cost of capital for every business. This is where the idea really gets stupid.

Let us suppose that the government starts taxing wealth at 2% annually, which might not seem too bad. Some percentage of shareholders of any public company will want to sell at least enough stock to pay the tax, and others will want to sell all their stock—and other financial assets, too. Whatever a company's dividend rate, if any, it now effectively pays 2% per year less than it did before.

You might think that is no great hardship, since real-estate taxes are often about 2-3% of the value of the house, and you don't see many people who can afford housing and the tax preferring to live out on the street. That is because protection from the elements is worth the tax. A stock, however, does you no good except as an investment. If it will now cost you 2% per year unless it goes up, why own it? And if nobody wants to own it, how will it go up? In fact, how will it stay much above zero?

Not everyone has to think that way, but given that stock prices are determined by the actions of a small number of people who buy or sell on a given day, the number of sellers will completely overwhelm buyers. Trillions of dollars of wealth will disappear quickly.

That will mean that 2% of newly destroyed wealth won't bring in as much tax revenue as expected. The following year, with sharply lower wealth, the tax rate might have to jump to, say, 5% to hit the revenue goal, which creates even more reason to hold no wealth. Defined-benefit pension funds, most of which already lack the assets they need to meet their obligations, would collapse and no doubt need more massive government tax increases, borrowing, or money printing to be rescued. Those counting on IRAs and other pension plans for their retirement may find that, with retirement, comes penury.

Bonds would be similarly affected. Whatever the wealth-tax rate, a bond would have to pay yearly interest higher than that rate to have a positive return and attract any buyers. The cost of capital would explode, since interest rates would shoot up above the wealth-tax rate, and companies would have to give up large pieces of the company to raise even the slightest amount of equity. Venture-capital investment and new-company formation would cease.

Another way of looking at it is this: The founder of Amazon is a multi-billionaire. If we wanted to tax his wealth to reduce it to below one billion, as some Progressives have proposed, that would force him to sell more than $100 billion of his assets, mostly Amazon stock. That would crush the stock price. Why would anyone want to invest in any inherently risky start-up, when one could buy Amazon at a massive discount to what is probably its inherent value?

There is no point in foregoing current consumption to save money and invest, and then be penalized for doing so. Initially, people will pretend they have less wealth to minimize their tax. Before long, they won't have to pretend. A tax that wipes out much of the nation's wealth and takes away the incentive to save and invest is not a sustainable way for a government to finance itself.

No question, taxes that slash savings and investment would succeed in one of their objectives, which is to reduce inequality. They will make the poor and middle class much poorer, but by wiping out big chunks of the country's wealth, they will also make the previously upper classes poor, too. If that is the kind of equality people want, then these taxes are a great way to achieve it.

In terms of sheer ability to raise money for the government without causing what is taxed to disappear, consumption taxes, such as sales taxes in the US and the similar Value Added Tax (VAT) in most other countries, are probably the best. People are not going to stop eating if food is taxed or put on old rags if clothing is taxed. Most of what most people buy are things they consider essential, so overall consumption would not be greatly diminished by consumption taxes.

The big drawback of consumption taxes of any kind is that it hits lower- and middle-class taxpayers much harder than higher-income people. The lower one's income, the greater the chance that one spends all of it. Thus, a consumption tax is effectively a tax on 100% of a poor person's income, and a smaller percentage of a high-income person's earnings. Higher-income people can and usually do spend more, though, so they would pay higher consumption taxes in total. Whether that meets the demand by some that "the rich pay their fair share" is anyone's guess.

Taxes on consumption can raise large amounts of money because most spending is consumption. A VAT would be a good idea for the US, but only in return for the end of payroll taxes and all income taxes, not in addition to them. Just adding it on will give the politicians an excuse to spend even more. That is what happened when VAT taxes spread rapidly through Europe starting in the late 1960s, without reductions of other taxes. The VAT added to government revenues, causing them to ramp up wasteful spending permanently to levels well above that of the US. All measures of Europe's living standards, economic growth, unemployment, and so forth have lagged that of the US ever since.

The US's big edge compared to Europe has been that our government, bloated as it is, is still smaller, relative to the private sector, which can still generate more wealth than our government can waste. Recent trends suggest we want to emulate Europe, rather than the other way around.

In any event, to discuss what tax is best to pay for the government is to answer the wrong question. We shouldn't accept a large and growing government as a given—and then fight over how to pay for it. Nothing is ever free; *somebody* always must pay for resources consumed. Any way to pay, either right away or with a lag, comes out of the living standards of the poor and middle class.

ENTANGLEMENT

• • •

THE MISTAKEN IMPRESSION THAT the economy does what it does, without being much affected by the government, leads to an incorrect syllogism that most Americans make when thinking about the problems of our society. Constantly reiterated by politicians, academics, and many economists, it goes something like this:

1) Problem X is wrong with our society. Lately, the most popular Problem X is income and wealth inequality, especially along racial lines, but other candidates for X include rising food, healthcare, energy, and tuition costs, rising rents and house prices in areas where good jobs are plentiful, climate change, the gender gap in pay and power in corporations, slow economic growth due to "secular stagnation," and other complaints.

2) Problem X involves money, so it must have some connection to the economy.

3) The US has a free-market economy, which means the free-market system must be the cause of Problem X.

4) Therefore, the government should have more control over society and the economy to solve Problem X.

Depending on one's viewpoint, what the government should do could mean anything—from more regulation, changes in tax rates or what it is that we tax, programs that effectively nationalize entire industries, breaking up big tech companies, and requiring that businesses have board members representing "stakeholders" who are not shareholders.

All proposed solutions for Problem X involve the government commandeering more money and/or power in society at the expense of the private sector. Whatever the problem, the proposed solution is more government dominance.

Even problems that seem more connected to the performance of the government itself than the economy—such as terrible inner-city public schools, rising crime rates, and deteriorating public infrastructure—are things which many believe could be ameliorated, if not entirely solved, if taxes on the rich were higher and the government had more money. As leftist New York City mayor Bill De Blasio said, *"Here's the truth. Brothers and sisters, there's plenty of money in the world. There's plenty of money in this city. It's just in the wrong hands."*

The problem with this logic is step #3. The US does *not* have a truly free-market economy. It has a free-market economy that is heavily controlled and shaped by the government. To be understood, it needs to be seen from the viewpoint of political economy, not just economics. Maybe Problem X does have a strong connection with free markets, but one can't conclude that without any consideration of what actions people are induced to take, or not take, by government laws and policies. Different rules would produce a different outcome.

Think of it in terms of sports. A typical basketball game might have one or both teams scoring something in the area of 100 points, a football team scores in the upper 20s, and a baseball team around 5 runs. Does that mean that basketball players are about four times more skilled than football players, who are about five or six times better than baseball players? Of course not. The scores are entirely a function of the rules of each game.

If professional baseball, in some misguided plan to make more money, wanted to change the rules so that the batter needed 4 strikes to be out, giving them more chances to get on base, average runs per game would soar, without any change in the quality of the hitters or pitchers. Strategies for players and teams would change to reflect the new rules, but games with both teams having double-digit scores would be the rule. One couldn't ignore the rule change and claim that suddenly batters got much better and pitchers worse.

Similarly, if there is some aspect of the US economy or society of which one disapproves, one must first make sure to examine the "rules of the game," i.e., the role of laws, regulations, subsidies, taxes, and the Fed's monetary policy, among other things, before saying that the problem is inherently the fault of the free market.

When one looks at the economy that way, mostly what one finds is people behaving exactly as one should expect, given a particular set of government-created constraints and incentives. If that behavior is dysfunctional, then those rules and incentives need to be changed to solve the problem.

This section covers how the private sector changes its behavior in response to government-created inducements. In some cases, that behavior is for the best. We should not want businesses to dump pollution onto land, into bodies of water, or into the air, so one can say the government's rules against them doing that is a benefit to society. We don't want people physically hurting others, threatening to do so, or stealing their property by force or fraud, not only because that is morally wrong, but because it takes away the incentive for people to work, be productive, to save and invest, or to engage in other behaviors that have a major positive effect on the wealth of a society.

But governments' laws and policies can also have a major impoverishing effect on a society to the extent that they induce us to do things that make us much poorer. That is never their ostensible purpose. Usually, their intent is help solve one problem, but the politicians or administrators who advocated for them either didn't understand or care about the negative effects that make some other problem worse, or they focused on the short-term benefit without considering the long-term cost.

Chapters 14-15 reiterate a flaw inherent in the construction of GDP, that it counts activity in the economy without any concern over whether that activity increases or decreases our living standards. A classic example is the building of pyramids in ancient Egypt – loads of employment, great for GDP, but what was in it for the average Egyptian? Not much. Before you start feeling superior to the ancients because we must be so much smarter, you'll see examples of things we do today, due to government rules and incentives, that are effectively the same thing in disguise. **Chapter 16** shows how government regulation of various industries and occupations, while occasionally useful, can be very harmful to our living standards and, in the case of healthcare, to our lives. **Chapter 17** shows how the free market reduces inequality, while government policies increase it. **Chapter 18** shows why our goal of helping future generations with programs to slow climate change, while certainly well intentioned, risks making them worse off.

CHAPTER 14

HOLES, PYRAMIDS, AND TAX LAWYERS

• • •

ONE OF THE FLAWS of focusing on maximizing GDP is that GDP is a measure of activity but not whether that activity results in increased output of value to anyone. Success by the GDP standard is measured by lots of people working and getting paid, not the result of that effort. People's living standards rise only if they can get the specific goods and services they want. If too many resources (materials, labor, management, capital) are devoted to producing output nobody really wants, what people do want will cost more, and living standards will be lower as a result.

Keynes famously suggested, only partially tongue-in-cheek, that to stimulate the economy, the UK government hire people to put money in jars and bury them deep in disused coal mines. The potential profit would attract businesses who would hire miners to dig through the rubble and retrieve the jars. The money spent on burying the jars is a government expense that is added to GDP. The spending and profits of the businesses whose employees retrieved the jars would also add to GDP. Many people would have jobs either digging holes or filling them up. There you go—a better economy (after all, the GDP is supposedly the economy, and the more, the better), all thanks to the benevolent government.

Except, what would anyone get out of this exercise? Nobody wants, in the sense of being willing to buy with their own money, either a hole or a filled-in hole. A lot of work would have to be done, money would be paid to people, but nothing of value to anyone would be produced.

Similarly, Keynesian economist Paul Krugman, in a TV interview with a few other talking heads in 2011, recommended a more modern parallel to Keynes' "bottles with money in a coal mine" thought experiment: *"If we discovered that space aliens were planning to attack, and we needed a massive buildup to counter the alien threat, and budgets and deficits took a secondary place to that, this slump would be over in 18 months. And if we made a mistake and discovered that it was fake, we'd be a better . . . "*

At that point another economist interrupted, but Krugman was clearly on his way to saying that we would be better off spending massive sums to protect against an imaginary threat, because that spending would add to economic activity. He later verified that interpretation: *"This is the kind of environment in which Keynes's hypothetical policy of burying currency in coal mines and letting the private sector dig it up—or my version, which involves faking a threat from nonexistent space aliens—becomes a good thing; spending is good, and while productive spending is best, unproductive spending is still better than nothing."*

Neither Keynes nor Krugman learned anything from the famous French economics journalist Frederic Bastiat (1801-1850.) He wrote about the "Broken Window Fallacy," which is the mistaken assertion that more spending is always good for the economy. His example is of some boys who, while playing ball, inadvertently break a window in a neighbor's house. The claim is made that this is good for the economy, because the homeowner will now have to buy a new pane of glass and have it installed, which provides more business for the glassmaker.

To use Bastiat's language, the purchase of the new window is "that which is seen." But, he says, we should always take into account "that which is unseen" but still must exist. In this case, because the homeowner had to buy a new window, he now has less money to buy something else, say, a new pair of shoes. His house is mended, but he doesn't have the shoes he would have had if the window had not been broken. The glassmaker comes out ahead, but both the homeowner and the shoemaker lose, so it is a net loss, not a gain or breakeven.

This is a simple concept, but it is astounding how few seem to understand it. With the very destructive Hurricane Ian hitting Florida not long ago, there was commentary about how this was good for the economy, because hundreds of thousands of people with severely damaged homes will have to fix them or buy new ones. The fact that those people would have to slash spending on other things wasn't considered.

For people to get what they want, others must produce that output. If people at work are doing something else instead, then the supply of what people want will be small and limited. I call that mechanism the *Pyramid Effect*. The economy of ancient Egypt shows how that works.

From its earliest days, Egypt was a prosperous country due to its agricultural productivity, which came from the rich soil brought down in the Nile floods every year. Being on the Mediterranean, farming was supplemented by fishing for a well-rounded diet, at a time when most other countries and tribes, not so blessed, struggled for subsistence.

Had today's macroeconomists been around at the time, they would have been delighted by Egypt's "infrastructure project" of building pyramids to give dead pharaohs a good sendoff into the afterlife. These were enormous projects, involving tens of thousands of workers in construction, many of them highly skilled artisans, plus numerous workers rounding up building materials and transporting them, and building and repairing the necessary ships, hoists, and other equipment.

Recently discovered ruins and papyri show the massive resources that Egypt devoted to pyramid construction. Materials such as granite, limestone, lumber, and especially copper were sourced from what is now Lebanon, Saudi Arabia, and other countries as well as in Egypt. Copper was essential for making tools in those days, and tests have shown that copper blades lost an inch of metal for every one to four inches of granite they cut. The Egyptians explored for copper, opened and ran mines, built ports, fleets of ships, barges, canals, and harbors to transport the copper to the pyramid sites, along with hundreds of furnaces to turn the copper into tools.

Conflating pyramid construction with Bible stories, we commonly think of the construction workforce as consisting of slaves, but discoveries of refuse pits from the barracks where many of the workers lived show that they had an almost royal diet, with generous servings of poultry, fish, honey, dates, and other delicacies of the time, suggesting that these were highly skilled and valued workers.

It is possible that some of the lower-skilled jobs were done by slaves, which fits in with the fact that there appears to be a vast number of what we would call middle managers at work to keep the projects going as planned. Even the slaves had to be fed, housed, and clothed as well as managed. Given the low level of productivity that existed 4600 years ago, they were expensive, too, even if they were not paid money.

It is hard for us to understand such an intense nationwide commitment to something whose benefits exist only in the religious realm. A comparison might be to certain medieval European towns that were not wealthy, but by working on the project for more than 100 years, constructed magnificent cathedrals. They weren't slaves—they were some of the most skilled craftspeople around at the time, and although paid, they probably felt that they would be getting some reward in heaven in addition to their salary on Earth for working on such a project.

We, therefore, shouldn't be cynical about the depth of religious conviction of ancient Egyptians, who may have felt it necessary for their pharaoh to be well placed in heaven after death for the same thing to happen to them, and were, therefore, willing to sacrifice what we consider decent living standards for that goal.

But look at the pyramid building from the point of view of an average Egyptian citizen, perhaps a fishmonger, farmer, carpenter, or other city dweller, and assume that they were not very devout and were more interested in improving their living standards as we think of them today.

Resources used in the construction were, by definition, unavailable to be used elsewhere in the economy. Someone wanting to hire a worker and use building materials to build or expand a house would have to pay up to do so, since supply of both labor and materials not needed for pyramids would be scarcer than if there weren't pyramids being built. Everybody was working hard, resources were being bought and deployed, and GDP would be high. But living standards would be low because output of what non-royal Egyptians wanted was low.

Remember, no pyramid workers took their pay, assuming it was greater than the free room and board offered slaves, and used the money to buy a piece of a pyramid. They would have wanted more and/or better food, clothing, housing, etc., just like every other Egyptian who had no connection to the pyramid-construction industry. Same thing for the stoneworkers, engineers, camel drivers, longshoremen, hoist builders, and managers on the pyramid projects.

Everyone wanted more or less the same consumer goods and services, but vast numbers were not producing them, nor were they producing trade goods that could be exchanged for output produced overseas in Greece, Phoenicia, and other relatively advanced societies.

Adding to demand while restricting supply made the prices for food and other items much higher than would have been the case had the government not been building pyramids.

All this had to have been disastrous to Egyptian living standards. Had GDP been calculated then, it would have soared to record heights, because government spending, no matter how worthless, counts in GDP. Aggregate demand would have been stimulated by all that spending, and mainstream macro's dreaded enemy, price deflation, would have been thoroughly defeated. Everything was exactly as our macro experts would have prescribed. The average Egyptian suffered badly as a result.

Think of how much wealthier and more powerful Egypt would have been had all those resources and all that hard work been used instead for higher food output and to build more irrigation canals, more grain storage, better housing, better port facilities and ships to enhance international trade, and other things to make life in Egypt before the afterlife much more rewarding. The history of the western world would likely have turned out very differently, with Egypt likely being the classical formative civilization of modern society and languages, rather than Greece and Rome.

The average Egyptian fishmonger and farmer paid for the pyramids twice—once when they were taxed to pay for constructing them, and once again when they had to pay higher prices for labor or any other resource for which they would easily be outbid by the government, which wanted the same resources for pyramid building and would use their tax money to outbid them. And the farmer and fishmonger were also competing for food, clothing, and other scarce consumer goods with pyramid workers, who didn't produce anything anyone would buy.

What is the relevance of this? Simply, our economy, for many years, has been filling up with the modern version of pyramid workers: an increasing percentage of the workforce who are well paid but produce neither goods and services anyone would voluntarily buy, nor output that foreigners would buy in return for output they produce that we want.

The cause is GGSP, the tremendous growth of government size and power. Spending trillions of dollars a year now, approaching half of GDP, the government buys goods and services that the politicians claim we want. Maybe we do want some of what the politicians buy, or maybe we don't, but the choice is not ours.

Besides about twenty million people working directly for the government, there are tens of millions of other people working at jobs whose original source of funding is related to government spending. One shouldn't try to be too accurate about that number, because the concept is fuzzy and inherently arbitrary as to what to count and what not.

We know that, for example, because of the massive power of the federal government, it is worth the while of great numbers of businesses, industry groups, and unions to employ lobbyists to influence the politicians to vote the right way on bills pertaining to themselves. Between the lobbyists and the employees of various think tanks and consulting groups who are lobbyists under a different name, the income levels of many counties in Virginia and Maryland near Washington, DC, are among the highest in the country, and rarely drop much, if at all, in recessions.

Most of those people are modern-day pyramid workers. No regular citizen has ever said, *Yes, I was thinking of taking a vacation trip, but instead I'll give that money to a lobbyist group so that laws, administrative policies, and mandatory reporting requirements affecting the widget industry don't add too much to widget makers' costs.*

The lobbyists all get well paid, but no matter how successful they are, their output is not something anyone other than a widget manufacturer would feel is worth spending their own money to accomplish. Now suppose a widget-industry lobbyist buys a new car. That seems to be a transaction purely in the private sector, yet the source of the lobbyist's salary was clearly government related.

If the politicians didn't run what is barely distinguishable from a mob extortion racket (*Nice widget industry you have there; it would be a shame if there were an excise tax on widgets, or excessive administrative restrictions and reporting obligations that would run up your costs*), the industry would not have felt it necessary to hire lobbyists for self-protection. It would have lower costs, the *Progress Mechanism* would push widget prices down, and living standards would rise.

If many industries were deregulated, or not preyed upon by politicians as the energy industries are lately in the name of climate change, then there would be many more people whose work instead would serve non-politicians by offering them output that they voluntarily choose to buy. More supply would reduce prices and increase living standards.

Most of us don't have much connection to the lobbying industry, but we all pay taxes of one sort or another and sometimes struggle to figure out what income tax we owe. Here is another example of the massive disconnect in society between pay levels and whether a person is providing others with what they genuinely want or whether they are satisfying artificial needs created by the government:

A bright friend in college went to a top law school and became a very successful corporate tax attorney. Retired now, he was a partner of a major law firm, advising businesses on how to minimize their taxes. His income was surely very high, but perfectly justifiable in that, whatever he charged, he probably saved his clients many times that in taxes. That was a good deal for them, and most people would view him as a productive citizen.

But from the point of view of society in general, his pay over the years was money wasted, in that there is no natural demand for tax advice, only artificial demand induced by a needlessly complex tax code. He wasn't well paid to solve any inherent problems in life or bottlenecks in the economy. Although certainly smart enough to have done well in any of these careers, he wasn't a doctor or medical researcher saving lives, or an engineer or scientist advancing knowledge or creating new products that might have benefited millions. Rather, he was well paid to solve a problem—interpreting and applying the complex tax code—that exists only because politicians prefer the code to be complicated.

The length of the tax code has been cited as being in the 75,000-plus-page range, but that is misleading because most of that consists of commentary and tax-court rulings. The current tax code itself is supposed to be merely 2,600 pages or so. But that is also misleading, in that there is so much ambiguity in the dense wording that one needs to read many additional pages of precedents and rulings to have a better idea of how the IRS or the courts are likely to interpret a given phrase in the code and apply it to a particular taxpayer.

Politicians love making the tax code ever more complicated, using deductions, credits, and penalties to get individuals or companies in some industry to make certain choices that allegedly are socially desirable. When tax rules apply to just some tiny segment of the tax-paying population, say, a special tax credit or penalty for widget makers who do or don't do something, it is easier for the politicians in power to fetch large campaign donations from the widget industry to keep those tax credits high or the penalties low, entirely unnoticed by 99% of the voters.

Until the 1930s, government was tiny by today's standards, and taxes were so low that it wasn't worth anyone's bother to spend much money or time minimizing them. The job of tax lawyer barely existed. If government were much smaller and taxes therefore much lower, the need for tax attorneys would be much lower. If politicians didn't prefer tax complexity to fuel their extortion/bribery racket, and instead we had a vastly simplified tax system with virtually no deductions or credits, there would have been little demand for my college friend to have the career that he did. He was effectively a pyramid worker, well paid to solve a problem that exists only because the government created it.

Multiply my friend's experience by the many hundreds of thousands of tax lawyers and accountants, all earning big sums, and that's at least $50B per year that is never counted as a cost of the government, but surely is. Over and above that, there is the time and effort people need to calculate their incomes, deductions, credits, and tax owed. Depending upon the value of that time, one might easily add anywhere from $50B up to many times that in costs to get the paperwork right. Whatever the number, it is big.

Remember, the total cost of these things are not just the checks we write to pay those accountants and lawyers, but the loss of output that we would have had, had all these people been working to give us what we truly want, not what the government makes us want.

Yes, Egypt's pyramids have been a great source of income to the country's tourist segment starting in Roman times, more than 2000 years after they were first constructed, and then again starting in the 1700s through the current day. However, the ROI to Egypt for constructing the pyramids was still deeply negative, weighting much more heavily the immediate losses to living standards versus the benefits to tourist income, even when discounted at a very low interest rate, since thousands of years passed before that income arrived.

CHAPTER 15

HOMEGROWN PYRAMIDS

• • •

A NCIENT EGYPT BUILT PYRAMIDS. For the lives of the average Egyptian of the time, it was all a colossal waste of money, not counting whatever psychic benefit they may have had knowing that their taxes went to assuring the current pharaoh's comfort and status in the afterlife. What reduced their living standards was that so many of the smartest and hardest working people in the country were working on the pyramids and diverting so many resources to that end, instead of providing the goods and services that fellow Egyptians would have wanted to live better lives, if they looked at life as we do today.

Given the country's immense natural advantages compared to everywhere else in the western ancient world, had Egypt made a priority of secular achievement as Rome did later, it would easily have been the richest country on the planet and could have afforded a military that made it the most powerful, with a dominance that might well have continued to this day.

Many people find it easy to be at least mildly contemptuous of those who lived in the past. They didn't have the astounding advances that we have from modern technology, medicine, transportation, and so forth. It is easy to notice mistakes and stupid practices in the past and think we are too smart to make those mistakes. But we are fallible humans, just like they were, not any smarter, and, often, we make the exact same mistakes, disguised enough that we don't realize it.

It turns out, unnoticed by anyone, we have been "building pyramids," too, not just what the government purchases, but with our own private money. Instead of about 118 massive pyramids that the Egyptians built, we have been building millions of them, much smaller, of course, and shaped somewhat differently. *We call them McMansions.*

What? An Egyptian pyramid had only a religious purpose, whereas we live in our houses, they protect us from the elements, they allow us to create a personal environment that we find attractive and that pleases us in many ways. Having a nice place to live is a major element in living standards that people want to be as high as they can afford.

All true. And we are so much wealthier today; our productivity advantage versus the ancients' is massive, so if we want to build, buy, or rent a fancy house or apartment, no peasants are going to starve to death because we chose to divert our limited food supplies to those in the building trades.

The comparison is somewhat far-fetched, but not entirely. The Egyptian pyramids, by our standards, were very expensive consumption, but we don't know enough about the theology behind them. It has been proposed that they were intended to launch the soul of a deceased pharaoh into heaven. If the Egyptians thought accomplishing that would lead to great prosperity or happiness for the people, then they may have thought of pyramids as a sound investment in national well-being.

Whether in the roughly 2000 years (about 2700 BCE to 700 BCE) when the Egyptians were building them, some minister suggested trying out a stripped-down, discount soul-launcher to increase resources available for living Egyptians, we just don't know, although in later years the pyramids were much smaller.

Most of us in western countries, where house prices have been going up at a strong rate for more than fifty years, with a few intervening crashes, think of our houses as investments. The truth is that housing in a developed country like the US is actually consumption, not investment. That sounds shocking. How can owning a home not be an investment?

Well, it is an investment in the colloquial sense of the word, as something you can buy and then sell later, hopefully for more than your cost plus anything you spent to maintain and improve it. But that is asset speculation, an exchange of ownership of an existing asset, where success as a speculation depends entirely upon its price at some future date when it is sold, rather than any favorable effect on the buyer's income or expenses before then.

The situation is different in underdeveloped countries. In some of them, many people live in shacks with no electricity, plumbing, or protection from disease-bearing insects. A new house that provides healthier living conditions, including being able to read at night, to store food in a refrigerator away from critters, and drink water untainted by sewage, will make the citizens healthier, more productive, and better able to earn a living. That makes new houses built to modern standards effectively a good business investment for them.

In the US, housing is counted in GDP as an investment. Despite its many flaws as a useful measurement, the developers of the GDP concept in the 1930s were probably right for calling housing an investment at that time. Much of the US had very poor housing until the 1950s or later. The US Census Bureau says that in 1940 31% of US houses had no running water, 35% no flush toilets, and 44% lacked either a shower or bathtub. A substantial percentage of houses, especially in rural areas, lacked electricity. For people in those houses, a new house with modern systems was truly an investment. Their lives would be healthier and wealthier by living in one rather than in the old shack.

That is no longer the case in the US and other developed countries. Close to 100% of the housing stock already has electricity, plumbing, and other modern conveniences. Moving from a perfectly fine small house to a fancy McMansion will not increase your lifespan, health, or earning capacity. Ongoing expenses for property taxes, insurance, mortgage interest, and maintenance will be higher in the McMansion. You may get pleasure from your new home in a variety of ways, but your disposable income after paying housing expenses will be lower than if you'd stayed in a more modest dwelling.

Still, in a world where the Fed is biased toward keeping interest rates excessively low for as long as possible, there is speculation potential. But the Fed is not a predictable market force, and sometimes, to save face from disasters caused by their previous interest-rate and monetary policies, it reverses and goes too far in the other direction, which adds to risk.

Besides the possibility of speculative gains, buying a nicer house in a more upscale neighborhood is no different from any other luxury consumption, in that your expenses increase, but you gain some pleasure. You could buy a yacht and cruise around or join an expensive golf club, and your lifestyle will also be upgraded if you enjoy those hobbies, but those also are luxury consumption, not investment in the economic sense. That may seem like a definitional quibble, but it is the key to understanding many of the problems that have hurt the economy of the US, the UK, and other countries where house prices have been rising quickly for decades.

But first, why has housing been such a great asset speculation for so long? Consider all the incentives that the US government uses to get people to put their savings into houses:

Tax advantage #1: deductibility of mortgage-interest expense, but not rent expense, from taxable income.

Tax advantage #2: favorable treatment of capital gains from the sale of a house. There have been some changes over the years in capital-gains taxes, but each $1 of profit from the sale of your house was either never taxed, or taxed at a much lower rate than $1 of capital gain from investing in a business.

Official subsidies for housing finance: government-sponsored enterprises (GSEs) like Fannie Mae, Freddie Mac, and FHLB, using their implied government guarantees to raise money at below-market rates to subsidize and guarantee mortgages.

Indirect subsidy #1: FDIC and FSLIC insurance, backed by the government, removing any incentive for depositors to care whether their money is at financial institutions run by prudent managers or crooks. Either way, they get paid in full up to a high limit if the bank fails. In fact, the more reckless or corrupt a bank's lending policies, such as lending to management's friends and relatives in return for kickbacks, the higher the interest rate the institution would happily pay to gather more deposits.

Indirect subsidy #2: Rules by banking regulators anointing Moody's, S&P, and Fitch as the only legitimate rating agencies, despite ample indications that they competed for business with securities packagers by offering to sell them bogus high ratings. Potential competitive rating agencies whose more-cautious models reflected more-accurate risk assessments have been effectively prevented by the government from entering the ratings business.

Speculative Stimulant #1: Although the ostensible intent is not to push house prices up, that is the predictable result of the combination of strict zoning, town planning, historical preservation, and other regulations restricting the addition of new housing in places people want to live. The consequent rapid rise in prices stimulated speculative greed.

Speculative Stimulant #2: Not a subsidy as such, but standard mortgages of the type guaranteed by the GSEs include no recourse to the borrowers' other assets if they fail to pay, which made buyers willing to pay more for a house, take on more debt, and then abandon it if its market value fell below the mortgage amount.

The Usual Suspect: Finally, there was the Fed, doing its usual thing of keeping interest rates too low for the entire bubble, until the very end, when all it took was a slight increase to topple the unsupportable price structure.

Why so much government pressure to stampede people into the housing bubble? Think of all the businesses and occupations that benefit from housing. Some that come to mind are: real-estate agents, mortgage brokers, developers, real-estate lawyers, bankers, appraisers, house inspectors, title company employees, dealers in mortgage paper, contractors, lobbyists for the GSEs, carpenters, plumbers, electricians and other building tradespeople, wood, concrete, brick and other building-materials manufacturers and their employees, truckers, manufacturers and retailers of home appliances, furniture, carpets, tiles, lumber, pool companies and all their employees, their suppliers and employees of their suppliers.

There are many people in these occupations or businesses in the districts of every member of Congress, and any politician hoping to be reelected would be unwise to oppose the housing juggernaut. Building more houses and having existing houses rise in value were therefore next to godliness for both political parties for decades.

In theory, the more houses built, the lower the appreciation of existing houses since there would be more supply relative to demand.

But rising house prices created buying panic among renters, who felt they had to buy soon or miss out on the gravy train forever. The supply of houses, especially with permitting-process delays, could not keep up with demand until prices got so high that there were few left who could afford them.

To most macroeconomists, the housing bubble was an unalloyed good. First, there was that long list of beneficiaries above. How can anything that benefits so many people be bad? Second, house-price appreciation generated rising real-estate taxes, which gave the local governments more money to spend. All the buying, selling, financing, building, manufacturing, and distribution creates income, and income creates income-tax revenue for the federal government.

Finally, people were getting rich from house appreciation, since all appreciation accrues to the owner, and the mortgage holder doesn't share in that. There was the general "wealth effect" of the higher prices. "My house is doing my saving for me" was a common refrain during the bubble.

Thinking they were relieved of the burden of saving, many people spent all their income, and others went further, taking out home-equity lines of credit—essentially variable rate mortgages using home equity for security—and spent that, too. All that spending is great for GDP, so what could possibly be the problem?

The problem was this: the housing bubble was an orgy of conspicuous consumption. Everyone thought that the house or condo they were buying would be a good investment, but they were not really investments at all—they were just consumption plus asset speculation, pretending to be investments.

True, a small percentage of buyers can gain financially from a house purchase even without any price appreciation. People whose kids' education is very important to them and who live in a town with poor public schools might gain by buying a costly house in a high-end suburb with better schools. The savings from not having to pay private-school tuition might more than cover the higher housing expenses. Similarly, people who sell investments or insurance to rich acquaintances might meet more of them in a high-end neighborhood.

For everyone else though, a more luxurious house means more happiness (maybe) and higher spending (definitely,) combined with an asset speculation.

There is nothing inherently wrong with spending money on consumption. The ability to do so easily if you wish is the very definition of a high living standard. Still, the future is always uncertain. The economy could turn bad in a way that harms your future income, or something happens that causes your expenses to rise more than you had anticipated. To avoid worry about possible future problems like those, it is good to have plenty of reserves set aside in case they are needed. And if there is something you can invest in that causes your savings to increase over the years, so much the better.

If the government is going to run deficits by spending heavily and pretending it costs nothing because taxes don't go up, and the deficits are accommodated by the Fed creating new money to purchase the debt to keep interest rates down, the value of the currency is going to drop against the various things that money can buy. When only rich people have access to most of the newly created money, which had largely been the case since the housing bubble collapse until the Covid stimulus checks, then house prices will indeed trend up and prove to be a good asset speculation.

The problem is that the more extravagant houses we build or renovate, the less capital we have for the kind of business investments that raise productivity and, therefore, our collective standard of living and future incomes.

In the years 2001 through 2007, people in the US bought about $3.5 trillion worth of new houses, most of that debt financed. Recall that debt-financed consumption makes one poorer. In other words, the housing boom—yes, the boom part, before there was any bust—kept reducing our net worth, while the temporary and fragile house price increases made us believe the opposite.

What we were doing all those years was taking on more debt to pay for our new, expensive hobby of living in fancy houses. We thought we were richer because the prices kept going up, so we increased our spending even more to celebrate. Prices can go down as well as up, as people discovered, but debt never goes down, unless one pays it off. Or one can go bankrupt to make the debt go away, but then one's assets go away, too.

The building of all those unneeded and extravagant McMansions made us less wealthy. The collapse of the bubble was the painful-but-necessary remedy for that massive blunder. It halted any further waste and freed up human and material resources to be redeployed in something more viable.

Historically, sharp economic downturns are almost always followed by sharp moves back up. Instead, after the housing crash until not long before the Covid lockdown economic disaster, we had a slow, struggling, pathetic recovery. This led to a large amount of bloviating on the subject of "secular stagnation," offering various reasons why the economy's growth was so much lower than any time in the post-WW2 period, not to mention the earlier era from country's founding to the 1930s.

Wikipedia's article on the secular stagnation, at least as of this writing, lists the various theories from major establishment economists like Larry Summers and Paul Krugman, who, being on the Keynesian side of orthodoxy, naturally thought the problem was not enough spending. Keep in mind that no one can prove correct any macro theories about why many things happen, and that includes the one that makes sense to me. It isn't on the Wikipedia list of possible secular stagnation causes yet, but it seems a much more plausible explanation than those that are.

For the ten years after the housing bubble collapsed, the US economy behaved as if we were a poorer country, with most people making little economic progress and much of the growth in incomes and net worth going only to the already-wealthy. The reason for that is, having borrowed trillions to pay for housing consumption, **we were, in fact, a poorer country.** We took on trillions in debt, and we didn't use it for anything that would increase our ability to service the debt. And we did it again during the next real-estate bubble of the Covid years. Debt-financed consumption always makes one poorer, and whether that is done by a government or by individuals doesn't alter that fact.

In a hypothetical alternative universe exactly like ours, except one in which the government and Fed did not try to stampede everyone into buying and building as much housing as they could possibly afford, those trillions spent during the bubble would have been available for other uses.

True, some of it might have been spent on housing anyway or on other consumption choices. However, given how widespread was the belief of home buyers that they were investing in an asset that would rise in value over time, it seems likely that, in this alternative universe, much of the trillions put into housing would have gone instead into capital for companies or deposits in banks that lent to them, and thence into business investments, intended to increase our net incomes, not just enhance our lifestyles.

Not all investments would have succeeded, but enough would that, compared to our actual universe of speculative real-estate bubbles pretending to be investment, we would have more successful companies, a better-educated populace, better healthcare, a greater share of world markets, higher incomes, and much-reduced poverty.

In that better universe, our houses wouldn't be as extravagant, and many more of us would suffer the indignity of preparing our sandwiches on Formica rather than on granite kitchen counters, but that drawback seems dwarfed by the benefits.

Instead, our politicians saw the biggest problem of the housing bubble as one of inequality, in that the middle and upper classes were getting rich, and we needed to change the regulations to let poor people participate in the Ponzi scheme as well. Banks and the GSEs were pressured to approve mortgages to the unqualified, who, being the last buyers before the collapse, soon thereafter had their years of savings wiped out.

The housing bubble shows that it is not just the Fed that damages the economy with short-term GDP worship. The same focus on aggregate spending with no concern about what the money is being spent on, thereby encouraging debt-financed consumption, is highly popular with nearly all governments.

China, for example, has put up massive ghost cities, with housing, manufacturing facilities, office space, and civic buildings for hundreds of thousands of people, but nobody ever lives or work there except a few security guards. All this construction gave them the GDP growth that they want but also soaring debt, which was spent on nothing of value, lowering their net worth.

This is what politicians the world over want to do anyway: spend heavily, pay for it with borrowed money so as not to have to raise taxes, and encourage consumers to overspend, too, creating a seemingly strong economy. Mainstream macro's GDP worship gives the politicians the intellectual authorization to do just that.

There is nothing inherently wrong with people buying homes. Some people can safely do so, if they have plenty of money and/or a secure job in a locale where, if they lost their job, they could find another one at similar pay.

Others must stretch to afford the purchase, or they have a job that, were they laid off, might require a move elsewhere to match. Those people would probably be better off renting.

The government should go back to its pre-1930s policy of being strictly neutral as to whether people buy or rent. You want to buy?

Great! You want to rent? Great! Whatever, do what you want, and, as a matter of policy, the government does not care. No tax breaks, subsidies, or favoritism toward one versus the other.

During all those decades when not caring whether you owned or rented was government policy, house prices were locally hot in some places and weak or stagnant in others, depending upon population growth and other forces that made for uneven regional economies within the country. But there was never a consistent sharp increase in house prices on a national basis until after the 1960s, when government stimulants to housing got larger, and the Fed became more aggressive at keeping rates below what the market would have had them, to stimulate more spending.

Despite the housing-bubble fiasco, the broad real-estate lobby remains powerful, right up there with the farm lobby, making it tough for any politician to challenge the vast subsidies it has secured. Over time, only a better understanding of economics, i.e., a rejection of our established wrong beliefs, might change that.

The claim is often made that the housing bubble was chugging along nicely, and it was only "greedy bankers" behaving badly that caused the collapse. That is nonsense. By 2007, US house prices got unaffordable almost everywhere relative to people's incomes. Prices were also too high relative to properties' going rental rates. The cash cost of servicing the mortgage plus paying property taxes and other expenses were far above any possible rental income, removing all except the richest and most patient speculators from the buying pool.

Not that there weren't plenty of greedy bankers cutting corners, just as there were plenty of greedy home buyers who lied about their incomes and other obligations to get mortgage approvals. This is what happens during bubbles—many people feel like chumps if they are earning money through honest work, when there is so much easier money beckoning in speculation.

Let's get cause and effect right. There was fraud because there was a bubble, not a bubble because there was fraud. There was no epidemic of car buyers lying to get loans at the time. Car prices weren't soaring; house prices were, so it was house buyers who were desperate to get approvals. Banks could make quick profits by placing mortgages, not car loans, into packages that could be flipped for a profit.

Worth repeating is that, to work properly, an economic system must recognize that the actors in the economy are humans. Humans regularly stampede toward or away from something when there is contagious greed or fear. If you intentionally create a stampede into buying houses, as the government and Fed did, then don't blame people for acting exactly as they were encouraged to do under the circumstances. Those who set up powerful incentives for people to commit fraud deserve the heaviest blame, not those who, like normal humans, responded as one would expect, given those incentives.

Why didn't all that investment help? Mainstream macroeconomists might object to this explanation of the housing bubble by saying that, even if we consider housing in the US to be more consumption than investment, there was also strong investment in the economy during the bubble years. Therefore, to say that the economy was distorted with debt-financed consumption is not correct.

That critique would again demonstrate a major flaw of mainstream macro, thinking in aggregates when the real world works in specifics. Whether in ancient Egypt or anywhere today, it isn't activity per se but what specific work people do that affects living standards. A company in the housing-products business putting up a large new factory in 2007 to increase output of things which soon would find little demand, is called investment. It was actually malinvestment, investment that was wasted. When there is a boom in asset prices somewhere in the economy, there will be lots of malinvestment.

First, there is investment to meet the needs of the bubble itself. The housing bubble generated strong demand for a variety of products—lumber, concrete, nails, and other building materials, tools, and equipment used to build a house. For the insides of houses, investment was needed to expand the production of furniture, carpet, appliances, and the like. Those companies that made those things invested to expand capacity since demand growth was relentless and seemingly sustainable.

Those who are getting rich on the bubble become big spenders, and industries that cater to them will also invest to expand because the demand is there. Many contractors, tradespeople, and those tapping their rising home equity with loans bought new SUVs and pickup trucks, so vehicle makers invested in new equipment and expanded capacity.

When the bubble ended, much of that investment was worthless. What we really needed at that point was what would have existed if we had never had the housing bubble. We needed more people who weren't up to their neck in debt. We needed more consumers who hadn't just lost their houses and years of savings to foreclosure. We needed companies with attractive innovations, and a workforce with people who had more skills than just the ability to swing a hammer.

But we didn't have those companies, we didn't have the technical advances, we didn't have the fruits of non-housing-related investment, we didn't have the right skills, because that capital was diverted to housing instead.

Similarly, it is likely that some percentage of the jobs "shipped overseas" went there, not because there was any great advantage manufacturing far away from the largest consumer market in the world, but because the capital that could have been invested in local manufacturing got diverted to serving the housing bubble instead.

It isn't the aggregate amount of money invested, but where exactly the investment money is being deployed that determines whether those investments make us richer or poorer. Savings and investment are absolutely necessary to create a rising standard of living, but they become a useless sacrifice of current consumption if all that the investment expands is the capacity to make more of what nobody wants.

That is what socialist countries do all the time, because central planners never have the valuable information generated by free market prices. That is what even a supposedly free-market economy like ours will do if bad government and central bank policies create powerful incentives for people to engage in debt-financed, capital-intensive asset speculation, instead of business investments that would have increased productivity and incomes. Those bad incentives kept house prices moving higher, and the desire of home buyers to get rich without having to work took over from there.

Nevertheless, nearly all macroeconomists cheered the politicians along, because as they see it, higher aggregate spending makes for a better economy. Whether that spending takes the form of investments in new technologies that will enhance living standards for years to come, or, as in the housing bubble, leveraged conspicuous consumption, makes no difference to mainstream economic theory.

But it should. Their failure to know the difference, and the consequent creation of incentives to encourage the wrong choice, is part of the cost to society of the deep misunderstanding of economics by economists.

• CHAPTER 16 •

INSTABILITY, REGULATION, AND THE FDA

• • •

S TARTING ABOUT A DECADE after its founding in 1913, the Fed made an error in judgment and has continued making the same error ever since. The mistake is not realizing that prices of absolutely everything, whether output (goods and services) or assets, reflect the supply and demand for dollars themselves, as well as for whatever is priced in dollars. The Fed doesn't appear to have ever learned that that one can't just look at placid consumer prices and assume that there is no excess of dollars around, if at the same time there is an asset bubble in process.

Bubbles are "fear of missing out" stampedes fueled by debt that take asset prices to unsustainable levels. When the tide turns, the value of the assets falls below the debt owed on them, and the owners could be wiped out financially if they can't service the debt. That's what happened in the late 1920s when the margin-fueled stock market bubble collapse initiated the Great Depression. There were similar stock-market bubbles in the late 1960s, the late 1980s, the late 1990s, and 2020-22. There were widespread real-estate bubbles in the US in the late 1980s, the first decade of this century, and most recently in 2020-22.

In every case the Fed, looking only at consumer prices that weren't showing much price inflation, concluded that interest rates weren't too low and money wasn't too easy, even as rapidly rising asset prices showed that people were happily borrowing dollars and quickly trading them for assets. This should have led the Fed to the opposite conclusion.

Another underlying cause of financial instability is US tax policy, namely the fact that interest expense (the cost of debt) is deductible for income-tax purposes, while the dividends on shares, which is part of the cost of equity, is not deductible. Just as the deductibility of mortgage-interest expense but not rent was an incentive for renters to buy houses, helping to fuel the housing bubbles, the deductibility of business-interest expense encourages businesses to borrow money instead of selling shares.

The difference is that, if a recession or some issue causes a business to lose money, it has the right to eliminate its dividend to save cash if it so chooses, but it is under contract to pay interest and principal on debt when due. Many companies end up going bankrupt that could have survived had their financing not been biased by the tax code to have more debt and less equity.

Free markets will always be somewhat unstable, in the sense that changes in public tastes and the arrival of innovative new products and business models cause declines in businesses whose products or services are no longer in sufficient demand. Companies go broke and their employees lose their jobs. Since the cause of that is the arrival of what is newer and better, which will need resources to expand, the turmoil is just a temporary price we pay for progress. To have otherwise viable companies go under because they were induced by monetary or tax policy to be too leveraged to survive a temporary economic setback is a needless loss to the economy.

The government also does a great deal of damage with other policies, incentives, and disincentives that never go through its budget, but cause people to waste money and take on extra risk that occasionally costs us dearly, as happened with the housing bubble.

Besides tax complexity that spawns millions of accountants and tax advisors working to solve problems that exist only because the government created them, another government failure is excessive regulation and licensing, which prevents many people from engaging in work serving others' needs and wants. Regulations are the rules with which existing businesses must comply. Licenses are given to individuals and businesses who qualify, and without which they cannot legally operate.

Regulation as a concept elicits wide reactions depending upon one's political viewpoint. Those who believe the free market is a dangerous enterprise in which evil people are constantly exploiting workers and consumers who are helpless without government protection, see more and tighter regulation as a solution to many perceived problems.

The opposite view is not against all regulation. One of the prerequisites for a free-market economy is the rule of law. Regulations, in many cases, are merely statements of how the law applies in specific circumstances.

For example, we know that restaurants have no right to make customers ill. No restaurant would ever want to do that, since they operate in a competitive field with tiny margins, and angry customers claiming on review websites they were poisoned is not good for business. Nevertheless, not all businesses are run by people who pay as close attention to details as they should.

Board of Health regulations about keeping the kitchen clean and foods properly refrigerated, plus occasional surprise inspections, seem a sensible way to avoid problems. That is more efficient than clogging up the courts with lawsuits by patrons who were sickened, requiring costly expert witnesses on both sides. Few restaurants are financially strong enough to pay any significant court judgments and are likely to go under, thereby compensating none of the victims.

Building codes are similar; they are statements of good practice that prevent unintended harm to building owners and occupants, and save everyone from costly lawsuits, as well as injuries or death.

If all regulations reduced unintentional wrongdoing, improved public health, or precluded other problems that would need expensive tort litigation to rectify, then few would object to them. The problem is that regulations often go very far beyond that point and, whatever their ostensible purpose, mainly protect entrenched suppliers in an industry from competition. We see that especially in occupational licensing, where, ostensibly to protect the public from damage caused by incompetent suppliers, a government will require large license fees and unreasonably extensive training before a person is allowed to engage in trades.

That includes many occupations where even the worst incompetence does little damage. Yes, incompetent surgeons and electricians can certainly do harm, but how bad can it be if one does business with an unlicensed and therefore possibly (but not necessarily) inferior florist, hair braider, lawn mower, or interior designer? Surely word of mouth and negative comments on review venues can handle this problem.

Many of the most egregious licensing requirements relate to service businesses that lower-income people can operate successfully in their homes with minimal capital and training. The license laws are very effective at keeping poor people poor and keeping the prices they must pay for certain services high.

Adding to the hurdles, you could be a very qualified and licensed person in an occupation in one state, and then must start almost from scratch with educational and other requirements should you move to another state. Fortunately, this is starting to break down, with Ohio most recently joining a handful of other states that accept licenses from other states as acceptable there, too.

Licensing rules are often outsourced to, say, the State Board of Cosmetology, whose decision-makers are all practitioners in that business. They have zero incentive to allow new people to compete with them, other than the risk of public shaming if their requirements for a license are too absurd. While regulators claim they are just trying to protect the public, the fact that many such boards spend most of their time rooting out unlicensed competitors suggests a different motive.

Even in fields such as medicine, where potential harm caused by unqualified practitioners can be severe, there has always been a strong element of "rent seeking" involved, i.e., using government power to help certain parties get money that they can't earn in a free, competitive market. In 1910, the openly racist (at the time) Progressive movement got together with the then all-white American Medical Association to put into effect the recommendations of the Flexner Report, ostensibly intended to upgrade medical education. Going forward, doctors could practice only if their degrees were from accredited schools.

Of the seven medical schools specializing in training African-American doctors, five of them failed to meet the AMA's accreditation standards and were forced to close. Since, in large areas of the country, African-Americans would be refused treatment or charged too much by white doctors, this led to untold death and suffering.

No doubt the five closed medical schools weren't as good as Johns Hopkins, but so what? By today's standards of medical practice, even Johns Hopkins in 1910 was awful. The closed medical schools had been educating African-American doctors who may not have been as knowledgeable about the then state-of-the-art in some things, but they certainly knew enough to set bones and provide many other useful treatments that they were now legally prevented from offering.

One of the many factors that makes medical care so expensive in the US remains a licensing system that requires years of very costly education for doctors and forbids less-well-trained people from competing with doctors on diagnoses and treatments that don't really require advanced training.

One would hope that, sometime in the next decade or so, an artificial-intelligence computer program operated by a minimally trained technician proves to be as good or better at diagnosing illnesses and suggesting treatments as a qualified physician. That would bring great savings to medical care, provided the program also can reliably determine which cases are too complex for itself and require a human physician to handle.

Another improvement would be to eliminate all state "Certificates of Need." In about half the states, if someone wants to put up a new hospital or expand an existing one, they effectively must get the approval of the existing hospitals in the area, who never have any reason to favor more competition. The concerns over the shortages of hospital beds during Covid, a major justification for the destructive lockdowns, was a consequence of expansion plans rejected because competitors made a case that existing capacity was sufficient.

For all they may complain about it in public, the biggest companies in many industries secretly prefer their industry to be highly regulated, because they can easily afford the large staff needed to comply with regulations. A small new competitor that might someday surpass the current leaders can't afford the necessary staff. The bigger companies also have the money for lobbying and other ways of influencing the regulators to set standards that benefit the established order versus allowing innovation.

Regulators would never admit that their function is to prevent the dominant companies from losing market share to innovative newcomers, and I doubt that is their intent, but that is the effect that many regulations have. Entire industries get frozen into place because new models for operating a business are not permitted by the regulations. For example, only because Uber set up in business without even attempting to register with local taxi commissions could it get started. Had it meekly gone to the commissions and applied to offer its service, without medallions, without directly employing any taxi drivers, it would have never been approved for business anywhere.

The protection that government regulation provides incumbents against change leads to corporate complacency. You see this in how regulated companies behave in terms of customer service, compared to those in unregulated industries. Ask people which companies they find to be the worst to deal with, and you'll see that nearly all are in highly regulated industries: electric, water, gas, or other utilities, phone and cable companies, hospitals, universities, insurance companies, banks, and other financial institutions.

Big drug companies are intensely regulated. They are allowed to sell a prescription drug only if it gets the FDA's approval, which can take years and billions of dollars in research and trials to achieve. That creates legal monopolies in many cases, and lacking competition, current or potential, the companies often price their products exactly as one would expect from government-protected monopolies.

The bad customer service list doesn't even count outfits that are actually run by the government, like a state's Department of Motor

Vehicles, the IRS, and the US Postal Service, which, like Amtrak, pretends to be a company, all of whose customer-service reputations are even worse than regulated companies. Regulated companies or government departments, these organizations don't have to worry about competitors and behave accordingly.

This also happens when the government anoints a company to be a sole supplier of some service that it previously handled, such as management of local rail transit. That is called privatization, but with no competition except perhaps at occasional contract-renewal negotiations, these companies behave little better than the government they replaced.

When we look at industries in the ostensibly private sector that are expensive, perform poorly, and that exacerbate inequality, three stand out: housing, college education, and healthcare. All three are highly entangled with the government.

We've covered housing, and, if the government had never had any involvement in it, house prices and rental prices would be substantially lower than they are today. Probably most people would be living in a place more modest than they presently do, in smaller houses with fewer decorative extravagances. Instead of struggling to pay their mortgage or rent, they would have higher living standards in other respects and have a higher level of savings. Those savings would fund more business investment, leading to higher innovation, productivity, and wages.

College has gotten ridiculously expensive due to the government. We've had a cycle wherein colleges raise fees, parents cry to the politicians that they need subsidies to pay for it, the government creates a new program or increases benefits in an existing one to give students and their parents more spending power, and colleges again raise their tuition fees to grab more money. The problem remains and becomes more costly.

People seem to think that there is something about healthcare that makes it need intensive government management, but that is not so. Healthcare is important, but no more important than people finding food to eat. Nobody can possibly accuse supermarkets of having high margins or excessive profits, just a level that brings a fair return on their invested capital. Their prices are rarely much more or less than that because the *Capital Cycle Mechanism* will bring in more competitors if profits are too high, and cause closures of the least-profitable stores if they are too low.

The same thing would be true in healthcare had it been allowed to develop on its own, with minimal government interference. Much of the structure of the industry today came from random, haphazard government rule-making that was never intended to be anything other than a short-term fix for some other problem altogether.

There is no inherent benefit to have health insurance offered by employers. One reason that insurance is more "sick care" than "healthcare" is that, as people move from job to job, they switch carriers and policies, and employers often switch insurance suppliers to get better deals. Insurance companies have no incentive to promote programs to increase fitness, weight management, and other services that will keep people alive and healthy longer because an insured person likely won't be their customer for very long. If people could buy their own insurance and keep it for many years regardless of their employer, then the insurance company would have a stronger incentive to help people stay healthy.

Employer-supplied healthcare exists only because during WW2, when there were wage and price controls, employees couldn't get raises at their existing jobs, but could switch companies to get higher pay in a new position. Businesses begged the government for some way to retain staff without breaking the law and were granted the right to offer health insurance to retain key employees, with that benefit counting as a business expense for tax purposes, but not counting as income to the recipient.

It is peculiar that solving an employment problem from eighty years ago, itself entirely a function of government-imposed wage controls, should determine how people handle large medical expenses today, but that is how it is.

Numerous aspects of the industry, all based on government rules, have combined to make healthcare vastly more expensive than it need be. A good example is the FDA, whose prime goal is to make sure that no medicine is ever marketed that causes those taking it to suffer harm. That's certainly a worthy goal, except that achieving it likely causes more harm than it prevents.

The cost of getting a drug approved by the FDA can easily be more than a billion dollars and spending that money doesn't guarantee approval. Not that it should, if harmful characteristics are discovered late in the approval process, but getting a drug through all the trials is so expensive that many drugs that might treat or cure fatal diseases are abandoned very early at the slightest setback, because the companies that invented them cannot afford to take such a large and risky bet.

Once again, we must look at not only what is seen, but what is not seen but which we know must exist. We see the great job the FDA has done in keeping bad products off the market, although it is too soon to be sure that the Covid vaccines won't have long-term negative effects. What is unseen, yet surely exist in large numbers, are people who died or suffered unnecessarily because the drugs that could have treated or cured them never made it to market, thwarted by the FDA's immensely costly approval process.

From the FDA's point of view, it knows that people who are harmed by bad drugs are seen, and the FDA will be severely blamed for approving a drug that, in retrospect, it should not have. What isn't seen is all those people who could have been helped or saved by various possible drugs whose inventors had to give up early. The FDA knows it will never be blamed for those deaths, because how can anyone know that an effective drug was prevented from existing?

Given those incentives, the FDA focuses on avoiding the mistake of giving approval when it should not have, because it was always held harmless for not giving approval when it should have. The FDA is strongly inclined to be strict as possible, constantly demanding more studies of drugs up for approval, because no amount of money spent by companies is too much if it keeps the FDA from being criticized.

With so few drugs making it over the FDA hurdle, those that do get approval often have monopolies—or close to them—in treating a disease. Their makers would have to charge a lot anyway to cover the costs of getting approval, but with costly FDA approval limiting or eliminating competition, they often can charge whatever they please.

People get upset, quite reasonably, when they see drug companies charging what seem like excessive amounts for certain drugs or raising prices at rates that far exceed inflation. The problem is not the free market, because those things don't happen in truly competitive markets. It happens only where the government makes competition nearly impossible.

The drug-approval process can be restructured in certain ways that will allow many more beneficial drugs on the market with minimal additional risk and much lower costs. This would take a while to describe and, realistically, is unlikely to be adopted until there is more basic understanding of the government's dominant role in causing healthcare to be so expensive. That is the purpose of this book—to get readers to appreciate just how costly government entanglement with the economy truly is.

CHAPTER 17

INEQUALITY

• • •

THE FIRST THING THAT usually comes up when one attempts to advocate free markets as the best economic system for creating widespread prosperity is the charge that free markets generate inequality, and that government control over markets is required to prevent a handful of people from owning just about everything.

The complaint is baseless. Free markets emerged and existed almost as if they were intentionally designed to do the opposite— enrich those who are the least wealthy.

That doesn't mean that there isn't plenty of inequality, but mainly in a way that most people don't mind. A famous movie or sports star, a brain surgeon, or a computer expert for a major tech company are all going to make a lot more money than the average person who doesn't have any special skills in great demand. The cop who works an extra 20 hours a week overtime on traffic control at construction sites, frequently in bad weather, is going to earn more than a fellow cop who doesn't. And an employee who has been at the same company for 20 years will have earned seniority raises that a new employee in the same position hasn't yet, even if the latter might be just as good at the job.

Do any of those inequalities bother people much? No. There seems to be a broad consensus of Americans on the topic of inequality, which is well considered and nuanced. Americans don't object to inequality of wealth or income where success is caused by someone working extra hours, extra hard, or extra smart, or because a person is naturally talented, or just provides many of us with good entertainment or catchy hit songs. We celebrate the person who risks their life savings starting up a new business and, after years of hard work, can sell it for millions.

We do object, however, when the reason for someone's success is considered fraudulent or undeserved, such as the preferential treatment of certain big financial institutions by the US Treasury and the Fed during the bust phase of the housing bubble. We also object when someone (other than ourselves, of course) gets an unfair edge through connections, as in the college-admissions scandal.

Related to that, we are uneasy about those with big inheritances; they don't really deserve that money, but we don't necessarily want to take away the right of their parents to bestow it upon their heirs, to the extent that the ability to do so was an important motivator in whatever the parents did that made them rich.

We know that rewarding achievement has been a key to the success of the US, but we want to reward true achievement, not unfair advantage. Although there will be disagreements on how this should apply in particular circumstances, we mostly share a sense of fairness that balances both true merit and equality of opportunity.

The best way to look at inequality is through the lens of living standards. What can lower-income/wealth people afford to buy, and how much of it? How does that compare to what middle- and upper-income/wealth people can afford? From that viewpoint, it is odd that the subject of inequality has become such an alleged problem, in that, contrary to common belief, the world has effectively become much more egalitarian over recent decades, regardless of what income or wealth statistics might say. Consider the basics of anyone's budget: food, clothing, and shelter.

Less than a century ago, there were major differences in the diets of the rich and the poor, with the latter—even in the US—sometimes literally starving, which is what is believed to have caused the death of Blind Alfred Reed, the singer/composer of this book's second epigraph, in 1956.

Nutritionists today criticize the diets of the poor, partially caused by the high prices and relative unavailability in poor neighborhoods of the natural, organic, higher-quality (and very pricey) ingredients they recommend. Still, because of massive productivity growth in agriculture that until recently pushed food prices down to record low levels relative to incomes, starvation, except in the poorest countries, is rare.

As for clothing, until late in the 20th century, it wasn't hard to know something about people's economic status by what they wore. Two men might both wear standard business suits and ties, but the less well-off man could not afford high-quality fabric and tailoring, and the difference was clear to upper-income people. (That has always been the whole point of social signals, which the upper-class notices but others don't, so the elite could tell who is "one of us.") The turn of China toward a more capitalistic economy and its entry into world trade, slashing what we had to pay for clothing, helped caused that distinction to disappear. It is not easy anymore to detect someone's class from their clothing.

If anyone in a developed country today is starving, it is probably because they are trying a fad diet. If two youngish guys are walking down the street in sneakers, shorts, T-shirt, hoodie, and baseball cap, one could be a low-paid clerk, the other an engineer/entrepreneur with shares in a tech company worth tens of millions, and, just looking at them, standing in the same line for the same takeout food, no one would know which was which.

The main reason for that is the ability of free markets to generate so much wealth that there is nothing one can do, in terms of day-to-day eating or clothing, that can possibly be a social demonstration of one's wealth. Can only the richest people afford some high-end baseball cap or mushrooms on their pizza? No. Of course, there will always be luxury foods whose existence is more due to rich people showing off that they can afford the finest, most expensive wines, caviar, and truffles. That is human nature, but it doesn't mean that those who can't afford those things can't find much less expensive foods just as pleasurable and nutritious.

And it is not just the ability of the clerk to eat and look exactly like the engineer that signifies their social near equality. It is also the reduced emphasis on visible signs of status in our society that allows high-paid engineers to not care if some friends or relatives met on the street might object that they are not upholding the dress standards appropriate for their income level.

Contrast that to England from well before Victorian times at least through WW1, when it was always essential for anyone middle class and above to not only dress appropriately, but also have the correct number and type of servants for their income and class or face social disapproval. Starting around the time of the Industrial Revolution, after centuries in which one's status in England remained stable because it depended upon birth family and birth order, society in the UK was scrambled by the rise of wealthy families with no social status. That created a popular demand from the upper crust for complex and largely unspoken social rules, table manners, and so forth that only the right people would know, and know to follow, to signal their status.

For example, a running gag in P.G. Wodehouse's many *Bertie and Jeeves* stories, which mostly take place in the 1910s-1930s, is set in motion by upper-class twit Bertie purchasing some article of clothing that his valet Jeeves felt was unacceptable for someone of Bertie's class. When Bertie, as always, required rescuing by Jeeves from some social fiasco of Bertie's own making, Jeeves would always exact as his reward the removal of the offending item from Bertie's wardrobe. Jeeves's social status, somewhat insecure since it depended upon that of his feckless master, made it more important to Jeeves than to Bertie that the latter maintain sartorial standards.

Other than the techie guy's ability to take fancy vacations and eat at luxury restaurants if he felt like doing so, the only significant difference between him and the clerk in their daily lives is likely their housing, where the techie's would be much more elaborate, expensive, and in a nicer area.

Very high housing prices have the government's hands all over them. Its tax and financing subsidies for home buyers and the Fed's decades-long downward pressure on interest rates artificially increased demand, while tough zoning and anti-development laws restricted housing supply. That made residences in many places unaffordable to anyone other than the very wealthy.

For some time, we have had a clamor from leftists that the government should crack down on free markets because of inequality, when the one item in which inequality is most clearly manifest is not food and clothing, which free markets have made egalitarian, but in housing, where the government and the Fed, not the free market, has caused the greatest inequality.

One can certainly find or create statistics that show great inequality in income and wealth, and, if so inclined, view this as the crime of the century, but in two of the most basic aspects of life, food and clothing, there is effectively no difference anymore between being rich or poor.

To get some perspective, read George Orwell's *Down and Out in Paris and London*. In the depth of the 1930s Depression, Orwell moved to Paris and tried to make his way there on what he could earn as an unskilled laborer. Although as yet unknown, he was already a very skilled writer and likely figured that, if nothing else, he could get some articles or a book out of it.

He worked as a dishwasher, and he and his coworkers, despite working in fine Paris restaurants, went days on almost no food. There and later in London, he lived among the poorest classes and, like them, made some money by picking up cigarette butts in the street, shaking the bits of remaining tobacco into some rolling paper, creating new cigarettes which could be sold for a penny or two. He and the others had very few clothes, and most of those and any other possessions were usually in pawn shops to raise money for a meal.

That was when "poor" was *really* poor. If Orwell could have stepped into a time machine and visited a present day developed country, he probably would not care how rich the rich are but would be astounded and shocked by how rich the poor are compared to the world he knew. Independent of statistics, inequality as actually experienced in day-to-day life in developed capitalist countries, except for government-created housing inequality, has never been less.

Where there still is huge inequality is between living standards in developed versus undeveloped countries, and between free-market and socialist countries. In many of the poorest countries, there is also great inequality between the elite and everyone else, usually connected to the very things that keep them poor, usually a kleptocratic government that exists to benefit only one set of families or a tribe or clan. They typically lack the rule of law, free speech, and the other prerequisites for free-market prosperity.

Also, keep in mind that all statistics used to measure inequality are highly suspect, since many of the numbers don't mean what they seem to say. For example, using household incomes or individual incomes will produce very different results. The number of workers in a household has a big impact on that, and those numbers change over time, often not at the same rate or direction for various income levels. Higher-income families often have two high-paid professionals bringing in money and may be intact. Low-income families usually don't have two wage earners, or two adults, or even one wage earner, due to divorce or other reasons. Comparisons of total household income will exaggerate the inequality versus a per-capita comparison.

Is the comparison between income groups pretax? Given the progressive income-tax rates in many states as well as at the federal level, that would be misleading. What about after tax? That is better, but lower or non-existent tax rates on lower-income groups are not the only benefits they receive. Are food stamps (now called SNAP) and the value of other programs counted? It gets complicated quickly.

The more something is taxed, the more it tends to disappear from the statistics. Changes in marginal tax rates have a big effect on reported income, with higher rates inducing business owners, who have more flexibility than regular workers, to delay income. Lower rates have the opposite effect. This is why, when there is some voluntary element to whether one takes income during a certain tax period, lower tax rates bring in more money to the government than higher rates do. Many of the trends in the reported incomes of the highest 10% of earners relative to median incomes, or similar statistics, are largely a function of responses to changes in income-tax rates.

An item that is easy for even the most disinterested researcher to get wrong is the value of benefits that come with a job. These have increased steadily over the years, partially mandated by law and partially voluntarily as businesses noticed that offering better health plans, parental leave, flex time, a congenial workplace atmosphere, and other benefits made it easier to recruit good employees.

Still, nothing can escape the fact that business owners won't pay employees more than their perceived worth to the business. If employees' benefits go up, that leaves less room for increases in paychecks. With most benefits not taxed as income, data from the IRS on people's incomes are not reliable guides to their true total pay package. The frequent claims one sees about how wage growth has lagged corporate profits usually fail to count the growth of benefits as part of employee compensation.

A common data flaw shows up in the reported incomes of executives whose pay includes stock options. One often sees headlines about the CEO of some company earning $50 million or some such large number in a given year. No question, top executives are well compensated in base salary, but those outsized numbers usually reflect a one-shot exercise of low-priced stock options received years earlier that paid off due to the company's success or just the Fed's constant pumping of financial-asset prices.

The inherent arbitrariness of calculating inflation figures, discussed earlier, is a godsend to any economist or politician who wants to assert anything at all about inequality and appear to back it up with statistics. Should you want to claim that the poor and/or middle classes are falling behind, make sure you adjust their rising earnings over the years with an index that says inflation has been high, thereby indicating that they have made little real progress. Or, if you want to claim their standard of living has kept up fine, adjust earnings with some other, slower-rising, inflation index, making the growth seem more real and less a matter of inflation.

There may be reasons why one of those indices is slightly more appropriate than the others, but none of them are inherently right. To justify picking one inflation measure over another produces a very technical discussion on statistical techniques which few will want to hear or read, even fewer will understand, and there still won't be a right answer. So, charge right ahead with your claim, and count on nobody noticing your trickery.

The master of using distorted statistics on income and wealth to make his case is the French economist Thomas Piketty, whose popular 2014 book, *Capital in the 21st Century*, claimed that the free market inherently leads to inequality of the unfair kind. Entire books have been written (not so much read, unfortunately) showing how he flogged the statistics mercilessly to force them to comply with his thesis. If you prefer to leave the math to others, just consider Piketty's ridiculous concept of the alleged mechanism that creates inequality in capitalism.

Piketty's big idea is "r" > "g," that "r," the rate of return on investments (ROI) is greater than "g," the growth rate of the economy, therefore the rich get richer. Piketty seems to think that "r" just gets issued to people on account of their having wealth, without them having to do anything to get it.

This is nonsense on multiple levels. There is no such thing as "r"—there is only some ROI, or none, or perhaps a loss on each investment. To consistently get much above the risk-free rate, one must be good at predicting which industries and companies will face increasing demand relative to supply for what they offer. That is what is likely to make profits rise. But that is just the first step.

One can do that, one also must correctly estimate future changes in supply as well as demand. The higher the valuations of companies that would benefit from strong anticipated demand, the greater the chance that start-ups and existing companies will find it easy to raise the capital to enter that business, because of the *Capital Cycle Mechanism*. That would, after a lag, increase supply relative to demand, leading to lower profits and valuations, despite rising demand.

Therefore, one must also know when to get out of a stock investment if competitive supply appears to be rising too fast, so as not to have a gain turn into a loss, a negative "r," which is very common in the real world, if not in Piketty-world.

Good investment judgment isn't a skill widely distributed, nor does it necessarily stick with anyone for their whole career. That is why investment managers are required to include the statement "Past performance is no guarantee of future results" in their ads. An investment manager who has done well for 25 years in a row could easily get nothing but losses starting in year 26.

This is also the basis of the Efficient Market Hypothesis (EMH), discussed previously. EMH argues that it is impossible to beat the market, that an investor should not try or pay anyone else to try. Instead, one should just allocate one's money in a diversified manner to index funds which charge minimal fees, based upon one's attitude toward risk, and hope for the best.

It is amusing to see left-leaning economists accept EMH as proven and use it as a reason to raise taxes on capital gains, since investors should not be rewarded for being "randomly lucky." Yet they also buy Piketty's claim that the richest people earn superior returns because they can afford to place their savings with the very best money managers who, contrary to EMH, know some mysterious secret of beating the market all the time.

One might think that the argument of this chapter, that inequality in living standards is much less than the extreme inequality claimed by those who regularly demand the government do something about it, contradicts my claim that the government and Fed are making inequality much worse. But both parts are true, and if we want to understand cause and effect correctly to adopt policies that enrich rather than impoverish society, we must disentangle the forces operating in the free market from those operating in governments.

The most powerful force for reducing inequality—raising the living standards of the less-well-off more than those of wealthier people—is the steady downward pressure on costs from business investment which, because of the *Progress Mechanism*, pushes prices down, allowing poorer people to get more of whatever it is they want to buy. It has no effect on the living standards of higher-income people because they already can afford to buy what they want. Lower prices add to their savings, but not their living standards, except perhaps in the future, if they invest wisely.

Business investment can do only so much, maybe push prices down 1% to 2% per year on average, but that adds up over time. Unfortunately, it has been decades since prices have gone down that much, and even years of flat prices have been rare. The good that the free market provides is overwhelmed by the damage the government and Fed do to the less well-off.

The cost of paying for the government itself keeps growing, as well as the cost in higher prices of the diversion of so many peoples' efforts away from producing output other people want to buy, toward "building pyramids" instead, i.e., producing output only politicians and their supporters want.

The Fed adds to the damage by imposing interest rates that are usually way too low, causing asset bubbles that increase the wealth of the asset-owning class, but not others'. That is often followed by inflation that reduces living standards of the less-well-off. Excessive inflation induces the Fed to raise interest rates too high, causing financial crashes that require years for recovery.

This needless volatility adds to risk in society, and risk is a cost that must be overcome to produce a profit, like every other cost to a business. Risk dissuades investment in innovative start-up companies, who typically lack the financial strength to handle weak economies. Some of the economic progress they might have created never gets a chance.

CHAPTER 18

DO WE TRULY CARE ABOUT
THE FUTURE?

• • •

D O WE TRULY CARE about future generations? One could say
"Absolutely yes," citing the actions taken to counteract climate
change. Our goal is to save those living some decades hence from
having to deal with reduced farm output, rising tides, and various
other possible negative developments from a hotter world. Doing
that will involve certain sacrifices in our living standards today,
but it shows others and ourselves that we care about our kids and
billions of others yet unborn.

The sacrifices, like the sacrifices of cattle in the days of the Bible
or ancient Rome, make us feel virtuous, but the situation is much
more complex than meets the eye.

Some of the sacrifices that we make do us no harm, save us
some money, or are good for our health, such as walking or biking
instead of driving, or bunching errands into one trip so we aren't

driving so much. But some of the sacrifices do cost us money, such as higher energy costs because of our discouraging or forbidding any expansion of oil production, refining, pipelines, or other transportation capacity. Food production and distribution are energy intensive, so those prices also rise, together harming the living standards of low-income people around the world, since food and energy are such a big part of their budgets.

The subsidies for wind, solar, battery-powered vehicles, and other forms of renewable energy technology are costly and are paid for the same way all government spending is—with a combination of taxes, borrowing (which increases future taxes), and money printing (which inflates prices as each dollar is worth less). Mandates requiring people to use more expensive technology, e.g., electric heat instead of natural gas, are not taxes as such but force people to spend more.

Compared to fossil fuels, renewables are almost always more expensive, even though the wind and sun are free, because of their high cost to build and install, plus the cost of getting power to the grid, relative to their output. Also, because their output is intermittent, fossil-fuel generating capacity must be maintained for when power is needed but there is no wind or sun.

Then there are the substantial subsidies for electric cars that, when one considers the diesel fuel consumed in mining, refining, and transporting battery materials, and the costs of expanding the country's electrical grid to service them, hardly benefit the climate at all. Subsidies count as spending, like all other government spending, and must be paid for by somebody, usually the poor, as discussed previously.

Net zero, producing no carbon emissions or taking CO2 out of the air equal to what we have put into it, for many people is a moral issue, like the goal of many religious people to commit zero sin. A few take the moral argument to its logical endpoint, that the importance of keeping the climate unaffected by human civilization is so great that the quality of human life, or even its continued existence on the planet, is unimportant by comparison.

I disagree with that extreme view for many reasons, but I'm no philosopher or theologian, and will leave that discussion to those who are. I think most people who favor measures to thwart climate change do so for what I would call economic and social reasons. They can imagine the Earth, before this century ends, afflicted with political and economic turmoil, with billions of people moving towards the poles to escape extreme heat, massive flooding, crop failures, wars over dwindling resources, and many other scourges.

There are various scenarios of how these might play out, but in economic terms they all can be described as a collapse of living standards, with all the negative political and social implications that would go along with that.

We want to forestall or prevent any of those problems, so that our grandkids can continue to lead increasingly prosperous lives as we have in recent centuries. There are two parts to that. We want to reduce future climate calamities and do so without harming the growth of incomes. Those two objectives, however, can clash. The sacrifices we make today in our living standards intended for the benefit of people living in the future might actually hurt, not help, their living standards.

That seems counterintuitive. Assuming the correctness of the scientific consensus on the role of human-caused CO_2 in raising worldwide temperatures, how could our efforts to reduce the amount of CO_2 in the air reduce future living standards?

Simple. Future living standards are not just a function of what we have to spend for protection against something bad—they also depend upon future incomes.

For any society, the growth of its income depends upon the growth of productivity, i.e., the ability to increase the value of output relative to the cost of inputs. The main force that does that is wise investment, i.e., not consuming all our income but using some for R&D, new products, new equipment, new processes, employee training, or anything else that raises productivity.

A society that consumes all its income has nothing left to invest. It might have the highest standard of living in the world, but if it doesn't invest, there is nothing that can be counted upon to make its future income rise.

If the world is going to keep reducing the number of people living in deep poverty, as it has been doing for more than a century, it is going to have to be the US and other developed countries who save and invest to make that happen. Only by steadily investing—and having investments made mainly by individuals and businesses who try to maximize their return relative to risk—can our savings increase productivity and thereby create rising incomes.

We don't have an infinite amount to invest. US savings in recent decades were rarely more than 10% of people's incomes, and lately, under the pressure of price inflation of basics that people can't give up, we've been saving less than 5% of our income. Living standards are sticky. When the cost of living increases, most people will keep buying what they did before, and reduce their savings. The recent surge of credit card debt suggests that many are now saving less than nothing. Businesses might still be saving, but having financially exhausted consumers suggests weaker business ahead and caution about investing their savings.

Here is the problem: to the extent that our climate politics make people pay more for energy, food, and everything else for which energy is a significant cost component, and taxes rise to service our massive deficits, our savings will stay very low or drop further, giving us less to invest. Reduced investment equals reduced income growth, and higher taxes on those who normally save will further reduce investment of the sort that increases productivity.

The bigger concern is that even if the total of savings available for investment does not decline, where exactly that money is invested makes a big difference. We saw that happen in the USSR, where there were massive savings relative to incomes compared to the US, but investment decisions were made by government workers whose decisions depended mainly on political considerations, not trying to get the highest possible risk-adjusted ROI. Without free-market prices to guide them, they couldn't have calculated where best to invest even if they wanted to do so.

Driven by massive government incentives, the US is, in effect, doing the same thing as the USSR did. R&D in the US has been shifting from the kind of investments that increase the value of output relative to the cost of inputs, i.e., productivity, toward investments aimed at technologies that produce the same outputs such as electricity, not less expensively, but actually more expensively and with less certainty if the sun isn't shining and the wind isn't blowing, but with less CO_2. That may be good for the climate, but does not increase productivity, which means no growth in incomes.

How will the shift from productivity enhancement to CO_2 diminishment as goals of our R&D investments play out over time? According to the database of the St. Louis branch of the Fed, real (adjusted for inflation) disposable (after-tax) income per capita since 1929 has grown by roughly 2% per year. If we could continue to grow at about the same pace, then, in 2073, fifty years from now, our per-capita incomes would grow from the current $45,000 to about $121,000, not counting any future inflation.

If, because of both reduced savings and investment, and R&D being directed away from what raises living standards toward what helps the climate, real incomes per capita grow at only 1% per year in the next 50 years instead of 2%, our real per-capita income in 50 years will be $74,000 each instead of $121,000. That is still $29,000 more than today, but $47,000 less than if we didn't divert business investment into climate investment.

If we don't make climate sacrifices, and our incomes continue to grow at about 2% per year, then we will have much higher income in 50 years, but we'll likely have to spend heavily to deal with a much warmer climate. If we do make climate sacrifices and reduce productive business investment, our climate costs in 50 years should be somewhat lower, but our incomes could be far lower.

My guess is that, even in a much-hotter climate, the cost of mitigation for the US will be far under the $19 trillion in annual differential in our aggregate incomes ($121,000-$74,000, times a very conservatively estimated 400 million people) we would gain by not sacrificing our living standards and growth potential.

Maybe we will have to spend a few trillion a year, but even as big as that is by today's standards, that will be easy to handle if 400 million of us are all earning $121,000 each, or about $48 trillion, not counting any inflation.

Maybe a few trillion per year for mitigation is too low. Moreover, these numbers refer only to the US. Just as we have some moral obligation to those living in the future after most of us are gone, we also have no right to make choices that will badly damage poorer countries, so we need to allow for the cost of alleviating damage to them caused by our choices.

Even so, many of our subsidies and policies to force people to substitute expensive "clean" energy for inexpensive fossil fuels will reduce our savings, while our green incentives will misdirect much of what savings we do have into projects that, whatever effect they have on the climate, won't increase our incomes as business investment generally does.

Put another way, the aggressive programs most Western countries have initiated in response to climate change will likely reduce the incomes of people living in the future much more than it will reduce the mitigation expense they would otherwise have to make, leaving them worse off.

The importance of high living standards for mitigating any bad effects of climate change can be seen by comparing the Netherlands with Bangladesh. The former has about 40% of its land below sea level, while Bangladesh has about 70% of its land no more than three meters above sea level. They both get occasional bad storms, but very few people die in the Netherlands because of its financial ability to protect its people, whereas thousands regularly die in floods every year in relatively poor Bangladesh.

You shouldn't think of a lower standard of living for the country in the future as meaning a billionaire then will be able to afford only a 125-foot yacht instead of a 175-footer. The very rich and the regular rich will not be affected much, because they always have financial reserves that can bridge any gaps between their income and what they want to spend in any year. It is the poor who will suffer.

If, 50 years from now, the US and other developed countries could have a few dozen more trillions of annual income, in today's dollars, by focusing on business investment rather than CO_2 reduction, that would come in handy dealing with even fairly serious climate change, should the more pessimistic climate models be correct.

There is widespread demand for extreme climate action now from people who romanticize today's climate, or that of 50 or 100 years ago, as being the absolute golden age of climate on Earth, and that no expense is too high to keep it at that level forever. Besides the inherent ridiculousness of that viewpoint, when it was only a few seconds ago in geologic time that much of the northern hemisphere was buried under glaciers, and humans managed to survive that, they should recognize that the cost of achieving their fantasy comes entirely out of the living standards of the lowest-income people today and everyone tomorrow.

Does this mean we should abandon our efforts to reduce the growth of CO_2 in the atmosphere? Not at all. But first we shouldn't make the Keynesian mistake of thinking in aggregates rather than specifics. We should look at each program individually.

If we list all the things we might do or are already doing to reduce climate change, they each have costs that are greater than sticking with how we would operate without any concern for climate. That must be the case, because if not, we would be doing them anyway.

For example, because it made economic sense, wind power for milling grain or pumping water for irrigation has been in use since the Middle Ages, long before anyone even knew what CO_2 was. Houses in hot climates for centuries have been designed to keep cool, and in cold climates to retain heat. No government mandates or subsidies were involved. People naturally chose the most cost-effective way to get something they wanted.

Every program or policy we have that takes climate into account is more costly than if it didn't, so every one of them will reduce savings and business investment to some extent. But if they are likely to have a big impact on CO_2 in the atmosphere relative to their cost, we will benefit by doing them, because they will reduce future costs more than future incomes. Programs with the opposite—having a high cost and minimal effect on the atmosphere—are terrible ideas and should not be undertaken.

Ignorance of this basic economic truth, that we should always want to maximize benefits and minimize costs, is widespread, as evidenced by the large numbers of countries and US states that have enacted laws to require net zero, or carbon neutrality, by some date, commonly about 20 years in the future. Net zero means that even programs that are extremely costly and have minuscule effects on the CO_2 in the air will still be pursued, if that is what it takes to reduce emissions from practically nothing to nothing.

Can you imagine the furor if a business that was nicely profitable with a decent percentage of the widget market said that, just as we hate carbon emissions and want to reduce them to zero, it hates the fact its competitors have any market share at all and wants to reduce that to zero. To do that, it will not just price its products at $0.00, but if necessary, pay people to take its products. For a little while, a company pursuing that strategy will indeed get 100% market share—at a cost of certain bankruptcy.

Net zero is no different; it is a policy choice that is bound to fail because it ignores the Law of Diminishing Returns. Is there a project or climate policy that won't cost us much and have a big effect on CO_2 in the air? Great, absolutely, let's do it! Projects whose costs are high and benefits low? Useless, a waste of good money, let's not.

The "Green New Deal," ostensibly a climate change program, celebrates as a benefit of its enormous costs the fact that millions of people would be employed doing various things that supposedly help the climate. Higher costs are *never* a plus; it is always higher *benefits* we want. Spending enormous sums (and that includes intentionally raising the price of fossil fuels), as the Green New Deal and similar programs advocate, to accomplish very little reduction of CO_2, will impoverish the least well-off of us and not do much to mitigate future climate expenses, which is the only possible benefit they might offer.

I don't want to make it seem like the fight against climate change is uniquely bad in any way. Still, as important as it is not to reduce future living standards with likely ineffective climate programs, even that is probably better than most of what the government wastes our money on—barely disguised payoffs to political supporters of whoever is in power. Let's get rid of that stuff first.

With climate-change spending, we have the good intention to live in a less-hot world. The lack of any attempt whatsoever to justify these costly programs based upon the expected ROI in terms of how much future mitigation expense will be reduced relative to how much people's incomes will be reduced by the lower business investment that these programs necessarily cause, suggests they are just the usual political-kickback bait in green costumes.

CHAPTER 19

CONCLUSION—USING
THE "P" WORD

• • •

THE PARADOX OF HOW Americans think of the free market is that those who criticize it most heavily from the left may be, unbeknownst to themselves, the biggest believers in its power to create prosperity.

Progressives want to pile multiple handicaps upon successful individual participants in free markets, such as higher taxes on wealth, income, inheritance, and capital gains. If enacted, these will reduce the savings and investment in society, in various ways:

- The government will use much of that additional tax money for increased consumption, waste, and misguided "investments."
- It will hand over more money to the politically connected, who will consume more.
- The wealthy will maintain their living standards despite higher taxes but reduce their savings and investment. The biggest

reduction will be in the very-high-risk, high-potential-return angel investing, since even in the rare case when big gains do occur, they will be taxed very heavily. That will slash the formation of innovative start-ups.

Progressives also want much heavier government regulation of businesses and their operations, as well as higher taxes on businesses and mandates that force companies to spend more to benefit employees and various unconnected "stakeholders." This will reduce businesses' profits and the inclination of savers to invest in them or banks to lend them money. Higher costs and the loss of financing would eliminate weak competitors, reducing supply, which will push prices up. Reduced savings will also raise interest rates and the cost of equity capital, making more business expansion and hiring not worth doing.

The Progressive program would likely lead to a severe recession, especially now that decades of Fed mismanagement has raised debt levels in the private sector, the government, and the Fed itself. Unwinding that leverage could kick off a steep and long-lasting economic downturn.

If Progressives understood economics, they would acknowledge this cost to society and try to show what benefits would be created by the policies they favor. But, to slightly paraphrase economist F.A. Hayek, if they understood economics, they wouldn't be Progressives.

The certain reduction in future incomes and living standards from their policies, let alone a financial crash and collapse, is something they never mention. That implies that Progressives could be, subconsciously, true believers in the power of the free market to generate wealth despite the increasing handicaps they want the government to place on it.

If so, they should contemplate just how much more wealth for society could be created by the savers, investors, and businesses without the government soaking and discouraging them so heavily.

Or, if Progressives don't subconsciously believe in the wealth-generating power of free markets, then they must be expert practitioners of magical thinking, that their intentions are so sincere and pure that their proposals won't interfere with cause and effect in the real world. A reduction in living standards is certain if we remove the incentives to create wealth, but somehow that won't happen under the Progressive program because they are really, really, sincere that they don't want that to happen.

Despite all that, many of the instincts and observations of Progressives and Populists, both left and right, are correct. They have their diagnosis right; it is their prescriptions that are all wrong. Our current political/economic system is indeed unfair to the poor, the working class, and the middle class. Their living standards are well below where they ought to be.

What Progressives and Populists get wrong, however, is why that is the case. Free markets are not the culprit. It is the immense costs of government and its policies that are to blame.

Because of the *Progress Mechanism,* the *Capital Cycle Mechanism,* and the *Grace of the Market,* free markets allow the masses of the non-rich to reap enormous benefits of what political economist Deirdre McCloskey calls "the great enrichment" of the last several hundred years. You can consume all your income, save and invest nothing, and your living standards will continue to rise over time from the benefits you get—better goods and services at lower prices—due to others innovating, working hard, saving money, and investing wisely.

But the forces of the free market that pressure down the prices and raise the living standards of lower income people by doing so have been overwhelmed by the inflationary consequences of rising government size and power. Those include:

1) The amounts the government takes in taxes.

2) What it must take in taxes in the future to service our rising debts and unfunded liabilities.

3) What it takes by stealth, by using newly created Fed money to pay bills, causing output- and asset-price inflation as more dollars are worth less each.

4) The additional inflation it creates by imposing costs and taxes upon businesses who, because of the *Capital Cycle Mechanism*, can raise prices to foist them off on customers.

5) Stampeding people into participating in asset speculation bubbles, since nobody wants to be a chump by not grabbing their share of the sure money, and then leaving those same people with assets of shaky value against which they have borrowed large sums.

6) Diverting so many people from working in jobs in which they produce goods or offer services that other people want, to become instead modern "pyramid workers," getting paid to do things that only the politically connected want.

7) Raising the cost of resources (labor, material, capital goods, management) to businesses and consumers as they must compete for access with the government.

All these things overwhelm the *Progress Mechanism* and push up consumer prices, harming the living standards of those with lower incomes and harming their future incomes by reducing what wealthier people can save, reducing business investment.

The only way to solve the problem, if Progressives really want to achieve their goals of helping the poor and downtrodden, is to shrink the government. We need to get it off the backs of lower-income people and let free-market economic growth enrich the poorest, as it always has.

There is no getting around using this unpleasant term, the "P" word: The government is a massive *parasite* that gets what it wants by forcing the lower economic classes to get less of what they want. This reduction in living standards is what provides the resources that the government and its cronies demand.

People usually get upset at the word "parasite" with reference to the government. Most people's image of the government doesn't include senators in the pockets of defense contractors, the farm lobby, the teachers' unions, the financial community, and other pressure groups. Rather, it is based on Norman Rockwell's images of teachers, social workers, the nice people at the post office, and even, until George Floyd, the kindly policemen.

And no question, there are many dedicated public employees throughout all levels of government. I have dealt with many myself, and I admire anyone who does what is right despite not having any economic incentive to do so, other than self-respect derived from their good character.

Nevertheless, the total of federal, state, and local spending in fiscal 2023 is estimated to be about $9.3 trillion, which works out to more than $28,000 per capita. If your household is four people, you are, in theory, responsible for paying for $112,000 of government spending, in addition to whatever you want to spend for yourself.

That is frightening, but also somewhat misleading, in that some government spending replaces your own. You don't need a private security detail because the government has the military, police, and courts. You don't need to be as generous to people in need because the government pays for a social safety net, and, if you are older than 65, the government pays for much of your healthcare. But vast portions of the budgets go to things you don't want, to which you would never voluntarily donate even a penny were someone passing a hat to fund them. But you pay for them anyway, like it or not.

Being a parasite is a common strategy in the natural world. A parasite lives on or in another organism (the host) and consumes nutrition at the latter's expense. That often causes disease and harms whatever organs of the host that are the weakest.

While we all bear some burden because of government's spending and diversion of resources and output to meet its selfish wants rather than our own, it is the economically weakest people, those with limited income and savings, whose living standards are most reduced by what it costs them in higher taxes, higher prices, and lower wages.

Trying to convince the parasite to prey more on stronger organs in the body never works. No matter how the government is financed, the result always turns out the same. We don't want to kill the parasite because it does do some useful things. Only by significantly shrinking the parasite can the weaker organs be restored to health.

There are no specific suggestions here of what specifically should be cut from the government budget because that deserves another, much longer, book. The point of this book isn't to name what most needs eliminating, just to show why so many things do.

The decision rule should be simple: **Does this program, policy, law, or cabinet department create so much value that it is worth making poor people reduce their living standards to pay for it? If not, eliminate it.**

Anything at all can seem justified if we think that either nobody pays for it (MMT) or "greedy billionaires and greedy corporations" will pay for it. That is why politicians rarely mention cost, never mention any ROI for the government's "investments," and make all discussions of government financing about finding some small segment of the population who we pretend we can make pay for everything so everyone else gets it for free.

The person or business who writes the tax check may appear to be the one paying, but as you've seen, the cost of government and its policies have a big impact on prices, and it is those who must cut back their living standards to pay those prices who are the ones really paying for the government.

If you think that a given program is worthwhile despite its cost being dumped on the backs of the poor, then put it on the "save" list. But most programs, many cabinet departments in their entirety, and most programs they fund probably won't pass that test. So, let's work toward eliminating them, not necessarily all at once, but we need to aim in that direction.

If we do so, yes, many people will lose their jobs, both government workers and those in the private sector whose jobs are subsidized by government spending. We can offer a safety net to tide them over for a while until they find other work. And nearly all will, due to the very positive effect on consumer demand from lower taxes, which will give people more to spend, and the positive effect on the living standards of the less wealthy that come from lower prices on what they want to buy. That will be caused by the transfer of millions of people from their old jobs "building pyramids" to producing goods and services that other people want and for which they will gladly spend their own money.

We should reduce taxes sharply as we shrink the government, roughly equal in dollar terms to the reduction in spending. Since lower-income people have been bearing the greatest burden of paying for the government, taxes that affect them most directly should be the first to be reduced and then eliminated. Those would be payroll taxes on what they earn and sales taxes on what they buy. The latter plus property taxes in the US go to states and local governments, which should be cutting their spending significantly, too.

Along with the worker's share of the payroll tax, the employer's share should be a high priority for reduction, freeing up more money for salaries or price cuts. Other business taxes and costly government mandates on companies should be next because they directly affect consumer prices.

It might seem that reducing both government spending and its payroll tax take equally would not reduce the deficit, but much of the higher after-tax earnings would be spent. Since every business would have their share of the payroll tax cut as well, competition would put downward pressure on the prices of everything, further enhancing living standards. All this will generate more taxable economic activity and help reduce the deficit.

Think about what happened with the opening of the Erie Canal, when sharply lower food costs in the East and sharply lower manufactured-goods prices in the West made everyone richer, and they spent accordingly. Just as the Appalachian Mountains were a physical bottleneck that kept both sides poor, our massive, parasitic government is a fiscal bottleneck doing the same thing today. If we really want to help those who have had to feed the parasite for so long, we must shrink it.

Another issue we'll have to consider is that the enormous government waste and induced malinvestment all over the world were mostly done with borrowed money. That requires care in the unwinding, but it must be confronted. We can't be condemned to having to live in a financially dangerous, over-leveraged society forever because it isn't easy to wind down heavy debts. To the extent we reduce government spending and cut taxes, the higher disposable incomes that result should allow us to steadily, if slowly, reduce them.

We also should drastically reduce the power of leading economists to impose their misconceived theories upon society. The Fed can hang around to help clear checks between banks and perform a few other useful functions, but we should carefully reduce its massive holdings of government and mortgage debt and get it out of the business of imposing interest rates and controlling the money supply based upon their hapless models.

Ultimately, the reason why the free market generates so much wealth, despite the parasitic drag of the government, is that it is the only economic system that is consistent with human nature. It accepts that people care about themselves and those who are close to them more than distant strangers. It accepts that people know themselves well enough to make specific choices that are better for them than what the government forces on them. It recognizes that people are willing to work hard, work smart, and fight to overcome pushback from status-quo beneficiaries when they innovate, provided they will be rewarded for doing these things.

In addition to a consonance with human nature, only the free market accepts the constraints of reality. Consumption consumes resources. Work can create new output, but only savings and business investment can create progress.

Without that growth in productivity, there is no growth in living standards. Free markets generate the knowledge and incentives to make that happen. Governments supplant economic knowledge with political considerations, and their incentives are directed at political success, not economic growth. If we care about the poor and middle classes, who bear the greatest burden of covering the government's costs, and if we care about the living standards of those living in the future, then we need to shrink the government.

CARD/KRUEGER: A DEEPLY FLAWED STUDY

• • •

IN 1994, ECONOMISTS DR. David Card and the late Dr. Alan Krueger published a study (C/K) of a "natural experiment." In April 1992, the minimum wage was raised in New Jersey to the highest in the nation, while the wage in Pennsylvania, next door, remained unchanged.

NBER working paper 10/1993: https://www.nber.org/system/files/working_papers/w4509/w4509.pdf

Card won a 2021 Nobel in Economics ("for his empirical contributions to labor economics"); Krueger almost certainly would have shared the prize were he still alive.

This appendix is a critique of C/K which points out three things about many, if not most, economic studies:

1. Even a widely celebrated study in macroeconomics can be just a mimicry of the scientific method and fail to prove what it claims.

2. Humans are not inanimate objects responding predictably to changes in the forces to which we are subject. We have volition and make our choices after considering many more factors and at a pace that no economist doing a study can ever know.

3. Economists can advance very far in their profession despite being unaware of how businesspeople think and operate.

The common-sense economic truth supposedly refuted by C/K is that, if a person thinks something isn't worth the money, they won't buy it. The fact that a person may be in business shouldn't change that. If the government demands that an employee be paid $X per hour and the owner or manager feels that the employee adds less than $X per hour in value, the owner will fire the employee as soon as practicable, or at least cut back their hours to only the busiest and most-productive ones.

Background: In early 1990, New Jersey passed a law increasing its minimum wage by 19%, to take effect in April 1992. Pennsylvania, next door, did not increase its minimum wage at the time. The C/K study checked employment levels in certain fast-food restaurants in both states from the period of 3 to 6 weeks before the law went into effect, i.e., in February and March 1992, and compared them to employment levels 7 to 8 months after the increase took effect. It claimed there was no significant difference in employment in those two periods in New Jersey vs. Pennsylvania and concluded that the increase in minimum wage in the former did not reduce employment.

This was a surprising result, because the law of demand in economics says that the higher the price of something, in this case, labor, the lower the demand, and the study appeared to contradict it. Although the authors were cautious in their claims, politicians and activist economists viewed C/K as giving them the green light to treat a proven economic law as optional and allowing them to require business owners to pay their unskilled workers whatever politicians thought appropriate.

While the study is thirty years old, it is still considered exemplary by the economics profession. Its co-author received the profession's highest award primarily for this study. According to the National Bureau of Economic Research, the study linked above has been cited over 4300 times in other studies. This is as influential a study as has ever been done in economics. While not a macroeconomic study as such, C/K certainly had macroeconomic effects, with widespread enactment of ever-higher minimum wages in the US and elsewhere in the world.

The laws of economics, as in any field, should be able to be overthrown, but only by thorough, comprehensive studies many times more powerful than C/K. Here are some of its flaws:

Flaw #1: Wrong Starting Point

The higher minimum wage law in NJ was passed in early 1990 but did not go into effect until April of 1992. It is plausible that the reason for the long delay was to give employers of low-skilled labor a good two years to prepare for sharply higher labor costs.

The C/K study was structured as a before-and-after picture: here is the employment level before the law went into effect; here it is after. But C/K's "before" was just a few weeks before the law went into effect in 1992. A better time to check the "before" level of employment was in early 1990, as soon as the law passed, when employers were served notice of what was to come.

Anyone who has ever even tried to think like a business owner would realize that, as soon as the law was passed, people who either owned a fast-food franchise, or were thinking of buying or starting up one in New Jersey, would know to assume higher costs after March of 1992. Many owners would start working at solving the problem right away since labor costs are a big percentage of their total costs. Some would have closed their businesses when the leases were up, and others would have reorganized their workflow to have the fewest possible workers once the wage hike went into effect.

No one can possibly know what percentage of owners made those kinds of changes in operations in advance of the effective date. But we know many (if not most) franchise owners must have done something. Many had their life savings invested, working 40+ hours per week to make a go of it. Fast-food franchises are a low-margin business that can't survive an increase in labor costs without responding in some fashion. The less successful owners would know that a legally mandated labor cost increase of 19% could force them to close.

But C/K didn't check employment levels until two years after the law passed, just a few weeks before the law went into effect—as if no franchise owner would do anything in advance. The data should have included restaurants that closed in the two years between announcement of the law and its going into effect, as well as those who reduced employment during that time through reorganizing workflow or automation. The C/K study should have assumed that businesspeople, for whom profit levels are not just interesting academic data, think and plan.

This flaw alone condemns the study. How can one compare "after" to "before," if "before" was long after many and likely most of the changes had been made?

Flaw #2: Cherry-Picking the Sample

This study did not cover all minimum wage employers in the area, or even all restaurants. It only covered certain fast-food restaurants. Did fast-food comprise most of the restaurant business in the area? No. The study quotes a government report from 1987 indicating that they represent about 25% of restaurant workers, which, in turn, were a subset of all workers affected by the new law. Fast-food was still gaining market share at the time, so that was probably higher than 25% by 1992.

The number of restaurant workers was probably quite a bit smaller than the number of retail-store workers in those pre-Amazon days, most of whom were also paid minimum wage or not much above. In the early 1990s, there were still many factories around using unskilled labor that hadn't yet encountered intense competition from China. Their employees were also predominantly minimum wage workers.

No attempt was made to survey stores, factories, or warehouses, another big employer of low wage workers. The authors also gave up on non-chain, mostly mom-and-pop restaurants, and the biggest fast-food chain, McDonald's, because, in both cases, the owners or managers were busy and would not take their surveys. If restaurants employed about one third of all minimum wage workers, fast food employed one third of those, and non-McDonald's chains employed three quarters of that category, then C/K was looking at only 8% of the market.

And not just any 8%. In recent years, many fast-food restaurant chains have struggled, but the 1980s and 1990s were periods of intense growth for that industry. The 1980s were known as the time of the "burger wars." McDonald's and Burger King spent vast amounts in TV advertising to gain share, with fast-growing newcomer Wendy's "Where's the Beef?" ad becoming a humorous catch phrase, a meme before the internet.

While their ads attacked each other, the collective effect of all that advertising and publicity was to increase the market share of all fast-food stores at the expense of one-of-a-kind sub shops, diners, and other mom-and-pop operations that lacked the marketing power, name recognition, novelty effect, and procurement and management savings of fast-food chains. Not to mention that the colloquial name for that category of restaurant was "greasy spoon," which made the clean, well-lighted fast-food places seem more attractive.

C/K therefore studied the fastest-growing segment of the restaurant industry. The 1990-91 recession likely knocked many non-chain competitors in New Jersey out of business, especially since their owners were aware of the impending sharp increase in their labor costs. The economy snapped back strongly in 1992 (contrary to the claim in the study), which must have helped fast-food demand and employment, as did the withdrawal of many mom-and-pop restaurants from the business.

Supporters of minimum-wage laws typically describe the C/K study as proving that increases in minimum wages don't reduce demand for labor. The best one can say about the study, even if it had no other flaws, is that, in one place, New Jersey, at one time, 1992, a sharp increase in the minimum wage did not affect employment at existing non-McDonald's fast-food restaurants, a tiny fraction of minimum-wage workers in New Jersey at the time.

That is a highly curated data point, to say the least, and is only one. One would need many of them to overthrow an established law of microeconomics: demand for something diminishes when its price goes up.

Flaw #3: Wrong Ending Point

Many, and likely most, franchise owners responded in some way to the mandated rise in minimum wages in the two years after the law was passed in early 1990 and before the C/K study began in February 1992, by making changes in business operations to reduce labor costs. Even then, they may not have done everything they hoped to do.

There may have been some who did what the study assumes they all did—nothing at all, until the increase went into effect in April 1992. Of these, what percentage of their complete response would have been completed in the eight months after the law went into effect and the study concluded?

We don't know, but it is certain that some percentage of the responses must have happened after the study was complete. That is because, for restaurants, retail, and mom-and-pop-owned businesses, occupancy costs are very significant, based on leases that run multiple years, and, most important, are personally guaranteed by the owner.

There were likely some owners who had a lease running until 1993 or beyond, whose business went into the red as soon as the higher minimum wage went into effect, while attempts at a price increase repelled some customers and couldn't cover the cost increase. Operating a business in the red is like working a job and getting paid less than nothing, not something anyone would voluntarily do.

Why didn't they close up shop right away? They didn't because the owner was personally on the hook to pay the rent until the end of the lease even if the business was no longer operating. The rent is a sunk cost which the owner can't avoid. The restaurant might still have been "profitable," not counting rent, which, for an owner, is not as bad as still having to pay the rent with no revenues at all.

But as soon as the lease term ends, the business would close and all employees would be laid off. Since leases are often written in years, not months, there had to have been at least some leases ending after the study's endpoint, and therefore not counted, understating the number of lost jobs.

On what basis did C/K decide that 7 to 8 months was enough time for the entire impact of the wage increase to have taken place? We don't know, and C/K makes no mention of checking how long the leases of the restaurants ran, so they must have been unaware of that issue, or chose to ignore it.

The sooner the study ended, the sooner they could publish. A quick end would also prevent the study from reaching a conclusion—an established law of economics still applies as it always has—that would not attract much notice.

Flaw #4: Ignoring Non-Wage Aspects of Work

Wages are not the only form of compensation, broadly defined, that people receive from a job. They get on-the-job training, particularly valuable to the unskilled and inexperienced workers paid minimum wages. They also get various fringe benefits and working conditions.

Some workers prefer the highest-possible wages and will put up with sweatshop conditions to get them. Others will be happier with lower wages but better non-wage benefits, like more schedule flexibility, a lower-pressure environment, better training and the chance for more responsibility, more time socializing with friendly workers and possible romantic partners, or freedom to take breaks and make personal phone calls.

Either model is fine if the business using it can attract the number and kind of employees it needs. Fast-food restaurants are too low-margin to offer both high pay and high non-wage benefits. Wages up generally means benefits and working conditions down. The C/K study made a limited attempt to check that out but couldn't go far because they ignored most of the non-wage benefits, which are hard to measure or value. Workers can tell the difference, but economists can't.

This raises a question: Do we want the government to force the sweatshop model on an industry? Why should workers be forbidden to work for lower pay in return for many non-monetary benefits, if that is what they prefer? Who are economists and politicians, who get paid well above the minimum wage, to decide for them?

Advocates of high minimum wages assume that all unskilled workers are wage-maximizing automatons. If we accept that workers are not robots but people, why not let them decide what employment model works best for themselves?

Another point, not C/K's job to address but one that deserves consideration: Wealthy people usually have good contacts and know how to place their children in unpaid internships, with the parents subsidizing their living expenses. At their jobs, these privileged kids get intensive training and exposure to potential employers and others who can help them in their careers.

Poor immigrants and inner-city kids don't have parents with those contacts or the ability to subsidize them even if they somehow could land an unpaid internship on their own. The only introduction to legal employment an unskilled, poor kid can get is through an entry-level, minimum-wage job. By forcing employers to pay them more than they are likely to be worth to a business, the law creates a major hurdle to their being hired.

Minimum-wage laws forbid a business hiring anyone below a certain wage unless the wage is zero and it is called "an internship." That gives an unfair edge to children of the wealthy and well connected. It isn't an insurmountable edge if hard-working, ambitious kids get a chance to prove themselves starting at the bottom, but minimum-wage laws cut off the bottom rungs of the ladder.

Flaw #5: Forgetting Who Pays

Because of the *Capital Cycle Mechanism*, any cost increases a business faces sooner or later get foisted onto its customers in higher prices, and/or on its employees in lower pay or benefits. Some fast-food restaurants probably were able to raise prices, not lose many customers, and earn enough to be reimbursed for the higher labor costs. Those that faced price resistance from the customers would have lower profits, and some of those would close. Reduced industry capacity relative to demand would allow the survivors to then raise prices and restore profits.

That is what happened in New Jersey after the law pushed up costs in 1992. According to C/K, prices rose by about 4%, which was more than which was more than was necessary to cover the increase in labor costs. That probably reflected the reduction in supply relative to demand, mostly from the mom-and-pops that were going under from fast-food competition. Minimum-wage advocates like to portray the laws as causing a transfer of money from businesses to workers, but after prices go up, it is really a transfer from a business's customers to those workers who weren't laid off. That raises two issues:

First, why are the customers of fast-food restaurants thought to be less in need of money than their employees? C/K didn't offer any reasons.

The other issue is, to the extent that customers were willing to pay more for fast food, what other output did they now buy less of? Most fast-food customers are not notably wealthy. If they kept paying more for fast food, and more for other output whose prices also went up to reflect higher mandated wages, then they probably had to cut back on some other goods and services, unless they also got a raise, which many did not. If they didn't have substantial savings as a buffer, they must have given up something. To think they didn't is to believe in magic. What did they give up, and what were the employment effects of their reduced demand for other things?

Suppose, for example, fast-food customers had to cut out their weekly bowling to pay for their lunches, to the point where the bowling alley had to lay off workers or shut down. Shouldn't that loss of employment count as an effect of the minimum-wage increase as much as anything happening at the restaurants? That would be true even if the pay of no bowling-alley workers were affected by the law.

True, it would be impossible without massive, intrusive surveys that few would answer with great accuracy, or at all, to determine where people no longer spent money to cover their higher fast-food spending, to allow the researchers to determine what happened to employment there. But do we want to get cause and effect correct, or just pretend we do?

My guess is most politicians don't really want to know the truth. To them, minimum wage increases are about getting more votes whether it is good for society or workers or not. Fine, let's just accept it as normal political pandering, and not have economists claiming that studies have shown mandated wage increases to be beneficial.

Flaw #6: Failing to Disaggregate

Even if C/K and similar studies could somehow have proven mandated increases in wages do not affect the numbers employed or hours worked, that does not settle the matter, because it ignores the question of who in society will get the minimum-wage jobs.

Minimum-wage laws, when first introduced in the US more than a century ago, were explicitly justified as designed to protect the white worker against black competition. Blacks at the time were, on average, less productive than whites. Their years as agricultural workers didn't give them the experience in non-farming jobs that whites had, and, at a time when workers were expected to provide their own tools, a carpenter who recently left farm employment lacked the capital to purchase the higher-quality tools that white carpenters owned. Minimum-wage laws, by taking away their ability to work for less per hour to compensate for the fact that they might have to work more hours to complete a job, succeeded, as planned, in slashing black employment.

Due to different factors today, such as a bad education from poor inner-city schools and their lack of role models with business experience in the homes in which they are raised, many unskilled blacks continue to be less-attractive job candidates than whites, if they must be paid the same starting wage. Moreover, the higher the minimum wage, the more attractive the jobs are to better-educated whites, who otherwise might not have applied.

High minimum wages make blacks and immigrants who are not proficient in English less likely to be hired in entry-level jobs, so they don't gain the initial experience they need to develop business careers. Being effectively barred from working legally, this gives them little choice but permanent welfare or crime, neither of which is good for them or society.

While it is true that minimum-wage laws were designed by Progressives who, at the time, were avowed racists, and today they are advocated by Progressives who are sincerely anti-racist, intentions make no difference. The earlier Progressives may have had vile beliefs, but they understood economics correctly. The laws were racist then, and, effectively, if not intentionally, are just as racist now.

ACKNOWLEDGMENTS

．．．

THIS BOOK GOT ITS start a dozen years ago in various email arguments with friends in the wake of the housing-bubble collapse in the US and the sovereign debt crisis in Europe. Some of these battles have continued to the present day. I always learn the most from people who disagree with me, and the two most wrong people in the world (they would disagree) who have forced me to improve my arguments the most have been Gary Gut and Bob Stolzberg. They are both very smart, and the book wouldn't exist without them, for which I greatly thank them.

Other people who have commented on parts or all of it and earlier versions include Jim Gerson, Bob Kricun, Peter Von Mertens, Nick Cumpsty, Mary Hamer, Maureen Rogers, Den White, Peter Aldrich, Chip Burke, Jim Sloman, Andy Snider, Harlan Rieur, Val Mayer, Jurgen Weiss, Bill Pike, Marc Tishler, Eileen Tishler, Rachel Turbet, Diana Himmelstein, Pamela Green, Fred Gerson, Tom Mylchreest, Andy Freeman, and the late Tom Reinhardt. Any parts of the book you don't like are my fault, not theirs.

I must also thank the excellent team at 1106 Design for whipping this book into shape, and Rachel Colbert for critiquing my work along the way. Most of all, I must thank my wife, Kathleen Rogers, the long suffering "economics widow," who has no problem disagreeing with me, and helped greatly that way as well as with the editing.